What is Missing?

▶ Draw what is missing in each picture.

1.

2.

3.

4.

5.

6.

Bone Mystery

Dog likes to make things. When he works, Dog often does things without thinking.

Yesterday, Dog made a table. When the table was done, he wanted to chew on a big bone. But his four bones were gone! Can you find Dog's bones?

▶ Underline the right answer.

1. What is the best name for the story?

   My Bones Are Missing!   Dog Works Hard

2. What does Dog often forget to do?

   play   think   chew

3. What happened to Dog's bones?

   They were stolen.   They were thrown out.   Dog used them.

4. What does "do things without thinking" mean?

   not think about what you do   chew on a nice big bone

5. Which thing was named in the story?

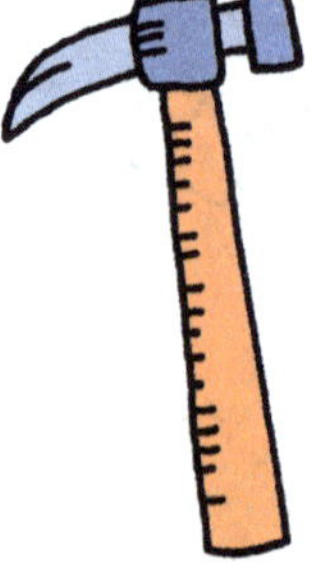

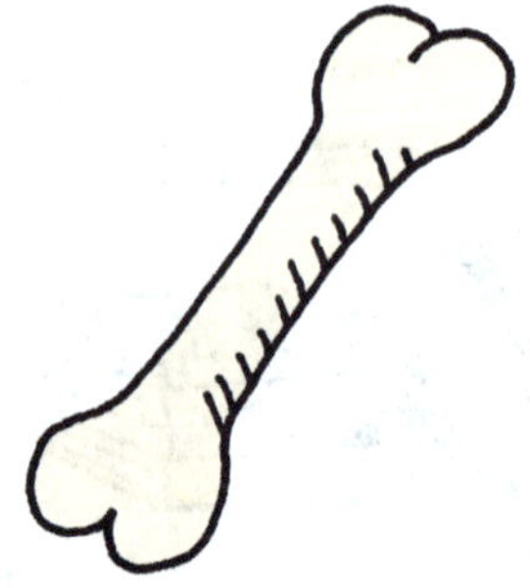

Mouse TV

Five white mice were on TV.
They had a show on Channel 3.

The first white mouse played a rat-ta-tat-tum.
The second white mouse began to hum.

The third white mouse tap-tapped his feet.
The fourth white mouse clapped out the beat.

The fifth white mouse sang about a cat.
Mouse TV—imagine that!

▶ Draw lines to show what the mice did.

hummed along

danced around

played a drum

sang a song

clapped his hands

What's Next?

▶ Underline what happens next.

1. Mick loves movies. He goes every time he has money. Mick got $5.00 from his uncle. What happens next?

2. PJ's mom gave her flower seeds. PJ made a garden. She planted the seeds every which way. What happens next?

3. Jerry forgets things. He took some books to show Andy. The kids were playing tag. Jerry played, too. Then it was time to go home. What happens next?

4. Mia's pup chewed her homework. He chewed a chair leg. Now he lives outside. Mia left her shoes in the yard. What happens next?

How Do You Use It?

▶ Write the correct words in the puzzle.

hose	path	shaker	shoe
shovel	rake	vase	ear

Across

1. Use it to pour salt.
3. Use it to dig.
5. Use it to walk in the woods.
6. Use it to put out fires.
7. Use it to listen.

Down

2. Use it to pile leaves.
3. Use it to cover your foot.
4. Use it for flowers.

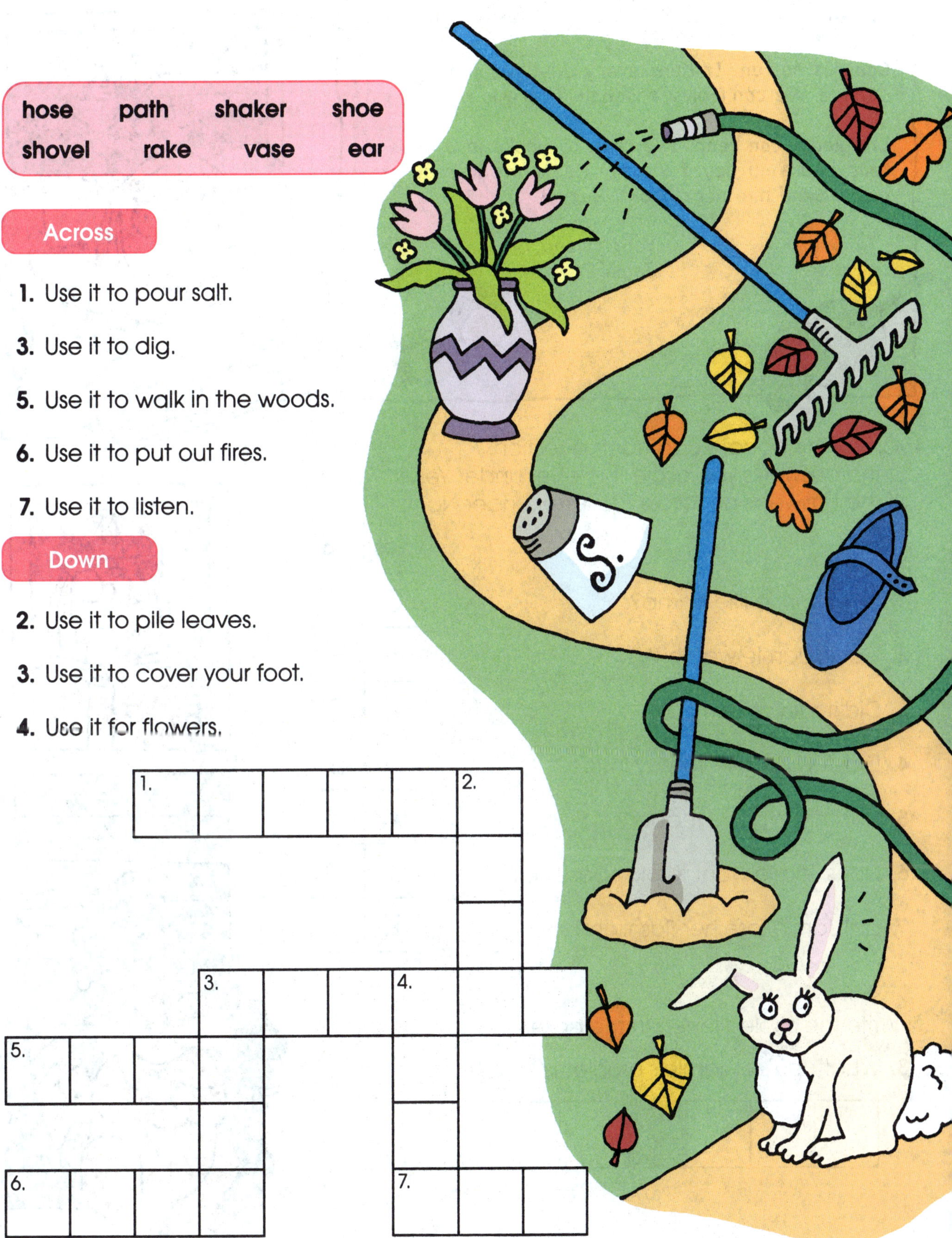

A Letter From Camp

Hi Jon! July 15

Camp is no fun. It rains every day! We can't go outside. We can't play baseball. There is no TV!

I'm glad I can read. I've read 10 books in 3 days. I read books all day. I use my flashlight to read at night. Send me more books. Hurry!

Your friend,
Jamie

▶ Crack the code! Read each question.
If the answer is yes, circle the letter under Yes.
If the answer is no, circle the letter under No.

	Yes	No
1. Does Jamie like camp?	O	T
2. Could Jamie watch TV?	L	H
3. Did it rain at camp?	E	D
4. Did Jamie have to stay inside?	R	B
5. Is Jamie a good reader?	A	O
6. Does Jamie want to play baseball?	I	O
7. Did Jamie lose her flashlight?	K	N

▶ Write the circled letters in the boxes.

8. What caused Jamie's problems?

			■				

Computer Cat

Computer Cat is a whiz on her computer. She can make drawings with her mouse. She can write long letters with the keys. She can write stories, too.

Computer Cat is writing a book. The book is about a cat using a computer. She will sell her book on TV! Would you buy it?

▶ Underline the right answer.

1. What is the story about?

   a cat who uses a computer   a cat and a mouse

2. Does Computer Cat draw pictures?   yes   no

3. Does Computer Cat chase her mouse?   yes   no

4. Does Computer Cat write letters?   yes   no

5. Which cat is Computer Cat?

Nightmare!

Henry was sleeping. He dreamed he was being chased through a jungle. A lion wanted to eat him! The lion was red. Then it was blue. Then it was yellow. But the lion's teeth were always white.

Finally, Henry woke up. He was glad the dream was over!

▶ Underline the right answer.

1. What is another good name for the story?

   Henry's Dream   Make-Believe Lions

2. What did Henry dream about?

   a lion chasing him   rainbows in the sky   going to bed

3. Where were Henry and the lion?

   in bed   in the jungle   on a rainbow

4. What is a nightmare?

   a bad dream   a lion   teeth

▶ Draw a line to the end of each sentence.

5. The lion   were always white.

   The lion's teeth   was red.

   Finally, Henry   woke up.

Plant a Tree

Dear Neighbors,

Will you help us keep the earth green? We want to plant trees in our neighborhood. We want a new tree in every yard. May we plant one in yours?

We will be planting next week. You can pick an oak tree, an elm tree, or a maple tree. The trees are free.

The Tree Club

▶ Underline the right answer.

1. What kind of writing is this?

   a funny story   a note   a birthday card

2. When is the Tree Club planting trees?

   last week   this week   next week

3. What kind of trees do they have?

   oak, maple, and ash   elm, ash, and maple   maple, oak, and elm

4. What will the trees do for the earth?

   keep it green   put one in your yard   trees are free

5. Which picture shows the Tree Club?

Save the Animals

The kids played a prank!
They hid the animals at the zoo.
They left a note, but the note is written in code.

Read the note to find out how many animals are missing.

▶ Follow the directions to read the note. Cross out the Cs, Ds, Js, and Qs.

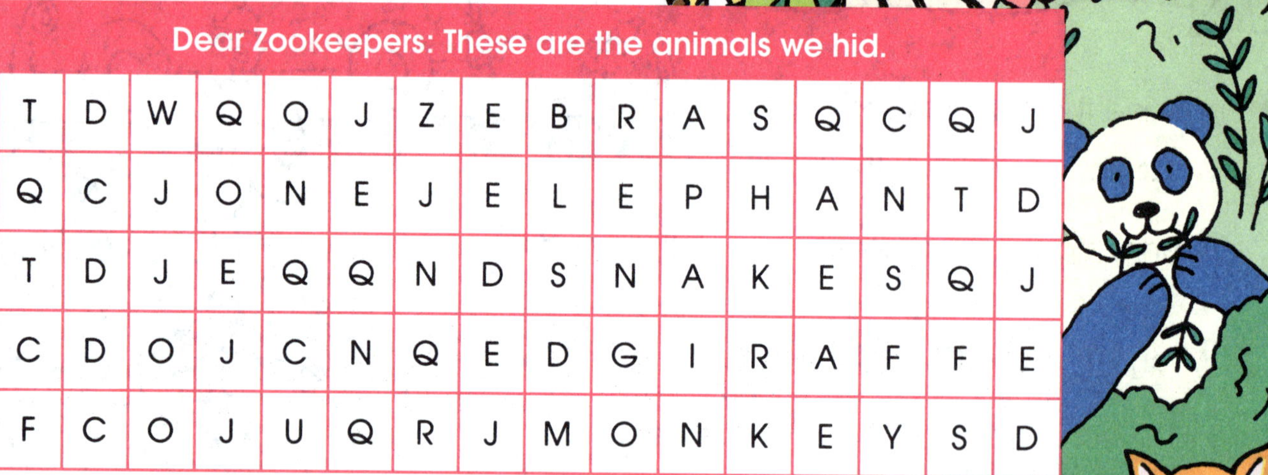

Dear Zookeepers: These are the animals we hid.

T	D	W	Q	O	J	Z	E	B	R	A	S	Q	C	Q	J
Q	C	J	O	N	E	J	E	L	E	P	H	A	N	T	D
T	D	J	E	Q	Q	N	D	S	N	A	K	E	S	Q	J
C	D	O	J	C	N	Q	E	D	G	I	R	A	F	F	E
F	C	O	J	U	Q	R	J	M	O	N	K	E	Y	S	D

▶ Draw your favorite missing animal.

Animal Puzzle

▶ Write the correct words in the puzzle.

anteater	bear	elephant	horse	
panda	seal	snake	zebra	monkey

Across

3. People can ride one.

4. Smokey is one.

7. Dumbo is one.

8. A teddy bear might be one.

9. This has no legs.

Down

1. This is like a chimp.

2. This looks like a horse with stripes.

5. This eats bugs.

6. This swims, but isn't a fish.

1. 2. 3. 4. 5. 6. 7. 8. 9.

Will You Play?

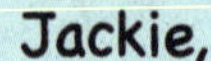

Jackie,

Will you play on our basketball team? You're a super shooter. We need players who can score.

We practice on Tuesdays at 7:00. Games are on Saturdays. Please come play with us!

Your friend,
Kris

▶ Underline the right answer.

1. What kind of writing is this?

   a funny story   a sign   a note

2. Who wrote it?

   Kris   Mom   Erica

3. Who is Kris?

   Jackie's aunt   Jackie's sister   Jackie's friend

4. What does Jackie do well?

   run   pass   shoot

5. When does the team practice?

   Tuesdays   Saturdays   every day

6. What does **super** mean?

   very good   very bad   very slow

Rhyming Riddles

▶ Finish each poem with a word that rhymes.
Use these words if you need help:

white day snow round running showers spring

1. Clouds fly high
   when the sun is bright.
   The very best clouds
   are fluffy and _____.

2. The hot days are best
   for swimming and sunning.
   But the cool days are better
   when I want to go _____.

3. It falls from the sky
   when the cold winds blow.
   I hope it stays awhile!
   I want to play in the _____.

4. I like the flowers growing.
   I like the birds that sing.
   I like the growing season.
   We call that season _____.

5. I like sunny days
   with snow on the ground.
   And I like the nights
   when the moon is so _____.

6. April brings rain.
   May brings flowers.
   But the color in May
   makes me like April _____.

7. Some days are foggy.
   Some days are gray.
   But I like the times
   when it's sunny all _____.

Make a Bank

Is there something you want to buy? Save your money! Make a bank. All you need is a plastic milk bottle, markers, and some tape.

Clean the milk bottle. Tape on the cap to keep your money safe. Have a grown-up help cut a slot for the money. Draw pictures on the bank. Then drop your money inside.

▶ Underline the right answers.

1. What do you need to make a bank?

new shoes	a milk bottle	some apples
some tape	a grown-up	some markers

▶ Put the steps in order. Write 1, 2, 3, 4, 5, and 6.

2.

☐	Drop your money in.	☐	Get a milk bottle.
☐	Draw pictures.	☐	Clean the bottle.
☐	Tape on the cap.	☐	Cut a slot.

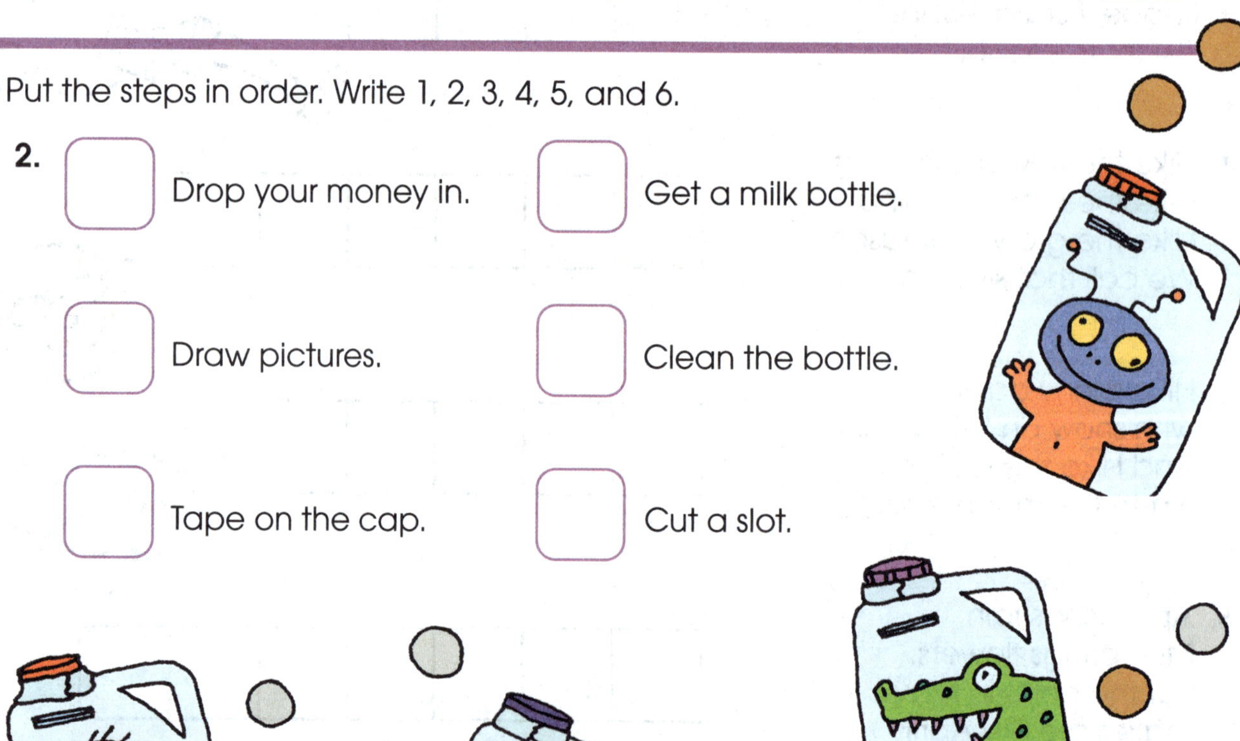

What Is a Sentence?

A **sentence** is a group of words that tells a complete thought. A sentence tells who or what is doing something and what happens.

kicks the ball

This is not a sentence. This group of words does not tell who is doing something.

Josie kicks the ball.

This is a sentence. It tells who is doing something and what she is doing.

▶ Write *yes* if the words make a sentence. Write *no* if the words do not make a sentence.

1. The game started on time. ________
2. The other team. ________
3. Then Ally made a goal. ________
4. I fell over the ball. ________
5. Cheered for their team. ________
6. Flew into the net. ________
7. Jason was our goalie. ________
8. The crowd in the stands. ________
9. Cheered after we won. ________
10. We will play again next week. ________

What Is a Subject?

The **subject** tells who or what the sentence is about. A **simple subject** tells about one person or thing. A **compound subject** tells about more than one person or thing.

Jorge plays the drums.

Jorge tells who this sentence is about. Jorge is a simple subject because it names only one person.

Drums and guitars are my favorite instruments.

Drums and guitars is a compound subject because it names more than one thing.

▶ Underline the subject in each sentence.
Circle *s* or *c* to show whether the subject is simple or compound.

1. Mr. Ramirez leads our school band. **s** **c**
2. The band plays at all the home games. **s** **c**
3. Cory and Rosa play the clarinet. **s** **c**
4. Jeannette teaches us how to march in step. **s** **c**
5. Leroy and his brother play the trumpet. **s** **c**
6. The bus takes us to games across town. **s** **c**
7. Our driver knows all our school songs. **s** **c**
8. Once Mia and I forgot our band uniforms. **s** **c**
9. Parents and students come to many games. **s** **c**
10. They like to hear the band play. **s** **c**

What Is a Predicate?

The **predicate** is the sentence part that tells what the subject does. The predicate always contains a verb.

The lion **hides** in the tall grass.

The words *hides in the tall grass* tell what the lion does. *Hides* is the verb.

A **simple predicate** tells about one thing the subject does. A **compound predicate** tells more than one thing the subject does.

The zebras **saw** the lion.

The words *saw the lion* are a simple predicate because they tell about one thing the subject did.

The lion **leaped** up and **chased** the zebras.

The words *leaped up and chased the zebras* are a compound predicate because they tell about two things the subject did.

▶ Underline the predicate in each sentence.
Circle *s* or *c* to show whether the predicate is simple or compound.

1. The sea turtle crawled out of the ocean. **s c**
2. She dug in the sand and laid her eggs. **s c**
3. Then she covered the eggs with sand. **s c**
4. The sun shone on the sand and warmed the eggs. **s c**
5. A snake dug up an egg and ate it. **s c**
6. People took some eggs for soup. **s c**
7. The rest of the eggs finally hatched. **s c**
8. The baby turtles climbed out of the sand. **s c**
9. They ran down the sand and swam into the sea. **s c**
10. Later they will come back and lay eggs. **s c**

What Is a Compound Sentence?

A **compound sentence** is two or more sentences joined by a comma and the word *and* or *but*.

The bus broke down. We were late for school.
The bus broke down, and we were late for school.

We were hungry. The cafeteria was closed.
We were hungry, but the cafeteria was closed.

▶ If a pair of sentences makes sense together, write a compound sentence using a comma and the word *and* or *but*. If the sentences do not make sense together, write *not a compound sentence*.

1. I like pizza. I hate mushrooms on it.

___

2. Greg dislikes pizza. He doesn't like hot dogs either.

___

3. We got pizza for the party. The weather was cold.

___

4. Dee makes her own pizza sauce. She buys crust.

___

5. Pizza has a lot of fat calories. It sure is good.

___

6. My mom doesn't eat pizza. Neither does my dad.

___

7. Pizza is a popular food. The grocery store closed.

___

Statements and Questions

A **statement** is a sentence that tells something.
A statement ends with a period. (**.**)

The rainstorm flooded our backyard**.**

A **question** is a sentence that asks something.
A question ends with a question mark. (**?**)

Did your yard flood, too**?**

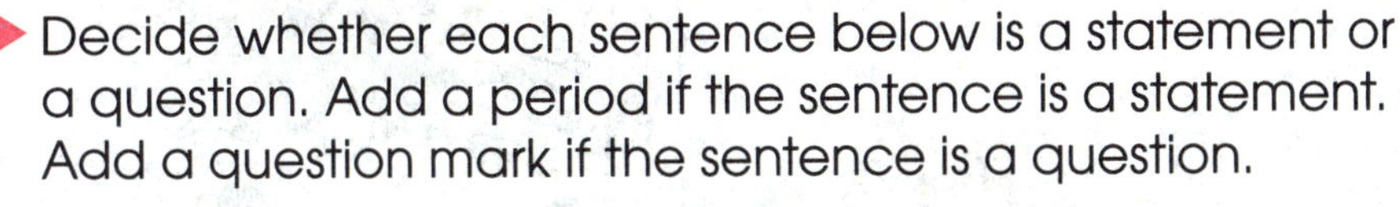

Decide whether each sentence below is a statement or a question. Add a period if the sentence is a statement. Add a question mark if the sentence is a question.

1. We heard thunder while we were eating ________
2. Mom ran to call our dog, Koko ________
3. Koko did not come ________
4. Where did Koko go ________
5. Was she hiding in the garage ________
6. Was she playing with the neighbor's dog ________
7. Suddenly we heard Koko's loud barking ________
8. My brother laughed and ran upstairs ________
9. Someone had shut Koko in a bedroom by mistake ________
10. Will she ever trust us again ________

Exclamations and Commands

An **exclamation** is a sentence that shows strong feeling. An exclamation ends with an exclamation point. (**!**)

What a terrific horror movie that was**!**

A **command** is a sentence that tells someone what to do. A command ends with a period. (**.**)

Come to the movie with me**.**

▶ Decide whether each sentence is an exclamation or a command. Write each sentence correctly.

1. don't give away the ending to the movie

____

2. yikes, it's an alien

____

3. wow, I was really scared

____

4. tell your friend what time the movie starts

____

5. pay for the popcorn at the food stand

____

6. oh, gross, there's gum on my shoe

____

7. cover your eyes at the scary parts

____

Context Clues

Sometimes the **context**, the words in a sentence or surrounding sentences, will help you understand a word you don't know.

The Milky Way galaxy is only one of many giant groups of stars.

If you don't know what *galaxy* means, you can figure out from the other words in the sentence that a galaxy is a giant group of stars.

▶ Circle the word or words that help you figure out the meaning of the underlined word or phrase. Then write the meaning.

1. I like looking at the constellations on a clear night. These star patterns have strange and interesting shapes.

____

2. They begin to show at dusk, just after sunset.

____

3. I really like the constellation of The Archer. I can almost see him shooting his bow and arrow.

____

4. Sometimes the stars seem to shimmer. It's as if they're on a switch that makes them brighter and dimmer.

____

5. The stars are an incredible distance away. It really is unbelievable how far from Earth they are.

____

6. Our solar system includes Earth, eight other planets, and the Sun.

____

Write a Book Report

When you write a book report, tell the important events, or **plot**, of the book. But don't give away the ending. Explain the most important idea. Write about the main **characters**, the people or animals in the book, and the **setting**, where and when the story takes place. Finally, give your opinion of the book or explain why someone might or might not like to read it.

▶ Read this book report about the book *Charlotte's Web* and answer the questions.

Charlotte's Web by E.B. White tells the story of a pig named Wilbur and how his life is changed by a spider named Charlotte.

The two animals live in a farmyard where they become friends. One day Wilbur hears that he will soon be killed for food. Charlotte says that she will save him and makes a clever plan. Learn whether her plan works in this book.

You'll never forget Wilbur and Charlotte. They show what true friends are like. There are other great characters, too, including a funny goose and a sneaky rat. This book is loaded with information about animals. Did you know that a spider can spin a complete web every day? Some parts of Charlotte's Web are sad, but I encourage everyone to read this wonderful book.

1. What is this book about?

____

2. Circle the paragraph that tells about the plot.

3. Write two things the book report writer likes about *Charlotte's Web*.

____

____

____

____

Plan Your Book Report

▶ Choose a book you would like to share with other people.
Plan your book report here.

Title: ______________________________

Author: ______________________________

Main Characters:

____

____

Setting: ____

Plot: What are the most important events?

____

____

____

____

Most important idea: What does the author want you to understand after you read this book?

____

____

____

Opinion: Your opinion is what you think or feel about the book. Are you glad you read the book or not? Would you suggest that other people read it?

____

____

____

Draft Your Book Report

▶ Reread the report on *Charlotte's Web* on page 22. Then reread your notes about the book you read. Now, write your report. Use uppercase letters for the important words in the title of your book. Use uppercase letters for the author's name and the names of characters or special places.

Be sure to

- use uppercase letters in the title and author's name
- tell about the plot and main idea
- tell whether you recommend the book

Title: ______________________

Author: ______________________

Revise Your Book Report

Proofreader's Marks

≡ Uppercase letter
⊙ Add period
ℓ Take out
^ Put in

▶ Read these examples. What is wrong? Use marks from the box to help you remember what to fix and how to fix it. Then write the examples correctly.

Title: James and the giant peach

____

Author: roald Dahl

____

▶ Cross out the sentences that do not give an opinion or reasons for an opinion. Use the ℓ.

I did not like this book. Most of the characters were silly. I did like the character Ally, because she was funny. I read another book by the same author once. The setting in this book was boring. Do all alien planets really look the same? The plot could have been more dramatic or scary. I had to stop reading because it was time for soccer practice.

▶ Revise your book report. Then check your book report.

Did you write the title using uppercase letters?	yes	no
Did you write the author's name correctly?	yes	no
Did you write about the characters?	yes	no
Did you write about the setting and the plot?	yes	no
Did you write your opinion of the book?	yes	no

Fix sentences that do not begin with uppercase letters and end with punctuation marks. Take out words or sentences that stray from the topic or do not make sense. Use the proofreader's marks to help you.

Publish Your Book Report

When you publish your writing, you share it with others. First make a final copy of your writing. Then choose one way to share it.

Choose a way to share your writing.

- Read your book report to your family.
- Give copies to friends to read.
- E-mail a copy.
- Work with friends to collect your reports into a book.

▶ Write the final copy of your book report here.

Title: ______________________________

Author: ______________________________

What Is a Noun?

A **noun** is a word that names a person, place, animal, or thing.

We are going to visit my **aunt**.	(person)
She lives in a **forest**.	(place)
She studies the **wolf**.	(animal)
She wrote a **book**.	(thing)

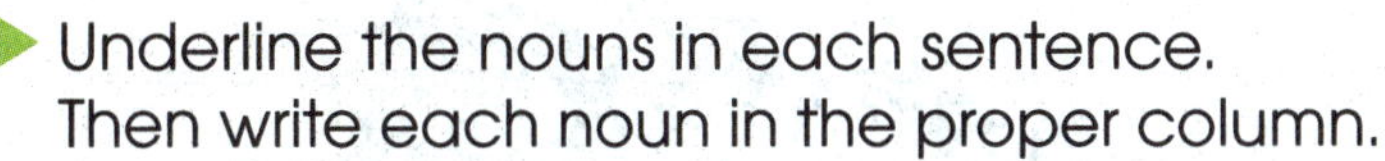

▶ Underline the nouns in each sentence.
Then write each noun in the proper column.

1. We went skiing out west.
2. I fell and broke my arm.
3. My brother took me to the hospital.
4. At the hospital, the doctor put on a cast.
5. I was glad to get home.
6. I played quietly with our dog.
7. My uncle asked if I wanted new skis.
8. I said I'd rather have a bike.

Person	Place	Animal	Thing

Singular and Plural Nouns

A **singular noun** names one person, place, animal, or thing. A **plural noun** names more than one person, place, animal, or thing. Many plural nouns are formed by adding s to the singular noun.

There is an apple **tree** outside my window.

There are lots of apple **trees** in the park.

▶ Write the plurals of the nouns under the blanks to complete each sentence.

1. I watched the ____________ (truck) unload at the store.
2. The ____________ (guy) carried in lots of ____________ (crate).
3. One was full of ____________ (banana).
4. The ____________ (clerk) put them out for the ____________ (customer).
5. Someone unloaded ____________ (apple) and ____________ (orange).
6. I kept waiting for the ____________ (lemon).
7. I love lemon ____________ (pie) and ____________ (cake).
8. Oh, I almost forgot to watch for ____________ (grape)!
9. I bought some fruit with my five ____________ (dollar).
10. I ate an apple and two ____________ (pear).

Plural Nouns with *es*

Some nouns have special endings. These are *s, ss, x, sh,* and *ch.*

The plurals for these nouns are formed by adding *es.*

dish ⟶ dish**es**

crash ⟶ crash**es**

Some nouns end in a consonant followed by *y.* To form the plurals for these nouns, change the *y* to *i* and add *es.*

cit**y** ⟶ cit**ies**

▶ Finish each sentence by writing the plurals of the nouns under the blanks.

1. Two ______________ (bus) took the four third-grade ______________ (class) to the park.

2. Mrs. Miller brought ______________ (box) of ______________ (lunch).

3. We took ______________ (dish) and ______________ (glass), too.

4. We sang and told ______________ (story) on the bus.

5. At the park I saw some ______________ (butterfly) on low ______________ (branch) and two ______________ (bunny) near a tree.

Proper Nouns

Proper nouns name particular people, places, animals, or things. Proper nouns begin with uppercase letters.

Name: Benito

Title: Mayor Ramsey

Place: Big Bend National Park

▶ Write each sentence correctly. Use uppercase letters to begin the proper nouns.

1. miss sampson asked about our summer vacations.

2. teddy and barb showed pictures of the everglades.

3. The tafts liked florida better than texas.

4. leroy saw wolves at yellowstone park.

5. eli and the cohens went canoeing in michigan.

6. roger's dad, doctor madison, helped a sick camper.

7. randy and maria loved the grand canyon.

8. The gurwitzes just escaped hurricane george.

Days, Months, and Holidays

Days, months, and holidays are proper nouns.

Monday

September

Passover

new year's day
april
monday
weekend
fourth of july
halloween
birthday
summer
thursday
thanksgiving

▶ Write a day, month, or holiday from the word box to match each description. Capitalize the proper nouns.

1. day after Wednesday ____________________

2. spooky holiday ____________________

3. season with no school ____________________

4. first weekday of school ____________________

5. holiday for starting over ____________________

6. day you were born ____________________

7. two days at end of week ____________________

8. holiday for the United States ____________________

9. fourth month of the year ____________________

10. holiday with pumpkin pie ____________________

Initials and Abbreviations

An **initial** is the first letter in the name of a person or place. Initials are uppercase letters and are followed by periods.

James Louis Potter ⟶ **J. L.** Potter ⟶ **J. L. P.**

An **abbreviation** is a shortened form of a word. Abbreviations begin with uppercase letters. They end with periods.

Doctor Jones ⟶ **Dr.** Jones Elm Street ⟶ Elm **St.**

▶ Write the underlined abbreviations or initials in each sentence correctly.

1. dr Roberts has an office on Dunham st

____

2. Tim Jones, jr, won the relay held at tl Wiley School.

____

3. mr Ramirez and ms Rosario both live on Harper ave

____

4. gp Bailey and Sons built the school on Belvoir blvd

____

5. gen Homer Watkins lives with mrs Watkins.

____

6. mr and mrs Bell live on Oak st near Bay ct

____

Possessive Nouns

A **possessive noun** shows ownership. Add an apostrophe (') and *s* to most singular nouns to make them possessive.

Jake**'s** backpack was lost in the flood.

Add an apostrophe after s in plural nouns to make them possessive.

The boy**s'** backpacks were lost in the flood.

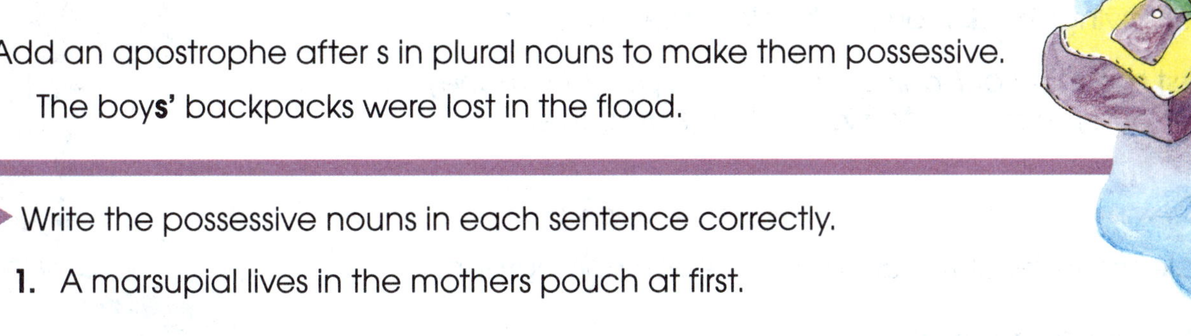

▶ Write the possessive nouns in each sentence correctly.

1. A marsupial lives in the mothers pouch at first.

 ____

2. Most other mammals mothers do not have a pouch.

 ____

3. The smallest marsupial is a rabbits size!

 ____

4. Kangaroos powerful hind legs help them move quickly.

 ____

5. These marsupials strong tails are used for balance.

 ____

6. A kangaroos fur is usually gray or red.

 ____

7. A kangaroo babys early life is warm and cozy.

 ____

8. The kangaroo is one of Australias best-known marsupials.

 ____

Homographs

Homographs are words that are spelled the same but have different meanings. Some homographs are also pronounced differently.

Our savings **bank** is on the **bank** of the Fox River.

The first meaning of *bank* is a place you put your money. The second meaning is the land alongside a river.

▶ Circle the letter of the definition of each homograph.

1. My friend Jack is at <u>bat</u>.
   a. small flying animal
   b. take a turn at trying to hit a ball

2. I hope he breaks his home run <u>record</u>.
   a. do something better than ever before
   b. put music on tape or CD

3. Is it a <u>fly</u> ball?
   a. insect with two wings
   b. baseball hit high in the air

4. No, it's out of the <u>park</u>!
   a. area of land
   b. leave a car in a garage or at the curb

▶ Write the meaning of the homographs.

5. Let's buy the top on the top shelf.

____

6. I long for thick, long hair.

____

7. Our dog leaves fall leaves all over the house.

____

8. Please watch my watch while I'm swimming.

____

Outlines

Writers use outlines to organize information for reports, articles, and other kinds of writing. The **title** of an outline gives the topic. The **main topics** are listed after Roman numerals and periods. The **subtopics**, or details about the main topics, follow uppercase letters and periods. Subtopics are indented.

Title: Two Ancient Reptiles

Main Topic: **I.** Alligator

Subtopics:
- **A.** Where it lives
- **B.** Characteristics
- **C.** Family life

Main Topic: **II.** Crocodile

Subtopics:
- **A.** Where it lives
- **B.** Characteristics
- **C.** Family life

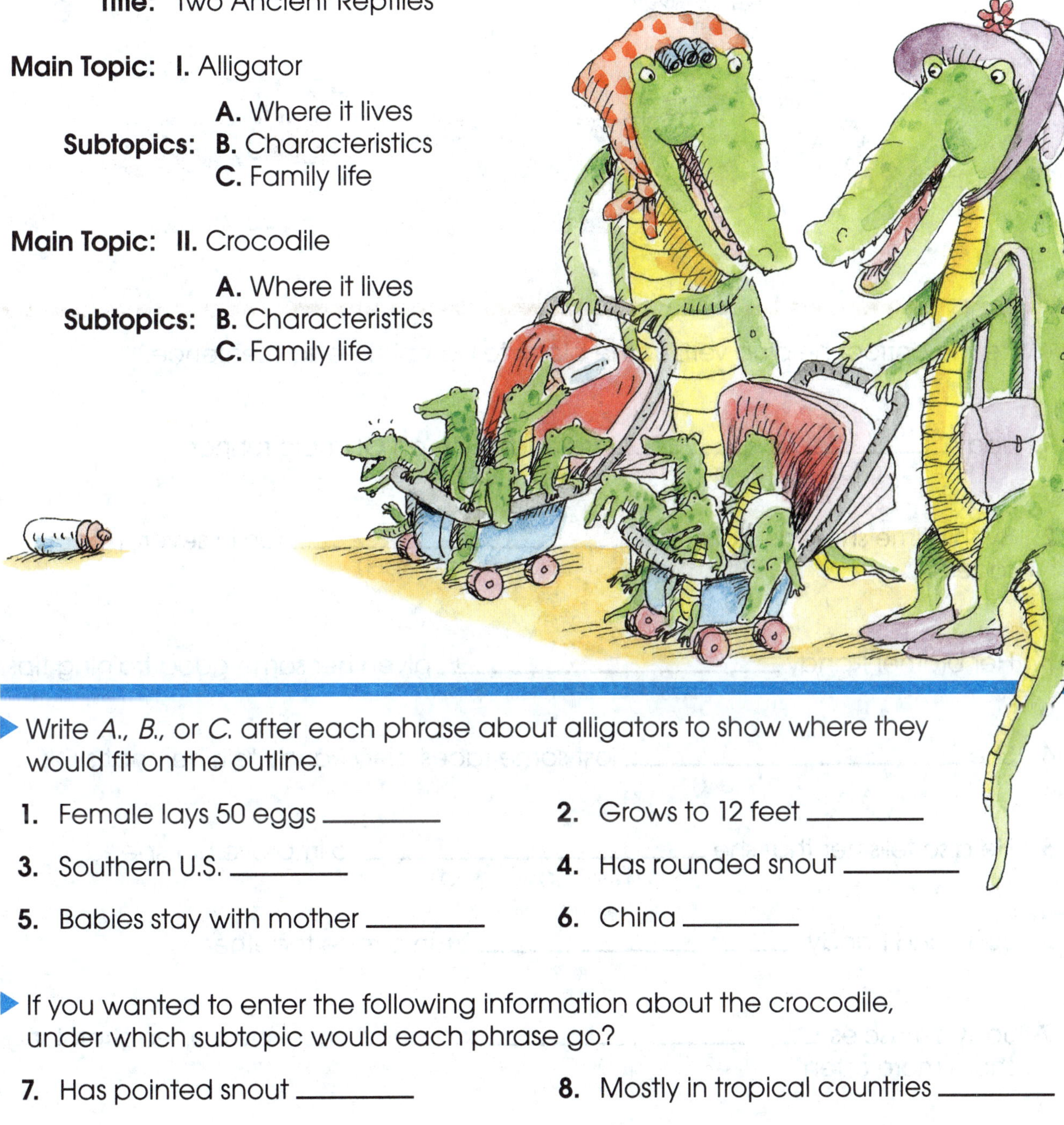

▶ Write *A.*, *B.*, or *C.* after each phrase about alligators to show where they would fit on the outline.

1. Female lays 50 eggs ________
2. Grows to 12 feet ________
3. Southern U.S. ________
4. Has rounded snout ________
5. Babies stay with mother ________
6. China ________

▶ If you wanted to enter the following information about the crocodile, under which subtopic would each phrase go?

7. Has pointed snout ________
8. Mostly in tropical countries ________
9. Grows to 21 feet ________
10. Babies hatch in 3½ months ________

Main and Helping Verbs

A **main verb** is the most important verb in the predicate. A **helping verb** works with the main verb. Some helping verbs are forms of the verb *have*.

Jody **has run** relays in track meets many times.

The helping verb *has* works with the main verb *run* to describe the action.

▶ Write the correct helping verb in the blank to complete each sentence.

1. Jody ______________ trained to be an Olympic runner.
(has, have, had)

2. By the time she was eight, she ______________ run in several local races.
(has, have, had)

3. Her brother Randy ______________ given her some good training tips.
(has, have, had)

4. She ______________ lost some races, and Randy tells her that's OK.
(has, have, had)

5. He also tells her that she ______________ to improve her speed.
(has, have, had)

6. Jody and Randy ______________ run a race together.
(has, have, had)

7. Jody's muscles ______________ loosened since she started stretching them more often.
(has, have, had)

8. We all ______________ watched Jody run in races.
(has, have, had)

Present and Past Tense

The tense of a verb tells when the action of a verb takes place. The **present tense** tells what is happening now or what happens regularly.

Our dog chews through a boot in two minutes.

The neighbor's dogs chew boots, too.

The **past tense** tells what already happened. Many verbs form their past tense by adding *ed*.

Clancy chewed my brother's notebook last night.

▶ Write *present* or *past* to describe the tense of the underlined verb in each sentence.

1. I <u>wash</u> my dog, Clancy, about once a month. ________________
2. He usually <u>likes</u> his bath. ________________
3. Sometimes he <u>barks</u> when he doesn't want a bath. ________________
4. Last week he <u>dashed</u> away from me before I could catch him. ________________
5. But I <u>dished</u> up some food to try to bring him back. ________________
6. He always <u>trots</u> back home when he smells his food. ________________
7. After I put the food down, I <u>waited</u> to grab him. ________________
8. After his bath, I <u>combed</u> him dry. ________________

The Verb *Be*

The verb *be* tells what something is or was. *Be* joins the subject to the predicate. Below are the present and past tenses of *be*.

Present: I **am** happy on the ice.
My sister **is** in the warming hut.
Her friends **are** roasting marshmallows.

Past: Last year, I **was** scared of falling.
Ice and snow **were** new to me.

▶ Write *present* or *past* after each sentence.

1. My skates are really perfect. ______________
2. They were a present from Aunt Tilda. ______________
3. I was sure I would like living where it snows. ______________
4. My brother and sister were not as certain. ______________
5. I am excited when I see dark clouds. ______________
6. That means snow is about to fall. ______________
7. The ice is frozen most of the winter. ______________
8. I am ready to skate after school any day. ______________
9. But homework and chores are ready for me. ______________
10. Oh well, my skates are ready when I am. ______________

Future Tense

The **future tense** of a verb tells what will happen tomorrow, next month, or any time to come. The future tense adds the helping verb *will* to the main verb.

Present: I **watch** the stars on a clear night.
Past: Last night I **watched** the Big Dipper.
Future: Tomorrow I **will watch** the full moon.

▶ Rewrite each sentence using the future tense of the underlined verb.

1. Our class <u>started</u> a school garden.

   ____

2. We <u>spend</u> time in our garden each week.

   ____

3. We think the flowers <u>make</u> the schoolyard pretty.

   ____

4. We also <u>grow</u> vegetables in the garden.

   ____

5. We <u>give</u> some vegetables to feed hungry people.

   ____

6. Suni <u>plants</u> beans.

   ____

7. I <u>pick</u> peas, and Grant <u>digs</u> carrots.

   ____

8. We all <u>weed</u> the garden regularly.

   ____

Irregular Verbs

Irregular verbs do not end with *ed* to show the past tense. Here are some irregular verbs.

Present	Past	Present	Past
come	came	go	went
do	did	run	ran
eat	ate	see	saw

▶ Complete each sentence by writing the correct tense.

1. We ____________________ to the neighborhood street fair on Sunday.
   (*go*, past)

2. Lots of people from around the city ____________________ to the fair each year.
   (*come*, present)

3. There is always lots to ____________________ and ____________________ .
   (*see*, present) (*do*, present)

4. Last year we ____________________ a relay to help raise money for a child care center.
   (*run*, past)

5. Then we ____________________ corn dogs until our parents
   (*eat*, past)
   ____________________ to get us.
   (*come*, past)

6. Often we ____________________ early to see the magic show.
   (*go*, present)

7. Once we ____________________ just in time to see the magician disappear.
   (*come*, past)

8. On Sunday we ____________________ too much and
   (*eat*, past)
   ____________________ too much and got very tired.
   (*do*, past)

9. Usually, when we get home, we don't ____________________ for days.
   (*eat*, present)

10. Our parents, who ____________________ with us one year, slept until ten the next day.
    (*come*, past)

Write a Persuasive Paragraph

When you write to persuade, you try to convince your readers to believe what you believe or to take action about something. Newspaper editorials and letters to the editor are examples of persuasive writing.

In a persuasive paragraph, you first write a **topic sentence** that explains what your paragraph is about. Then you write some **reasons** you hold your opinion. Finally, you may **restate** your feelings and ask readers to agree with you or to do something.

▶ Read this persuasive paragraph and answer the questions.

Building a new office building at the corner of Elm St. and Superior St. would be a terrible mistake! This office building and its parking lot would ruin the park that's between Superior and Terrace. There are many beautiful old trees that would be cut down. These trees and green space are homes for birds and animals. The park is a place for walking, running, playing ball, and learning about nature. Last week our class studied water life in the creek in the park. There are other places to put office buildings, but there are very few park areas left. Please come to the City Council meeting next week and speak up to save the park!

1. About what does the writer have a strong opinion?

____

2. What does the writer think the office building will do?

____

3. Why does the writer think the park should be saved?

____

____

4. What does the writer want readers to do?

____

Plan Your Persuasive Paragraph

Think of something about which you have strong feelings or a strong opinion. Perhaps you want the school lunchroom to have more healthful meals. Maybe you love animals and want to tell people to take better care of their pets. Or perhaps you like someone who is running for office and want to tell readers why.

▶ Plan your persuasive paragraph here.

Topic: ______________________________

Opinions and feelings about the topic:

____

____

____

Reasons and/or facts to back up your opinion:

____

____

____

What should readers do or believe?

____

____

____

Draft Your Persuasive Paragraph

Reread the paragraph about the park on page 41. Notice that the writer uses words that signal opinions, such as "I think" and "I believe." The writer states her opinion clearly. She doesn't want to see an office building go up, and she gives several reasons why.

Be sure to

- use uppercase letters to begin sentences and the names of people and places
- write complete sentences
- give your opinion and back it up
- suggest what readers can do if they share your opinion

▶ Write a draft of your persuasive paragraph.

Revise Your Persuasive Paragraph

▶ Read these examples. What is missing? Use marks from the box to show corrections. Then write the examples correctly.

Proofreader's Marks

≡ Uppercase letter
⊙ Add period
ﻭ Take out
^ Put in

I believe jan parker should be elected student council president. She listens to everybody and has good leadership qualities. Who could do a better job

___

___

___

▶ Look at these sentences. Take out the sentences that do not state an opinion or give reasons for an opinion. Use the ﻭ.

I think Adele Smith deserves the Athlete of the Year award. She runs and swims. She plays soccer and basketball. She lives on our street. She keeps her grades up, too. I feel she is the best athlete this school has ever had. Please vote for her! The next soccer game is Friday.

▶ Revise your persuasive paragraph. Then check your paragraph.

Did you use uppercase letters to begin sentences?	yes	no
Did you use uppercase letters for proper names?	yes	no
Did you state your opinion clearly?	yes	no
Did you use phrases such as "I believe"?	yes	no
Did you give reasons for your opinion?	yes	no
Did you ask readers to take some action?	yes	no

Fix sentences that do not begin with uppercase letters and end with end marks. Take out words or sentences that do not add to the meaning. Use proofreader's marks to help you.

Publish Your Persuasive Paragraph

When you publish your writing, share it with others. First make a final copy of your writing. Then choose one way to share it.

▶ Write the final copy of your persuasive paragraph here.

Choose a way to share your writing.

- If your opinion is about something at school, send your paragraph in letter form to the editor of the school newspaper.
- If your opinion is about something in the community, send it to the editor of the community newspaper.
- If your opinion is about something important to your classmates, read it to them and ask for other examples of persuasive writing on the same subject.

What Is a Pronoun?

A **pronoun** is a word that takes the place of a noun.

Jamie knows all about snakes. **He** knows all about snakes.

He takes the place of *Jamie*.

Singular pronouns: *I, me, you, he, she, him, her, it*
Plural pronouns: *we, us, they, them, you*

▶ Underline the pronouns.

The class is studying animals. We saw a movie about snakes today. I don't know why people are frightened of snakes. They are fascinating animals. You could not race the fastest snakes and win, since they can move up to twelve miles per hour. We saw a big python in the movie that was as big around as a person's leg. Tania said it was really gross. But then we saw a close-up of the snake's scales. Tania said the colors and patterns were pretty. Now she thinks snakes are neat. It seems to me that snakes probably think we are the scary ones.

▶ Write two or three sentences about snakes. Include some pronouns.

___

___

___

___

___

___

___

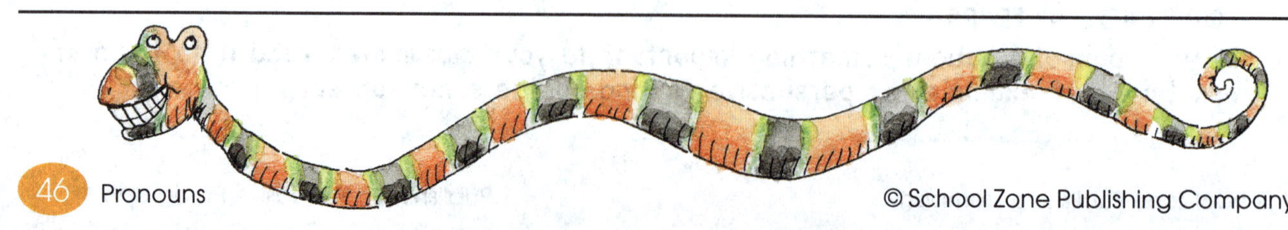

Subject Pronouns

A **subject pronoun** takes the place of a noun or nouns in the subject of a sentence.

The oldest son plays the trumpet. **He** plays it very loud.

He takes the place of *the oldest son*.

Some subject pronouns: *he, she, it, you, we, they*

▶ Write a pronoun in each blank to replace the underlined word or words.

Ramon was excited because Ramon ________________ was going to play in the band at a football game for the first time. He polished his trumpet until the trumpet ________________ gleamed. Then he blew a few notes to see how the notes ________________ sounded. Ramon's friend Rosa came to practice with him. Rosa ________________ plays the clarinet. The two players practiced the school fight song. They did not like the way the school fight song ________________ sounded. So they practiced over and over. Finally Rosa and Ramon ________________ were satisfied.

Rosa said Rosa ________________ would meet Ramon at the band bus. Ramon said Ramon ________________ would be there. The two kids hoped their parents would come to the game. Their parents ________________ particularly like to hear the trumpet and clarinet.

Object Pronouns

An **object pronoun** takes the place of a noun or nouns in the predicate of a sentence.

Some object pronouns: *me, you, him, her, it, us, them*

Max watched **the shark video**. Max enjoyed **it**.

It takes the place of *the shark video*.

▶ Write an object pronoun to complete each rhyme.

1. This belongs to Joe and Clem.

   Yes, I'll give the book to ________________ .

2. Look, did Marcy get a hit?

   Wow, she really blasted ________________ !

3. The spotted dog ran up to Jim.

   Every day it waits for ________________ .

4. I brought some cookies and some tea.

   So come and have a snack with ________________ .

5. Your shoes are pretty. Are they new?

   They look so very fine on ________________ .

6. Lashanda sleeps and doesn't stir.

   We'll try not to awaken ________________ .

7. Leroy's jacket doesn't fit.

   Perhaps now he'll get rid of ________________ .

I and *Me*

I is a subject pronoun that takes the place of your name. *Me* is an object pronoun that takes the place of your name. When you write about another person and yourself, always name yourself last.

Mom and I picked out our new computer.
Mom taught **me** to use the computer.

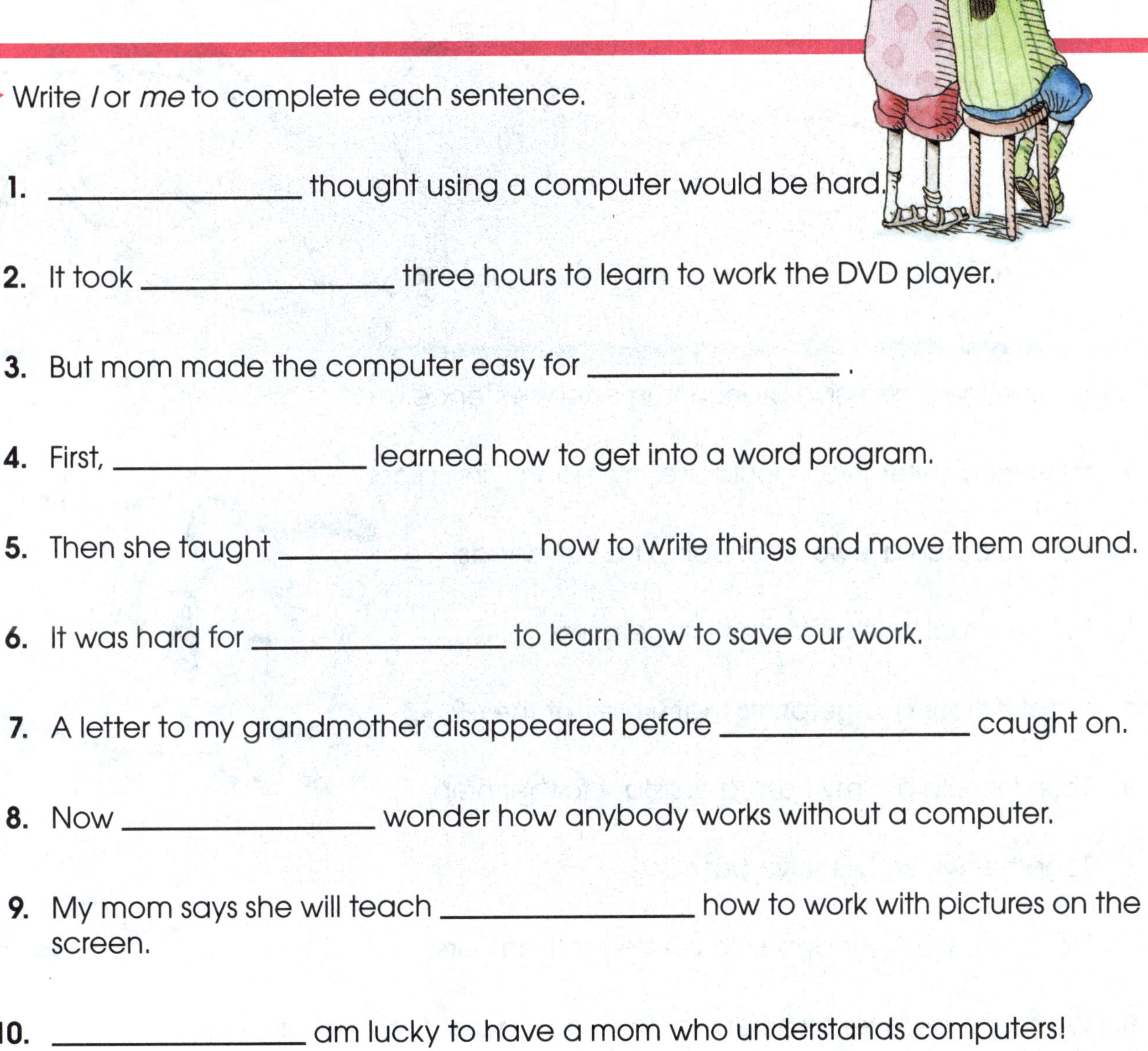

▶ Write *I* or *me* to complete each sentence.

1. ________________ thought using a computer would be hard.

2. It took ________________ three hours to learn to work the DVD player.

3. But mom made the computer easy for ________________ .

4. First, ________________ learned how to get into a word program.

5. Then she taught ________________ how to write things and move them around.

6. It was hard for ________________ to learn how to save our work.

7. A letter to my grandmother disappeared before ________________ caught on.

8. Now ________________ wonder how anybody works without a computer.

9. My mom says she will teach ________________ how to work with pictures on the screen.

10. ________________ am lucky to have a mom who understands computers!

Possessive Pronouns

A **possessive pronoun** shows ownership. Some possessive pronouns take the place of nouns. These are *my, your, his, her, its, our, your,* and *their.*

These are **my** skates. Those are **your** boots.

Other possessive pronouns can stand alone. These are *mine, yours, his, hers, ours, yours,* and *theirs.*

These are my skates. These skates are **mine**.
That is your magic marker. That magic marker is **yours**.

▶ Underline the possessive pronouns in each sentence.

1. If I were a detective, I could use my magnifying glass.
2. I could catch a jewel thief doing his evil deeds.
3. I would track thieves by their fingerprints.
4. What if I found fingerprints that were not theirs?
5. Then I would ask my trusted assistant for her help.
6. Together we would solve our case.
7. No detective agency would be better than ours!
8. We might discover a secret plot to kidnap a general and his family.
9. Of course, not all the glory would be mine.
10. Some would be hers.

Direct Quotes

A direct quote shows the exact words someone says. Quotation marks (" ") come before and after the speaker's words. A comma, question mark, or exclamation point comes after the speaker's exact words and before the rest of the sentence.

"We're going through an asteroid path," said the captain.
"There's one now," cried the first officer. "Look out!"

▶ Add quotation marks to the sentences.

1. Go to warp speed! shouted the captain.
2. I can't, answered the first officer. Our warp engines are down.
3. Does anybody have any ideas? asked the captain.
4. The engineer replied, We could reverse the engines to push the ship backward.
5. Try it! ordered the captain. We have to try everything!
6. It's working! yelled the first officer.
7. We're going backward, but the asteroid is still too close, she added.
8. Suddenly the engineer cried, The warp engines are back up. Let's get out of here!
9. Please steer clear of asteroids for a while, sighed the captain. That's an order.
10. Is anybody hungry? asked the cook. It's time for lunch.

Using Quotation Marks for Titles

Use quotation marks when you write the titles of stories, poems, songs, or articles.

I love One Direction's "What Makes You Beautiful."
My young sister likes "Hakuna Matata" from *The Lion King*.

▶ Place quotation marks correctly in each sentence.

1. Did you read the editorial Why Vote? in today's paper?
2. Yes, and I liked the letter to the editor entitled The Responsibilities of a Citizen.
3. I think Candle in the Wind is a very sad song.
4. But the article The Death of a Princess was much sadder.
5. I've always loved Rocky Mountain High by John Denver.
6. I prefer Take Me Home, Country Roads myself.
7. The poem Steam Shovel compares the machine to a dinosaur.
8. Yes, and the poem Garden Hose compares the hose to a snake.
9. There's a piece in the paper today called Save the Park.
10. That's because last week someone wrote Build the Mall.
11. Is The Telltale Heart one of Edgar Allen Poe's short stories?
12. Yes, but Jack London wrote To Build a Fire.

▶ Write a note to a friend telling about your current favorite songs or a good story you have read recently.

____

____

____

What Is an Adjective?

An **adjective** is a word that describes a noun.

Luke is reading about **ancient** animals.
These **fascinating** creatures are now **extinct**.

▶ Circle the adjectives that describe the underlined nouns.

1. The word dinosaur means "terrible lizard."
2. Dinosaurs were probably the biggest animals that ever lived on land.
3. These huge dinosaurs were excellent walkers.
4. Their thundering footsteps could probably be heard over a large area.
5. The smaller animals could run fast.
6. One kind of adult dinosaur was the size of a chicken!
7. Young dinosaurs stayed in muddy nests.
8. Dinosaurs had sharp eyesight and keen hearing.

9. Some dinosaurs ate huge, leafy ferns.
10. Both meat eaters and plant eaters lived when Earth had a warmer climate.
11. Scientists do not know if dinosaurs were gray or green.
12. Perhaps a cooler climate caused dinosaurs to die out.
13. Maybe a plunging asteroid helped them along.
14. Some scientists believe that yesterday's dinosaur is related to today's bird.
15. New facts about these amazing animals appear regularly.

▶ Write a sentence about dinosaurs that includes one or more adjectives.

____

Adjectives That Tell How Many and What Kind

Some adjectives tell how many or what kind.

We won **three** tickets to a **magic** show.

The word *three* tells how many. *Magic* tells what kind.

▶ Circle the adjectives that describe the underlined nouns.

1. The tall magician was dressed in a white coat.
2. First, he raised his long, black wand.
3. Then he made several red scarves appear from his sleeve!
4. Next he spoke a few magic words and the scarves disappeared!
5. Would he do the famous trick with the two locked cabinets?
6. No, instead he wrapped many heavy chains around him.
7. Then his two assistants dropped him into a huge water tank!
8. Of course he got loose in one minute.
9. Then he took a grand bow.

▶ Write adjectives that tell how many or what kind to complete each sentence.

10. I saw ________________ squirrels and ________________ robins in the park last week.
11. The squirrels were eating and burying ________________ nuts.
12. A ________________ dog ran after the squirrels.
13. They scurried into the ________________ trees and chattered.
14. Suddenly, ________________ gulls soared over the ________________ lake.
15. I had ________________ hours of ________________ homework to do, so I headed home.

Articles

A, *an*, and *the* are called **articles**.

A and *an* refer to any person, place, animal, or thing.

A is used before nouns that begin with consonant sounds.

Let's have **a** party!

An is used before nouns that begin with vowel sounds.

That's **an** awesome idea!

The refers to a specific person, place, animal, or thing.

The party will be at my house. You bring **the** games.

▶ Write the correct article in each sentence.

1. I've never planned __________ (a, an) party before.

2. I have __________ (a, an) idea that I think __________ (the, an) guests will like.

3. We'll have __________ (the, an) party at __________ (a, an) roller rink.

4. Everyone will get __________ (a, an) invitation soon.

5. Should we have __________ (the, a) regular cake or __________ (a, an) ice-cream cake?

6. Or should we just order __________ (a, an) huge pizza with everything?

7. Let's all chip in for __________ (the, an) gift for Joe.

8. I know he'd like __________ (a, an) astronomy T-shirt with Earth and all __________ (the, a) planets on it.

Adjectives That Compare

Adjectives that end with *er* compare two people, places, animals, or things. Some adjectives add the word *more* to compare two.

Padre Island is **bigger** than many other national seashores.
To me, Isle Royale is **more thrilling** than Padre Island.

Adjectives that end with *est* compare more than two people, places, animals, or things. Some adjectives add the word *most* to compare more than two.

Carlsbad Caverns is our **darkest** national park.
It has the **most interesting** underground caves.

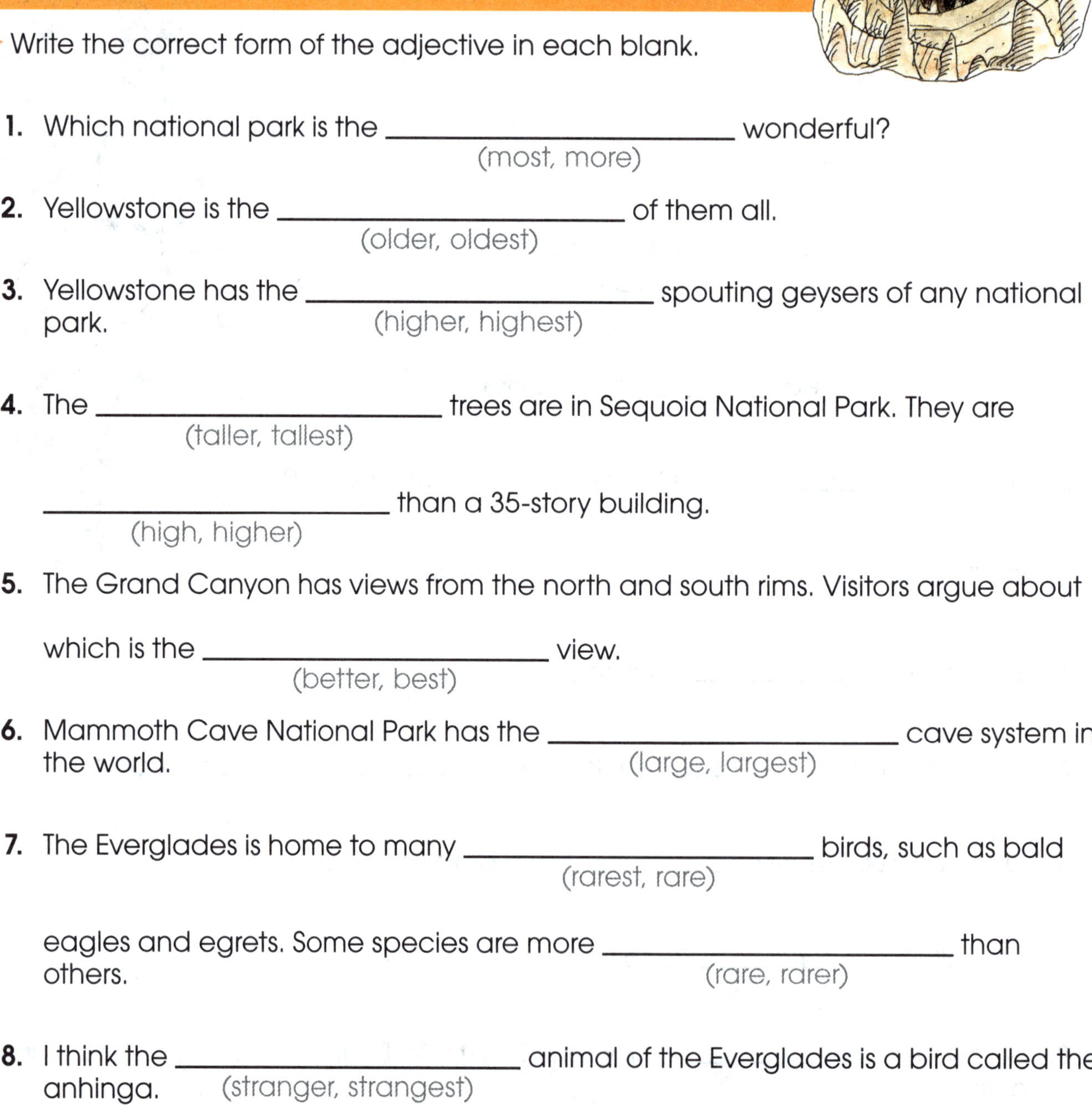

▶ Write the correct form of the adjective in each blank.

1. Which national park is the ______________________ wonderful?
   (most, more)

2. Yellowstone is the ______________________ of them all.
   (older, oldest)

3. Yellowstone has the ______________________ spouting geysers of any national park.
   (higher, highest)

4. The ______________________ trees are in Sequoia National Park. They are
   (taller, tallest)

   ______________________ than a 35-story building.
   (high, higher)

5. The Grand Canyon has views from the north and south rims. Visitors argue about

   which is the ______________________ view.
   (better, best)

6. Mammoth Cave National Park has the ______________________ cave system in the world.
   (large, largest)

7. The Everglades is home to many ______________________ birds, such as bald
   (rarest, rare)

   eagles and egrets. Some species are more ______________________ than others.
   (rare, rarer)

8. I think the ______________________ animal of the Everglades is a bird called the anhinga.
   (stranger, strangest)

Write a Story

Characters are the people or animals in a story. Most stories have a **setting**, where and when the story takes place. A story has a **plot**, what happens in the story.

The beginning of a story introduces the main character or characters and describes a problem they have. The beginning usually describes the setting. The middle of the story tells what the characters do to solve the problem. The end of the story tells how the characters do (or do not) solve the problem.

▶ Read this short story and answer the questions.

Shelter in a Storm

I didn't expect to be a hero that weekend last year. It just happened. When the sudden snowstorm blew out of the mountains, we knew our plans for camping were lost.

"Whew, I can hardly see," gasped Jerry, as we struggled up the mountain. "Where did you say that cabin was, Andy?"

"I don't remember exactly," I yelled, my heart beating fast. "I was only there once."

"We have to keep going," shouted Ashley over the howling wind.

We plodded on, our legs and feet growing heavier and heavier. I tried to keep a picture of the cabin in my mind. My family hiked there on a clear day. Today we couldn't see more than a few inches in front of us.

"Andy, do you see anything familiar?" asked Ashley, shivering. "I don't think I can go on much longer."

"There," I shouted. "Come on guys, only a few more yards." We fell through the cabin door and hurried to light a fire. Then we took off our cold outer clothing and wrapped ourselves in blankets. The cabin was stocked with dry food, so we wouldn't starve. We would just wait out the storm.

1. Who are the characters?

____

2. What is the setting?

____

3. What is the plot?

____

Plan Your Story

What should your story be about? What have you done lately that could be part of a story? Have you read any articles or books that gave you story ideas?

▶ Write some ideas below.

Story Ideas:

___

___

___

▶ Choose one of your ideas. Now plan your story.

Setting: ___

___

Main Character(s): ___

___

___

___

Plot: What happens to the characters in the story? What are the main events? How does one event cause another one?

___

___

___

Draft Your Story

Reread the short story on page 57. Then reread your notes about the story you are writing.

Remember to

- introduce the characters
- describe the setting
- include a plot with a beginning, middle, and end
- put quotation marks around characters' exact words

▶ Write your first draft.

Title: ______________________________

Author: ______________________________

Revise Your Story

▶ Read this example. Use the proofreader's marks from the box to make corrections.

"Throw it over here! yelled Marcia.

No, throw it here!" shouted tony. the two children

were playing football with their father.

Suddenly mr. Vento tripped and fell. Ouch, he

hollered. I think I broke my leg!

Proofreader's Marks

≡ Uppercase letter

⊙ Add period

[Indent

^ Put in

▶ Revise your story.

Did you create a setting for your story?	yes	no
Did you introduce the characters and tell something about them?	yes	no
Does your story have a beginning, middle, and end?	yes	no

Add parts to your story that you forgot. Make other changes so that your story is just the way you want it.

▶ Proofread your story.

Did you use uppercase letters to begin sentences and characters' names?	yes	no
Did you use quotation marks around the exact words characters said?	yes	no

Use proofreader's marks to make corrections.

Publish Your Story

Choose a way to share your writing.

- Read your story to some friends or relatives.
- Give a copy of your story to someone.
- E-mail a copy to a relative or friend in another town or state.
- Combine efforts with some friends to produce a collection of your short stories.

▶ Write the final copy of your story. Use a second sheet of paper if you need to.

Title: ______________________________

Author: ______________________________

____

____

____

____

____

____

____

____

____

____

____

What Is an Adverb?

An **adverb** is a word that tells about, or **describes**, a verb. Adverbs can tell when, where, or how.

The cat will leap **soon**.	when
She will leap **down** on the dog.	where
The cat **carefully** plans her leaps.	how

▶ Underline the adverb in each sentence. On each blank, tell whether the adverb tells when, where, or how.

1. Our dog, Muffin, was snoring noisily. ____________
2. The cat, Rami, eyed him cautiously. ____________
3. Rami sometimes misjudged her leaps. ____________
4. She might jump over Muffin. ____________
5. Then he would wake suddenly and yawn. ____________
6. If she leaped too close, he would bite her. ____________
7. He bit playfully, so she wasn't afraid. ____________
8. Still, Rami preferred to land near Muffin. ____________
9. Then she would yowl loudly and wake him up. ____________
10. Finally, they would chase madly after each other. ____________

▶ Write several sentences about something you and your family like to do together. Use adverbs that tell how, when, and where.

____

____

____

____

Adverbs That Tell How

Many adverbs tell *how* an action takes place. These adverbs usually end with *ly*. If a word ends in *y*, change the *y* to *i* and add *ly*.

The spy crept **secretly** into the fort.
Does anyone do homework **happily**?

▶ In each blank, write the adverb form of the word in parentheses.

1. I will die (immediate) ______________________ if I climb that hill.
2. No, I think you just get tired (quick) ______________________.
3. Well, I was (complete) ______________________ bushed after the hike.
4. Let's leave (prompt) ______________________ at 7:30 a.m. tomorrow.
5. We'll have to leave (quiet) ______________________ or we'll wake Mom.
6. She would be (extreme) ______________________ mad if we did that.
7. I can (easy) ______________________ leave the house by jumping out my window!
8. No, you'd be walking (painful) ______________________ all day.

▶ Make adverbs from these adjectives

9. icy ______________________	10. cool ______________________
11. impatient ______________________	12. slow ______________________
13. unhappy ______________________	14. safe ______________________

Good and *Well*

Good is an adjective that tells what kind. When used after an action verb, *well* is an adverb that tells how. *Well* is an adjective when it is used after a linking verb such as *is*, *feels*, or *seems*.

Alien is a **good** movie. It has a **good** cast. (adjective)
The special effects are done **well**. (adverb)
But I didn't feel very **well** after I saw it. (adjective)

Write *adjective* or *adverb* to identify each underlined word.

1. The new student is a good soccer player. ____________
2. Yes, she played well in the tryouts. ____________
3. We need a good goalie. ____________
4. Yes, Angie is good but she has been ill. ____________
5. I hope she will be well soon. ____________
6. She didn't feel very well yesterday when I talked to her. ____________
7. She said she was watching a good video. ____________
8. But she definitely did not think her medicine was good! ____________
9. How well do you think the team will do tonight? ____________
10. We will all play as well as we can. ____________
11. But will that be good enough? ____________
12. I hope so, or I won't feel very well! ____________

Adverbs That Tell Where

Some adverbs tell where or in what direction.

Where did the cat go? She ran over **there**.

▶ Underline the adverb in each sentence.

1. My dog, Frodo, hates to come inside on a nice day.
2. He runs down to the lake to hide.
3. I have looked everywhere for Frodo.
4. Once he stayed behind me so I would not see him.
5. Most days he runs far ahead of me.
6. I don't think he would ever run away.
7. But I worry about Frodo getting lost outside.
8. That's why I try to stay close to him.
9. Oh, there he goes up to the house.
10. If he wants to go inside, he must be hungry!

▶ Write several sentences of your own. Include some of the adverbs you underlined in the sentences above.

____

____

____

____

____

Adverbs That Tell When

Some adverbs tell when.

We went to the rock concert **yesterday**.
The group will also be performing **today**.

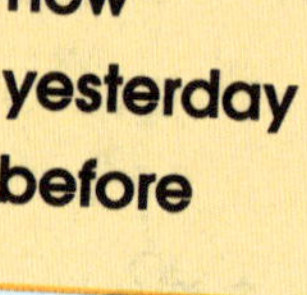

▶ Use an adverb from the box to complete each rhyme.

1. Will we ever see the full moon?

   In the east, it will rise ______________________ .

2. Have you seen an alligator?

   Stick around, we'll see one ______________________ .

3. Do you see my uncle's cow?

   There it is, I see it ______________________ .

4. Have you heard from Dan and Jay?

   Yes, we saw them ______________________ .

5. I want to call my puppy Freddy.

   Look, he knows his name ______________________ .

6. Here's some cake, if you want more.

   Thanks, I'll drink some milk ______________________ .

Adverbs That Compare

Adverbs that compare two actions end with *er.* Adverbs that compare three or more actions end with *est.*

The game started **late** last night.
The game last week started even **later**.
The homecoming game started **latest** of all.

▶ Write the correct form of the adverb in parentheses to complete each group of sentences.

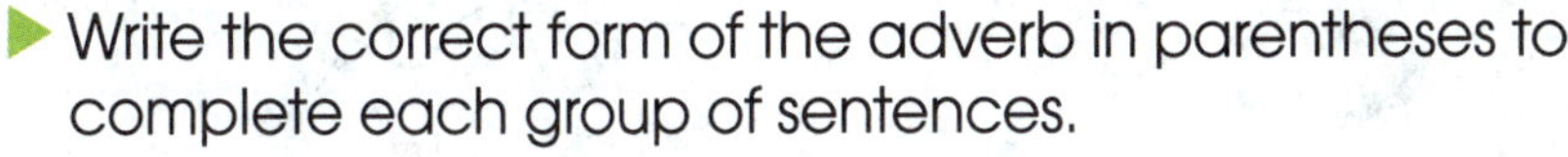

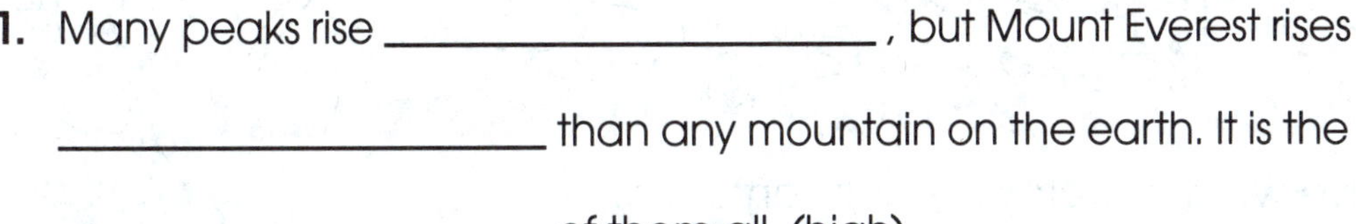

1. Many peaks rise ______________________, but Mount Everest rises ______________________ than any mountain on the earth. It is the ______________________ of them all. (high)

2. My dog runs ______________________ than yours. You may think yours runs ______________________, but mine runs the ______________________ of any dog on our street. (fast)

3. Abdul plays ______________________ than any member of our team. I thought I played the ______________________ of anyone, but Abdul shows me that I only play ______________________. (hard)

4. I grew ______________________ over the summer, but many of my friends grew even ______________________. Sandy grew the ______________________ of all of us. (tall)

5. The Halloween party will start ______________________. Last year it started the ______________________ of any year. If we get ready early, this year's party will start ______________________ than last year. (soon)

Negative Words

No and *not* are negative words. *No* is often an adjective.

I have **no** luck shopping for clothes.

Not is an adverb.

I do **not** mind going to stores.

Some other negative words are *none, never, nothing, no one,* and *nobody.*

▶ Write the negative word or words in each sentence.

1. Nothing I see comes in the right color. ____________________
2. Sometimes I do not like the fabric. ____________________
3. Often none of the things I like are in my size. ____________________
4. Last week, nobody would wait on me. ____________________
5. No one else seems to have problems shopping. ____________________
6. Liu never comes home from shopping empty-handed. ____________________
7. There is nowhere she likes more than Bonn's. ____________________
8. None of my friends will shop for clothes with me. ____________________
9. Too bad there are no shopping classes! ____________________
10. But I guess that's not the solution. ____________________

Adverbs or Adjectives?

An adverb tells about a verb. An adjective tells about a noun or pronoun.

The **tiny** puppy barked **constantly**.

The word *tiny* is an adjective that tells about the noun *puppy*. The word *constantly* tells when or how about the verb *barked*.

▶ Circle the adjectives and underline the adverbs in each sentence.

1. The ideas for many common inventions may have come from animals.
2. The turtle has solid, armor plates for protection. Humans use tanks that move slowly and carry soldiers safely.
3. The rattlesnake shakes its loud rattle if an enemy walks nearby. People can protect their homes with noisy alarms to warn of burglars.
4. Birds carefully avoid the bright red ladybug, which contains poison. Red signals warn traffic to stop regularly.
5. Insects and birds fly easily by rapidly beating their wings. Air moves over a wing on an airplane and causes the wing to move upward.
6. Beavers have large, sharp teeth for cutting down trees. People use chisels to shape wood carefully.
7. Bats make high sounds that bounce against small insects. These echoes help bats locate food instantly. People use sonar, a sound system for locating objects underwater.
8. Ducks have soft, downy feathers which trap layers of warm air. Their young can sleep comfortably. People make special material in the same way for campers to wear outside.

Contractions

A **contraction** is a short way to write two words. The words are joined and a letter or letters are left out. An apostrophe (') takes the place of the left-out letter or letters.

I **do not** know his name. I **don't** know his name.

Some common contractions with *not* are **aren't** (are not), **can't** (can not), **isn't** (is not), **doesn't** (does not), **don't** (do not), **shouldn't** (should not), **haven't** (have not), **hasn't** (has not), and **couldn't** (could not). The contraction **won't** is short for *will not*.

She **will not** be home. She **won't** be home.

Write the contraction for the underlined words in each sentence.

1. Does not ________________ it seem that life is full of rules?
2. The traffic signs say do not ________________ walk.
3. And we should not ________________ dive into the deep end.
4. It is not ________________ proper to talk with your mouth full.
5. In the woods, we can not ________________ leave the path.
6. During the test, we could not ________________ ask questions.
7. And we will not ________________ watch TV before we study.
8. Do not ________________ the rules ever change?
9. Are not ________________ we old enough to make up our own?
10. Why could not ________________ someone write some new ones?
11. Who does not ________________ have some good ideas?
12. Why have not ________________ we thought of this before?

Conjunctions

A **conjunction** is a word that joins words, sentence parts, or sentences. Common conjunctions are *and, or,* and *but.* When you join two sentences together with conjunctions, use a comma before the conjunction.

I like to run, **but** I am too slow for the track team.
The best wrestler is Aaron, **and** everyone knows it.
The fastest swimmer is Katie, **or** maybe it's Mimi.

▶ Write *and, or,* or *but* to connect each pair of sentences to make the most sense.

1. Should we go skating? Should we play catch?

____

2. Ben is going to the gym. I want to go with him.

____

3. We could use the treadmill. We could use the weights.

____

4. I could be as strong as Ben. I don't work out regularly.

____

5. Tammi likes to play hockey best. Sometimes she plays soccer.

____

6. Tammi likes to play goalie. Andy likes to be a forward.

____

7. Let's go outside and practice. We could watch sports on TV.

____

8. I love to play sports. I like to watch them, too.

____

Dictionary: Entries and Entry Words

Dictionaries list the meanings, pronunciations, and parts of speech of words. The words that are defined in dictionaries, the entry words, appear in alphabetical order. Look at the **entry**, the **entry word**, and the information about it, for the word *dribble*.

drib•ble (drib´əl) **verb 1** to flow in drops or a trickle. *Water dribbled from the pipe.* **2** in basketball or soccer, to control the ball while kicking or bouncing it. — **drib´bled drib´bling** — **noun 1** a small drop. **2** the act of dribbling a ball.

▶ Now examine this entry.

scheme (skēm) **noun 1** a plan in which things are carefully put together. *the color scheme of a house.* **2** a plan or program, often secret or dishonest. *a scheme for getting people to give money.* **verb** to make secret dishonest plans; to plot. *Sue is always scheming to avoid her homework.* — **schemed, schem´ing** — **schem´er noun**

1. Which parts of speech can *scheme* be? ______

2. How many syllables does *scheme* have? ______

3. Does *scheme* rhyme with *beam* or *hem*? ______

4. Use the word *scheme* as a verb in a sentence. ______

______

______

Dictionary: Guide Words

Guide words help you find entry words in a dictionary. Guide words tell you the first and last words on a dictionary page. The other words on the page are in alphabetical order between these words.

guide words

cheetah	107	chicken
chee•tah (*che tə*) **noun 1** a swift leopard-like animal of Africa and South Asia		**chess** (*ches*) **noun 1** a game played on a checkerboard by two players, using a variety

You would expect to find the entry words *cherry, chest,* and *chew* on this page because all three words fall alphabetically between *cheetah* and *chicken.* But you would not find the words *cheese* or *child* on this page. *Cheese* comes before *cheetah* in the alphabet and *child* comes after *chicken.*

▶ Write the words from the word box that you would find on a dictionary page with the guide words *snail* and *snowfall.*

sniff		sneeze
snack		snake
snowstorm		snore
snuggle		snarl
sneak		snowplow
snapshot		snorkel

snail	565	snowfall

1. ____________________

2. ____________________

3. ____________________

4. ____________________

5. ____________________

6. ____________________

7. ____________________

8. ____________________

Dictionary: Pronunciation Key

A **pronunciation key** in a dictionary shows you how to pronounce entry words.

Pronunciation Key

a add	**i** it	**o͞o** pool
ā ace	**ī** ice	**u** up
â care	**o** odd	**û** burn
ä palm	**ō** open	**yo͞o** fuse
e end	**ô** order	**oi** oil
ē equal	**o͝o** took	

ə = **a** in above, **e** in sicken, **i** in possible, **o** in melon, **u** in circus

Look at each phonetic spelling. Use the pronunciation key to decide which of the three words it spells. Write the word in the blank.

1. (al´i ga´tər) (allergy, alibi, alligator) ____________________
2. (as´tə roid´) (asterisk, asteroid, astonish) ____________________
3. (bliz´ərd) (blister, blizzard, blazer) ____________________
4. (gi tär´) (gutter, guitar, gather) ____________________
5. (mag´nit) (magnet, magic, magazine) ____________________
6. (prə pel´ər) (property, propeller, properly) ____________________
7. (sat´ərn) (Saturday, sudden, Saturn) ____________________
8. (snāk) (snack, sink, snake) ____________________

Words with Long *a*

Long *a* words may be spelled *a_e, ai,* or *ay.*

▶ Write the correct words in the puzzle.

stray	brain
spray	trail
place	snake
plain	locate
paint	decay
mistake	whale

Across

2. wander away

5. error

6. rot

7. not fancy

8. a path or track

10. a large sea mammal

Down

1. a reptile

2. tiny drops; mist

3. mind

4. find the position of

7. a particular area

9. a liquid form for coloring

Words with Long *e*

Long *e* words may be spelled *e, ee, ea,* or *ey.*

▶ Write the correct word to finish each sentence. Then circle the word in the puzzle.

valley	**agree**	**degree**
speed	**season**	**freeze**
east	**neon**	**grease**
money	**female**	**turkey**

G	M	O	N	E	Y	V	F	Q	C
W	G	G	F	R	E	E	Z	E	V
D	E	G	R	E	E	H	E	A	A
A	S	P	E	E	D	L	A	B	L
G	R	H	I	A	A	L	R	N	L
R	V	O	E	M	S	S	J	E	E
E	N	G	E	L	S	T	E	O	Y
E	W	F	S	E	A	S	O	N	E
T	U	R	K	E	Y	E	S	K	M

1. The first paper ________________ was probably made in China.

2. A ________________ spider of average size lays about 100 eggs.

3. The sun rises in the ________________ .

4. Highway signs show the ________________ limit.

5. ________________ is used to make lighted signs.

6. Towns are often located in a ________________ .

7. Do we all ________________ to leave by 9:00?

8. Before you add the cake batter, ________________ the pan.

9. ________________ is often served at Thanksgiving.

10. We ________________ food to preserve it.

11. To what ________________ do you want to succeed?

12. Changes of ________________ are caused by movements of the earth around the sun.

Words with Long *i*

Long *i* words may be spelled *i, i_e,* or *y.*

▶ Write the correct word to finish each sentence. Then write the word in the puzzle.

beside	**shy**
deny	**child**
silent	**icy**
mild	**invite**
divide	**kindly**
rhyme	**lilac**
pilot	**sign**

1. 2. 3. 4. 5. 6. 7. 8. 9. 10. 11. 12. 13.

Across

2. We planted ________________ bushes in our garden.
4. The empty house was ________________ .
5. ________________ is the opposite of multiply.
8. The ________________ child would not talk to us.
9. Be sure to ________________ your new friends to lunch.
12. The winter storm made the roads ________________ .
13. His niece is an only ________________ .

Down

1. My sister wants to be an airplane ________________ .
3. Everyone treated the new student ________________ .
6. Reggie did not ________________ he took the last cookie.
7. Put your suitcase ________________ the others.
8. There is a new stop ________________ on our street.
10. The words "look" and "book" ________________ .
11. Hawaii has a sunny, ________________ climate.

Words with Long *o*

Long *o* words may be spelled *o, o_e,* or *oa.*

▶ Write the correct words in the puzzle.

ago	goal
ocean	slope
vote	robot
coast	float
globe	lonely
obey	tomato

Across

1. end; aim

2. a great body of salty water

6. slant

7. a rounded, red fruit

10. a machine that often looks like a person

11. follow the rules

Down

1. a round object

3. in the past

4. shoreline of seas

5. having no friends

8. to choose in an election

9. what a boat does

Words with Long *u*

Long *u* words may be spelled *u, u_e,* or *ue*.

▶ Write the correct word to finish each sentence. Then circle the word in the puzzle.

pupil	value
human	useful
fuel	future
amuse	usual
perfume	units
regular	refuse

V R P U P I L R S
A U E P U N I T S
L S R E G U L A R
U E F U E L H M E
E F U S U A L U F
H U M A N C B S U
D L E Y S M N E S
R S C F U T U R E

1. Mr. Hanns has room for one more ________________ in his class.

2. This baseball card has little ________________ .

3. We gave Mom ________________ for Mother's Day.

4. Grandmother brought a new toy to ________________ the baby.

5. A dictionary is a ________________ source of information.

6. The jet needs ________________ before it can leave.

7. Students need to plan for their ________________ .

8. The ________________ voice is feared by wild animals.

9. After the storm, we had school as ________________ .

10. Six o'clock is our ________________ dinner hour.

11. The offer of extra credit was too good to ________________ .

12. The book was divided into 12 ________________ of study.

Words with *c*, *ss*, and *sc*

The *s* sound may be spelled *c*, *ss*, or *sc*.

▶ Write the correct word to finish each sentence. Then circle the word in the puzzle.

press	**scent**
scene	**scissors**
center	**address**
lesson	**dance**
ounces	**pencil**

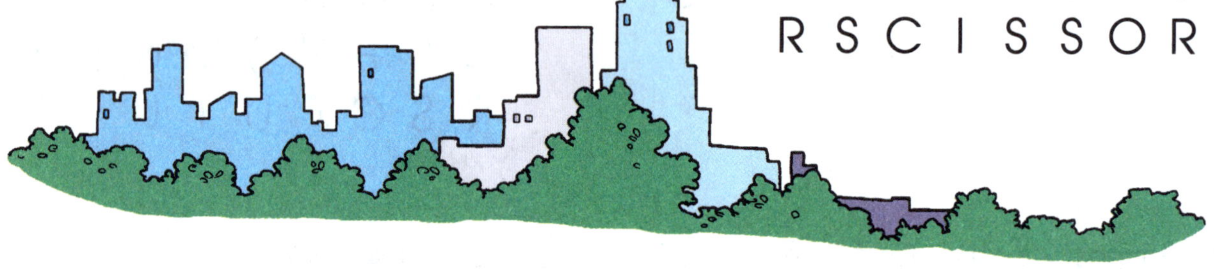

1. There are 16 ________________ in a pound.
2. We use ________________ to cut paper.
3. Ballet is a kind of ________________ .
4. The park is located in the ________________ of the city.
5. It is time for his piano ________________ .
6. The ________________ on the postcard is beautiful.
7. Her perfume has a pleasant ________________ .
8. The lead of the ________________ broke.
9. Before Jed moved, he gave me his new ________________ .
10. There is a button to ________________ for help.

Words with *j*, *g*, and *dge*

The *j* sound may be spelled *j*, *g*, or *dge*.

▶ Write the correct word to finish each sentence.
Then write the word in the puzzle.

budge	jest
jelly	germs
subject	giant
fudge	engine
gentle	ledge

1. 2. 3. 4. 5. 6. 7. 8. 9.

Across

3. Her favorite ______________ in school is math.

5. Some ______________ can cause disease.

6. The door was stuck and would not ______________ .

7. It was a warm evening with a ______________ breeze.

8. Apple ______________ tastes good on toast.

9. The author is a ______________ in his field.

Down

1. Birds like to sit on the window ______________ .

2. Her mother made ______________ for the party.

4. A train ______________ is very powerful.

8. I hoped my ______________ would make her laugh.

Adding *s* and *es*

Add *s* to the end of most words to name more than one.
Add *es* to words ending in *ch, ss, sh,* or *x.*

▶ Add the correct ending to the words to finish each sentence. Then write the word in the puzzle.

match	tax
wish	fox
dish	nickel
friend	hunch
flash	pass

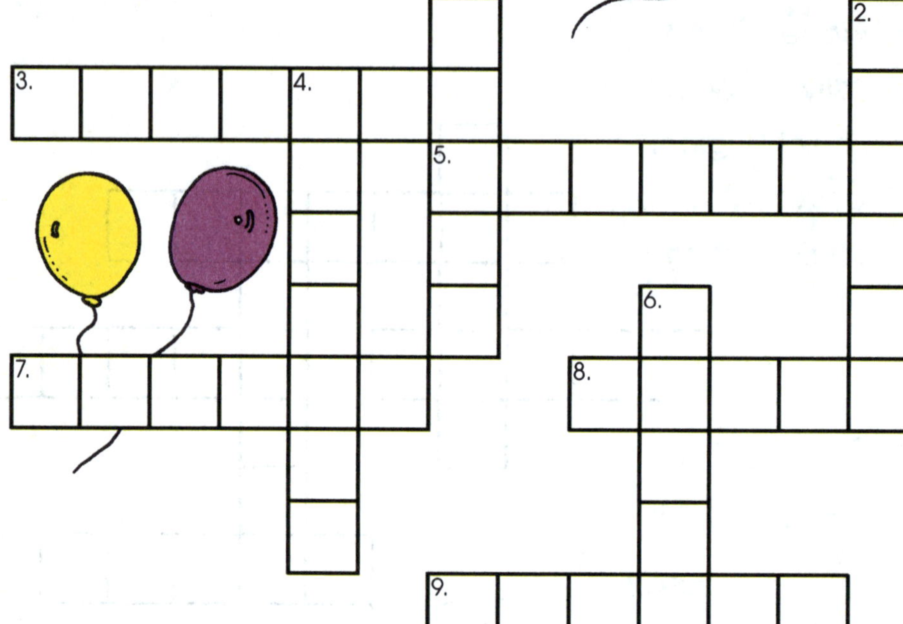

Across

1. ________________ are related to dogs and wolves.

3. We invited all our ________________ to the party.

5. Sometimes our ________________ can help us.

7. The genie granted their ________________.

8. Citizens pay ________________ on their income.

9. He may go after he washes the ________________.

Down

1. There were ________________ of lightning during the storm.

2. We all received free ________________ to the game.

4. Five ________________ equal one quarter.

6. We used several ________________ to light the fire.

Words with *f*, *ph*, *ff*, and *gh*

The *f* sound may be spelled *f*, *ph*, *ff*, or *gh*.

▶ Write the correct word to finish each sentence.
Then circle the word in the puzzle.

laugh	**telephone**
coffee	**trophy**
rough	**alphabet**
forest	**enough**
office	**finger**

K R B G Z N Y D S T
T D F O R E S T E T
F E R O U G H B O R
I E L P V B A V F O
N N Z E T H R M F P
G O R M P J Y B I H
E U P L X H L K C Y
R G A H F R O R E Q
G H L A U G H N S H
T C O F F E E C E Y

1. Many kinds of animals live in the ______________ .

2. Her silly joke made us ______________ .

3. Our school won the football ______________ .

4. He pinched his ______________ in the door.

5. There are 26 letters in our ______________ .

6. Do we have ______________ pizza for everybody?

7. Dad likes to dunk doughnuts in his ______________ .

8. Will you answer the ______________ , please?

9. The school ______________ is closed today.

10. The gravel road was very ______________ .

Consonant Digraphs: *ch, sh, th, wh*

A consonant digraph is two consonants written together to spell one sound, such as *ch, sh, th,* or *wh*.

▶ Write the correct words in the puzzle.

chest	**cloth**
thick	**choose**
author	**share**
leash	**whim**
wheat	**both**

Across

2. upper front part of the body

4. pick from a group

5. someone who writes books

7. a kind of grass that bears grain

8. not thin

Down

1. a strap to lead or hold an animal

3. use or have with others

4. material made by weaving

6. one and the other

7. a sudden wish or idea

Vowel Sounds with *r*

The vowel sound with *r* has the same sound in the words *her, turn,* and *bird.* This vowel sound with *r* may be spelled *er, ur,* or *ir.*

▶ Write the correct word to finish each sentence. Then circle the word in the puzzle.

thirsty	serve
shirt	dirty
every	further
curve	verb
surprise	burned

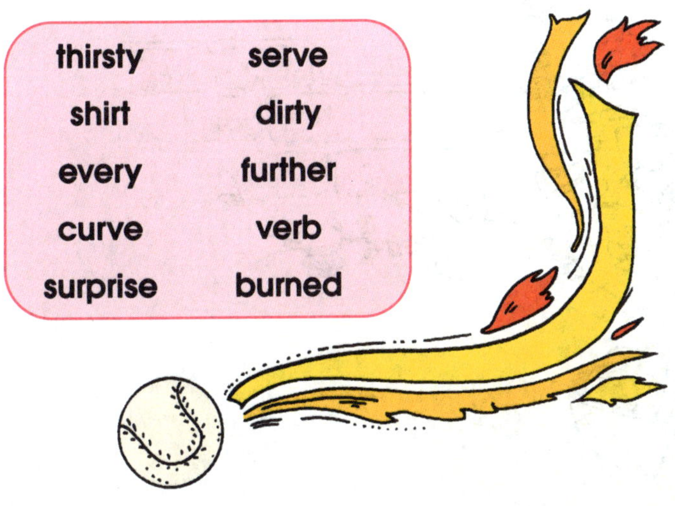

K R B U R N E D S
T F V E R B E B U
H C U R V E V C R
I S E R V E E O P
R D I R T Y R M R
S T R L T H Y B I
T R O T E W E C S
Y R S H I R T R E

1. A ________________ is often an action word.

2. The pitcher threw a ________________ ball.

3. His pants got ________________ when he fell.

4. The robber was caught by ________________ .

5. The old factory ________________ to the ground.

6. We will not discuss it ________________ .

7. Eating peanuts makes me ________________ .

8. He spent ________________ dime he had.

9. What shall we ________________ for dinner?

10. Matt tore his ________________ on the fence.

Vowel Sounds with *r*

The vowel sound with *r* in *star* is spelled *ar*.
The vowel sound with *r* in *horn* is spelled *or*.

▶ Write the correct word to finish each sentence.

market	morning
sport	smart
labor	thorns
apart	orange
garden	start

1. Baseball is my favorite ___ ___ ___ ___ ___.
2. The car would not ___ ___ ___ ___ ___.
3. There are weeds in our ___ ___ ___ ___ ___ ___.
4. Would you like a section of an ___ ___ ___ ___ ___ ___?
5. Laying bricks is hard ___ ___ ___ ___ ___.
6. Teachers are ___ ___ ___ ___ ___.
7. The book fell ___ ___ ___ ___ ___.
8. We will leave early tomorrow ___ ___ ___ ___ ___ ___ ___.
9. Our class took a trip to the fish ___ ___ ___ ___ ___ ___.
10. Be careful of a rose's ___ ___ ___ ___ ___ ___.

Words with *au* and *aw*

These words have the vowel sound in *ball*.
This vowel sound may be spelled *au* or *aw*.

▶ Write the correct word to finish each sentence.

crawl	**fault**
gauze	**lawn**
pause	**awful**
thaw	**taught**
dawn	**autumn**

1. The accident was not his _ _ _ _ _.

2. We waited for the ice to _ _ _ _.

3. The baby is learning to _ _ _ _ _.

4. His favorite season is _ _ _ _ _ _.

5. Before the play began, there was a _ _ _ _ _.

6. She wrapped the cut with _ _ _ _ _.

7. It's time to mow the _ _ _ _.

8. The food tasted _ _ _ _ _.

9. He recited a poem he was _ _ _ _ _ _.

10. We all stayed up until _ _ _ _.

Words with *oi* and *oy*

The words below have the same vowel sound as in the word *boy*. This vowel sound may be spelled *oi* or *oy*.

▶ Write the correct word to finish each sentence. Then write the word in the puzzle.

noise	loyal
oyster	voyage
choice	voice
employ	annoy
point	enjoy

AHOY

1. 2.
3.
4.
5.
6.
7.
8.

Across

1. The men were ________________ to their commander.
3. Did you ________________ your trip?
4. What was the ________________ of his question?
5. The ________________ by sea took seven days.
7. We had a ________________ of fish or beef for dinner.
8. An ________________ is a sea animal.

Down

2. Cindy hid the pencil to ________________ her brother.
3. How many people does the company ________________ ?
5. He lost his ________________ after cheering so much.
6. The sudden ________________ woke the baby.

Words with *ou* and *ow*

These words have the vowel sound in *out*.
This vowel sound may be spelled *ou* or *ow*.

▶ Write the correct word to finish each sentence.

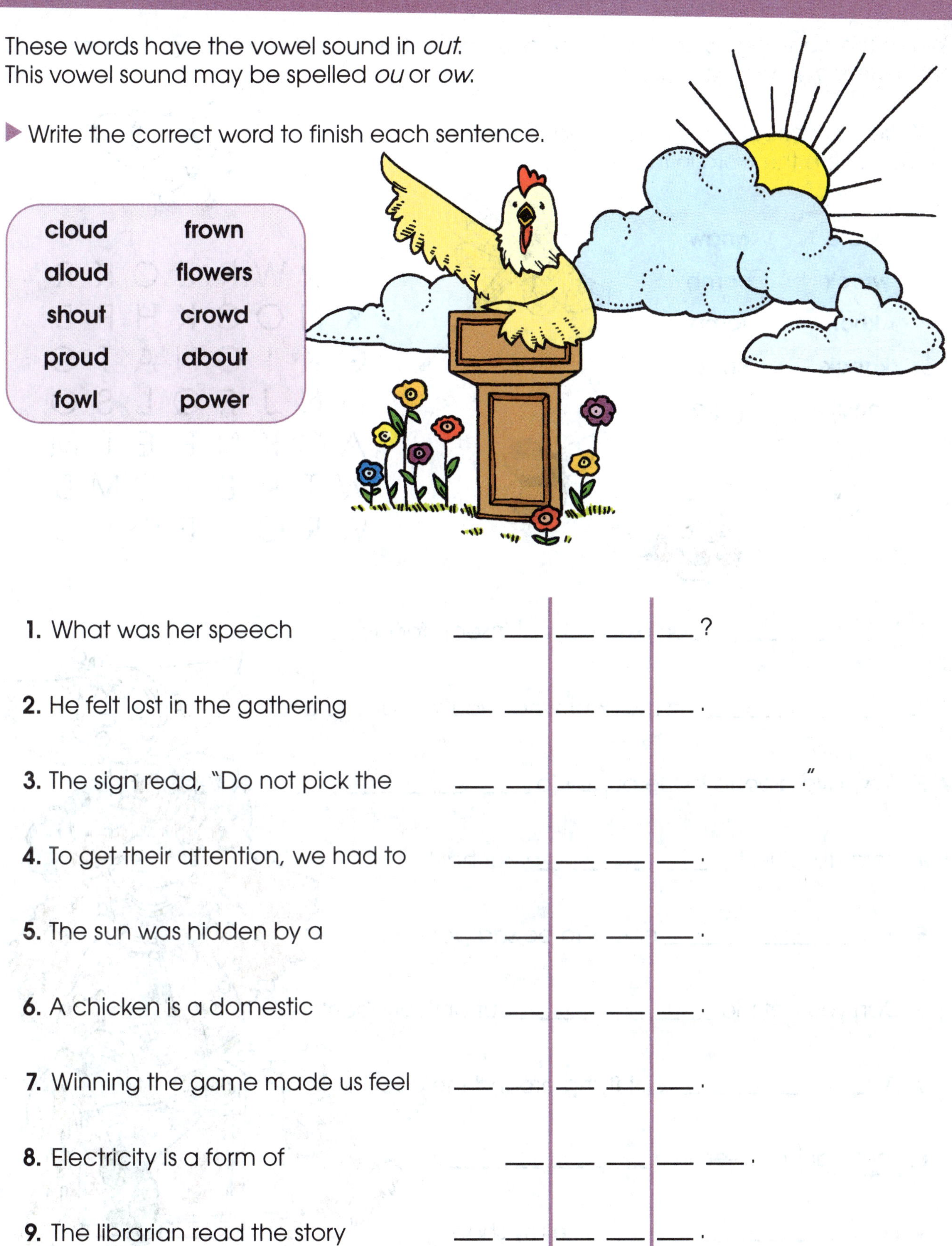

cloud	frown
aloud	flowers
shout	crowd
proud	about
fowl	power

1. What was her speech ___ ___ ___ ___ ___?
2. He felt lost in the gathering ___ ___ ___ ___ ___.
3. The sign read, "Do not pick the ___ ___ ___ ___ ___ ___ ___."
4. To get their attention, we had to ___ ___ ___ ___ ___.
5. The sun was hidden by a ___ ___ ___ ___ ___.
6. A chicken is a domestic ___ ___ ___ ___.
7. Winning the game made us feel ___ ___ ___ ___ ___.
8. Electricity is a form of ___ ___ ___ ___ ___.
9. The librarian read the story ___ ___ ___ ___ ___.
10. His antics made the teacher ___ ___ ___ ___ ___.

Silent Consonants

When the consonants *gn, kn, mb,* and *wr* are written together in a single syllable, the letters *g, k, b,* and *w* are silent.

▶ Write the correct word to finish each sentence. Then circle the word in the puzzle.

wrote	**gnaw**
wreck	**comb**
knot	**tomb**
knock	**kneel**
gnat	**knife**

K	R	W	R	E	C	K	R
K	N	O	C	K	H	P	B
G	K	I	G	N	A	T	C
N	N	J	F	Q	L	S	O
A	O	K	N	E	E	L	M
W	T	R	L	T	O	M	B
W	R	O	T	E	W	F	C

1. I ________________ an essay about insects for class.

2. ________________ on my door when you're ready to go.

3. We gave a bone to the puppy to ________________ .

4. Hold still while I ________________ your hair!

5. This ________________ needs to be sharpened.

6. Can you get the ________________ out of this ribbon?

7. A ________________ kept flying around the pear.

8. That car has been in a ________________ .

9. I had to ________________ to tie my shoe.

10. President Grant's ________________ is in New York City.

Words with Long *a* and *e*

The long *a* sound may be spelled *eigh*.
The long *e* sound may be spell *ei* or *ie*.

▶ Write the correct word to finish each sentence. Then write the word in the puzzle.

weigh	**niece**
believe	**ceiling**
receive	**deceive**
sleigh	**relief**
field	**eight**

1. 2. 3. 4. 5. 6. 7. 8. 9. 10.

Across

2. It was a ________________ to get out of the cold.
4. His ________________ arrived by plane.
7. How much does an elephant ________________ ?
9. Camouflage helps ________________ enemies.
10. I ________________ he told the truth.

Down

1. The snowy night was perfect for a ________________ ride.
3. Did you ________________ the tickets for the play?
5. Four plus four equals ________________ .
6. The football ________________ is muddy today.
8. The kitchen ________________ needs to be painted.

Adding *ed* and *ing*

When verbs have a consonant-*y* ending, change the *y* to *i* and add *ed*.

hurry → **hurried**

▶ Write the correct spelling of the words to finish each sentence.

carry	**copy**	**try**
deny	**bury**	**marry**

1. He ________________ the suitcase upstairs.

2. She ________________ to fix the broken doll.

3. Sam ________________ breaking the dish.

4. She was ________________ last June.

5. When their pet turtle died, they ________________ it.

6. He ________________ his name by tracing it.

When verbs have a silent *e* ending, drop the letter *e* and add *ing*.

make → **making**

smile	**rise**	**drive**
vote	**write**	**excite**

7. We will be ________________ to Yellowstone Park.

8. The sun will be ________________ in the east.

9. The tennis match was ________________ .

10. Mom is ________________ a letter to my sister.

11. Which candidate are you ________________ for?

12. We took a picture of her ________________ .

Words with Long *o*

The long *o* sound may be spelled *o, o_e, oa,* or *ow.*

▶ Write the correct words in the puzzle.

borrow	**protect**
growth	**hollow**
cocoa	**most**
broke	**global**
pillow	**roast**

Across

1. having no money
2. a way to cook
3. the process of growing
5. used to cushion the head while sleeping
6. used to make a chocolate beverage
7. the greatest amount

Down

1. to use something temporarily that belongs to someone else with his or her permission
3. worldwide
4. an unfilled space inside something
5. guard

Comparisons

To compare two people or things, add *er* to the ending of a word. To compare more than two people or things, add *est*. Change the *y* to *i* before adding *er* or *est* to words that have a consonant-*y* ending.

tricky → **trickier** → **trickiest**

▶ Add the correct ending to the words to finish each sentence. Then circle the word in the puzzle.

happy	**fast**
pretty	**clean**
soft	**short**
sweet	**noisy**
rough	**busy**

```
H R F A S T E S T L T S
C A S H O R T E R S T R
L S P R E T T I E S T O
E H F P R F D T L H S U
A F U J I Z E M F L O G
N U M H P E Q N C B F H
E L P D W Y S S M N T E
R B U S I E S T T F E R
N O I S I E R C T Y R S
```

1. He is happy at Thanksgiving and Halloween, but ________________ at Christmas.
2. Is this pillow harder or ________________ than yours?
3. Those lovely flowers are the ________________ I've seen.
4. A five-year-old is ________________ than a ten-year-old.
5. People with two jobs are the ________________ of all.
6. This kind of apple tastes the ________________ of all.
7. Traveling by jet is the ________________ way to go.
8. The floor is ________________ since we mopped it.
9. You can hear that traffic is ________________ during the day than at night.
10. The brick road is bumpier, or ________________, than the highway.

Prefixes

The letter groups *un, re, in,* and *dis* are prefixes. When added to the beginning of a word, they change the meaning of the word.

▶ Write the correct words in the puzzle.

un means **not**
re means **again**
in means **into** and sometimes **not**
dis means **lack of**

untied	rewrite
unhappy	dislike
incorrect	renew
disagree	rebuild
indirect	unjust

Across

3. make or become new again

4. not correct; wrong

6. not tied

8. differ; argue

Down

1. not straightforward

2. not just; unfair

3. write again

5. build again

6. not happy; sad

7. not like; hate

Suffixes

The letter groups *ful, less,* and *ly* are suffixes. When added to the end of a word, they change the meaning of the word.

▶ Write the correct word to finish each sentence.
Then circle the word in the puzzle.

ful means **full of**
ly means **how**
less means **not having**

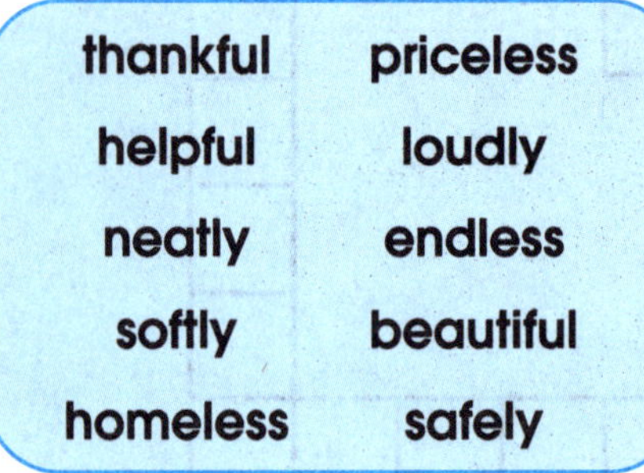

B A P R I C E L E S S L W
Y E S R N J H L G F E O H
T S A R E G L C N V N U O
X O F U A V R W R F D D M
C F E Z T W G X B D L L E
S T L C L I H R T S E Y L
D L Y T Y Y F K Q Y S Q E
C Y P J K M G U K C S X S
S T H E L P F U L F H R S
D C T H A N K F U L T K T

1. Snowflakes fell ________________, covering everything in white.
2. The tornado left many families ________________.
3. The view from the mountain was ________________.
4. She called ________________ for help.
5. The suitcase was packed ________________.
6. The highway appeared to be ________________.
7. His art is ________________.
8. The pilot landed the plane ________________.
9. The pilgrims were ________________ for their blessings.
10. My mother found the store clerk very ________________.

Antonyms

Antonyms are words with opposite meanings.

big, little

▶ Write the antonym for the bold word in each sentence. Then circle the word in the puzzle.

laugh	**sour**
short	**easy**
light	**start**
big	**lose**
dirty	**slow**

L A U G H P Q S
O L B I G V H L
S O U R N O L O
E H N C R E I W
C T P T K A G X
S T A R T S H R
D I R T Y Y T K

1. My father is a **tall** man. ________________

2. Did you **find** your money? ________________

3. It is time to **stop** the game. ________________

4. The lemonade is too **sweet**. ________________

5. The story made him **cry**. ________________

6. I thought the test was **hard**. ________________

7. The horse was **fast**. ________________

8. Is your shirt **clean**? ________________

9. The package was **heavy**. ________________

10. Her dog is **small**. ________________

Synonyms

Synonyms are words with almost the same meaning.

look, see

▶ Write the synonym for the bold word in each sentence. Then write the word in the puzzle.

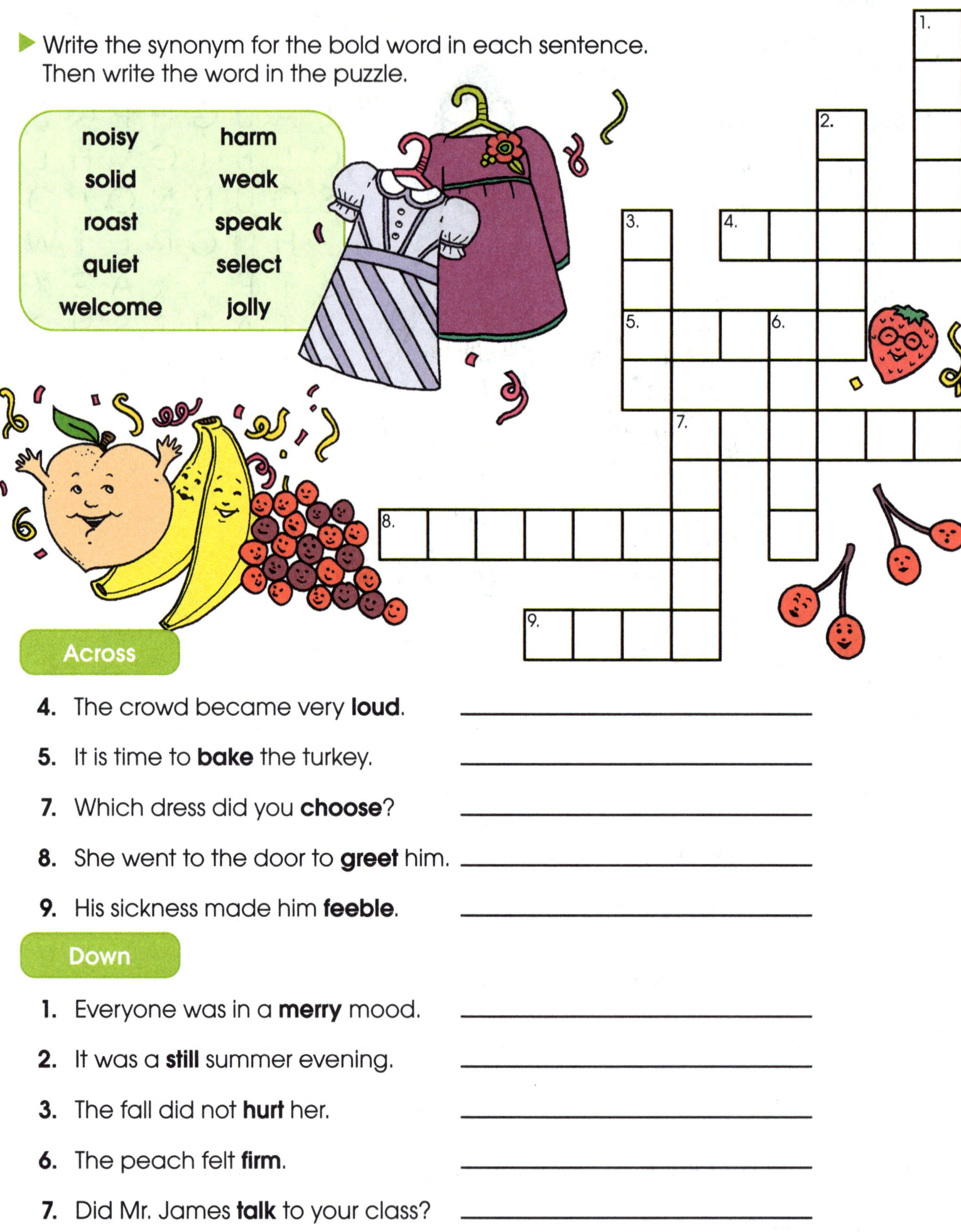

Across

4. The crowd became very **loud**. ________________

5. It is time to **bake** the turkey. ________________

7. Which dress did you **choose**? ________________

8. She went to the door to **greet** him. ________________

9. His sickness made him **feeble**. ________________

Down

1. Everyone was in a **merry** mood. ________________

2. It was a **still** summer evening. ________________

3. The fall did not **hurt** her. ________________

6. The peach felt **firm**. ________________

7. Did Mr. James **talk** to your class? ________________

Homophones

Homophones are words pronounced alike, but with different spellings and meanings.

to, too, two

▶ Write the correct homophone to finish each sentence.
Then circle the word in the puzzle.

peace	**write**
piece	**weak**
there	**week**
their	**hear**
right	**here**

S	R	G	F	H	E	A	R	H
P	I	T	T	W	H	T	B	W
E	G	T	H	E	H	R	Q	R
A	H	N	C	E	L	S	P	I
C	T	P	I	K	R	X	M	T
E	H	R	K	J	H	E	R	E
P	I	E	C	E	W	E	A	K

1. After the quarrel, there was ________________ and quiet.
2. Would you like a ________________ of pie?
3. They lost ________________ tickets to the game.
4. How do you get ________________ ?
5. ________________ a letter to tell me about your trip.
6. How many answers did you get ________________ ?
7. His vacation begins next ________________ .
8. The flu left her feeling ________________ .
9. I could not ________________ what she said.
10. Did you get ________________ on time?

Adding *es*

To spell the plural of a word ending in *f* or *fe*, change the *f* or *fe* to *v* and add *es*.

loaf → **loaves**

▶ Write the correct spelling to finish each sentence.
Then write the word in the puzzle.

knife	**life**
calf	**leaf**
elf	**wife**
half	**shelf**

Across

1. Firefighters save many ________________ .
3. ________________ are young cows or bulls.
4. There are many folklore stories about ________________ .
5. The ________________ are filled with books.
7. The ________________ need to be sharpened.

Down

1. ________________ can be used for mulch.
2. Henry the Eighth had many ________________ .
6. Two ________________ make a whole.

Verb Endings

Most verbs are not changed when *ed* or *ing* is added.
Double the final consonant before adding *ed* or *ing* to one-syllable verbs that have a vowel-consonant ending.

flip → **flipping**

▶ Write the correct word to finish each sentence.
Then circle the word in the puzzle.

melt	**slam**
walk	**carry**
slip	**reach**
point	**trot**
drip	**step**

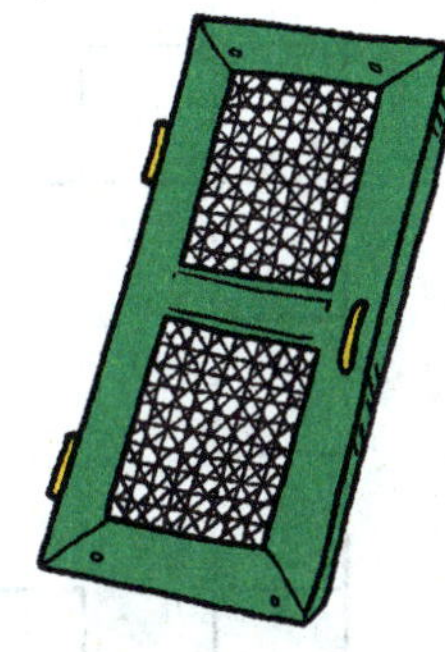

S A M E L T E D C H B

C R S T E P P E D D G

R E L L H W C Q E R P

W A I C A O R T F I O

A C P L K M T M H P I

L H P K J O M L R P N

K I E N R C T I C I T

E N D T V R G K N N E

D G C A R R Y I N G D

1. The screen door kept ________________ in the wind.

2. The horses ________________ to the barn.

3. The glass ________________ out of his hands.

4. The snow ________________ by April.

5. The ship is ________________ a load of ore.

6. They ________________ 10 miles to town.

7. Brad's teacher ________________ out his spelling mistake.

8. The baby was ________________ for her rattle when it fell.

9. The ________________ faucet kept me awake.

10. He ________________ into a puddle when he got out of the car.

Irregular Verbs

Some verbs do not spell the past tense by adding *ed*.

▶ Write the correct word to finish each sentence. Then write the word in the puzzle.

grow - grew	**swing - swung**
fight - fought	**write - wrote**
freeze - froze	**drive - drove**
feel - felt	**leave - left**
tear - tore	

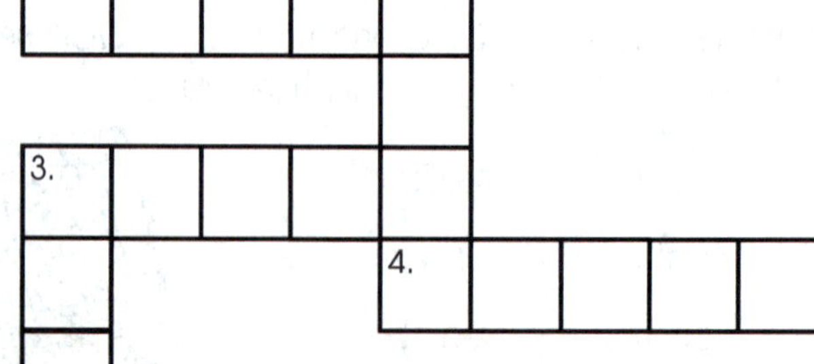

Across

1. Sydney ________________ at the ball.

3. The water in the pond ________________ last night.

4. Abraham Lincoln ________________ the Gettysburg Address.

6. Dad ________________ his keys on the counter.

8. He ________________ his pants while playing ball.

Down

2. His hair ________________ too long.

3. Our forefathers ________________ for freedom.

5. On our vacation, we ________________ to the mountains.

7. Matt ________________ under his bed for his slippers.

Idioms

Idioms are expressions or phrases that do not mean what they seem to say.

You crack me up! means **You make me laugh.**

▶ Draw a line to match each idiom with its meaning.

Idiom	Meaning
1. all tied up	flatter
2. butter up	be quiet
3. a piece of cake	make every effort
4. walking on air	tell a secret
5. bend over backwards	easy
6. bite your tongue	got angry
7. top banana	asleep
8. blow your top	lead person
9. spill the beans	busy
10. out like a light	happy

Book Drop!

▶ Write each title next to the correct category.

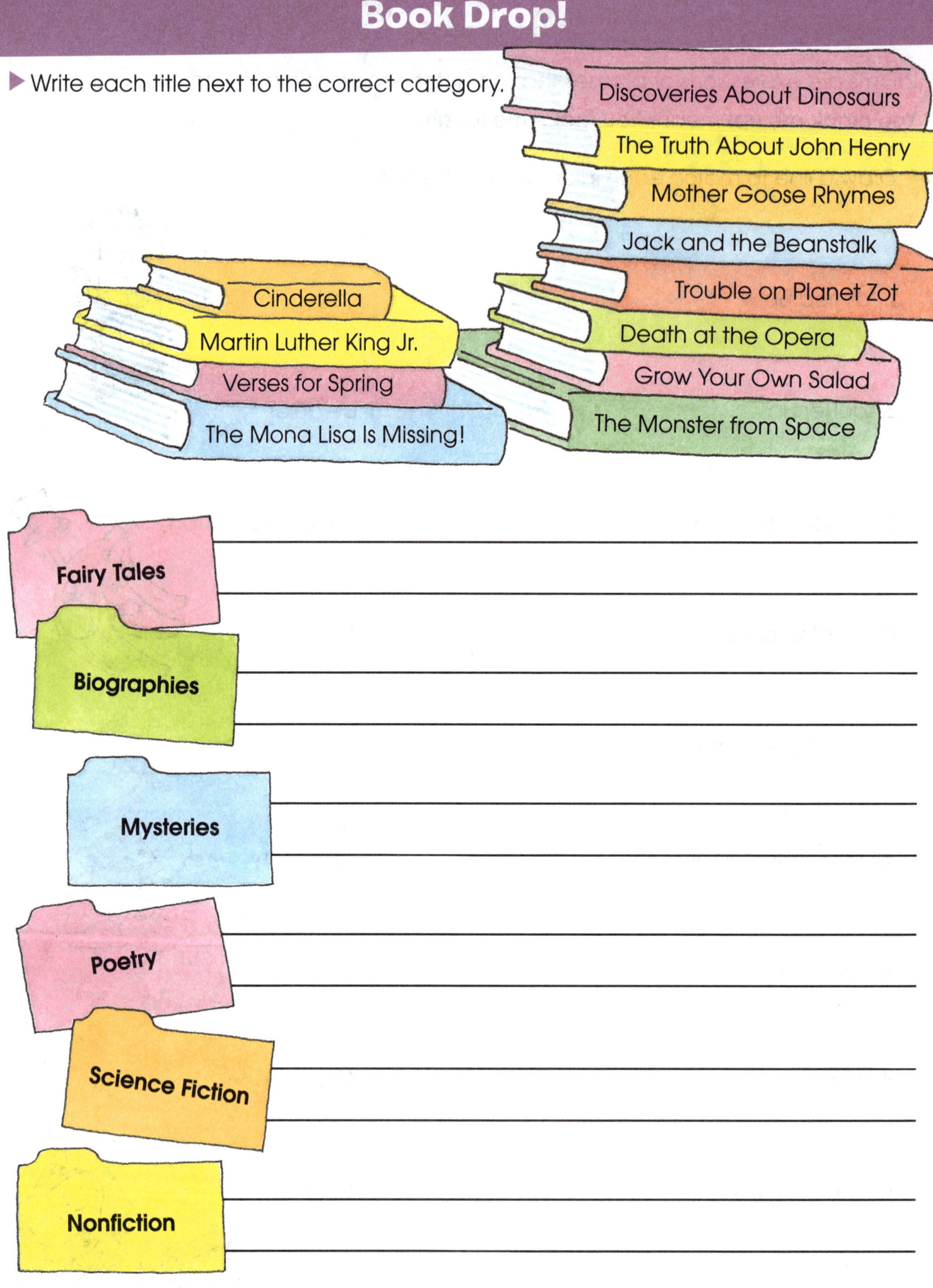

Word Toss

▶ Write the parts of speech in the proper bins.

Alphabet Sort

▶ For each group of words, write the word that is **NOT** in alphabetical order in the puzzle. Then read the message in the boxes.

1. bench branch bunch batch crunch
2. hand hat head habit helicopter
3. shatter shed ship school shutter
4. cake checkers cabin chop creamy
5. tack trim trip tooth tuck
6. bright bring brown baseball bumpy
7. carton drum doghouse doorbell drag
8. sting string stuck sweater spring
9. crib cracker crayon creep crest
10. different doghouse drag dragon doorbell
11. answer apple argue artist another

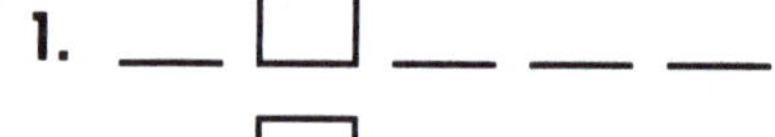

1. ___ ☐ ___ ___ ___
2. ___ ___ ☐ ___ ___
3. ___ ☐ ___ ___ ___ ___
4. ☐ ___ ___ ___ ___
5. ___ ___ ___ ___ ☐
6. ___ ___ ___ ___ ___ ☐ ___ ___
7. ___ ___ ___ ☐
8. ___ ☐ ___ ___ ___ ___
9. ___ ___ ☐ ___
10. ___ ☐ ___ ___ ___ ___ ___ ___
11. ___ ☐ ___ ___ ___ ___ ___

Now and Then

Write the past tense of each word in the puzzle

1. dig
2. go
3. do
4. send
5. grow
6. lose
7. build
8. sell
9. think
10. say
11. understand

Under Construction

▶ Add a **prefix** or **suffix** to each of the words below to make a new word.

Some common prefixes and suffixes are *dis-*, *un-*, *re-*, *-ness*, *-less*, *-ful*, and *-ly*.

mother ________

honest ________

fear ________

quiet ________

beautiful ________

slow ________

able ________

paint ________

comfortable ________

thought ________

year ________

good ________

care ________

kind ________

joy ________

quick ________

agree ________

write ________

continue ________

happy ________

Synonym Roundup

▶ Draw lassos from the cowpunchers to the synonyms.
(Synonyms are words that have the same or nearly the same meanings.)
One lasso is drawn for you.

If I Just Had a Pepper!

▶ Write what each worker uses.

gavel
oven
scalpel
van
glove
blueprint
computer
telescope
tractor
trowel
camera
brush

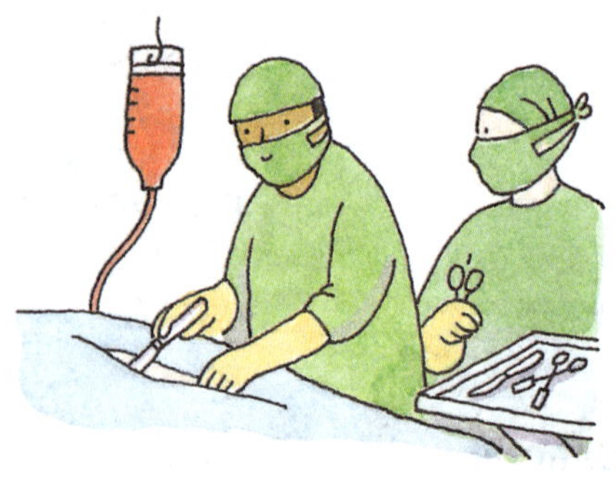

The Great Outdoors

Compound words are two words joined to make one word. The two words might be clues to the meaning of the compound word, but not always.

foot + print = footprint
A footprint is a print made by a foot.

butter + fly = butterfly
You know that butter does not fly!

▶ Put together two small words from each side of the diagram. Write the compound words in the center.

skate	____________________	**corn**
sand	____________________	**ball**
pop	____________________	**glasses**
sun	____________________	**box**
play	____________________	**board**
base	____________________	**ground**

Mind Bender
Invent some three-part compound words such as headphonewire, breakfasttime, and highwaylane.

All Shook Up

A **noun** is a word that names a person, place, or thing.

person	**place**	**thing**
scientist	laboratory	discovery

It's a Fact!
Lightning is a flash of light in the sky. An electrical current flows between clouds or between clouds and Earth to make the bright light.

Take a closer look at these nouns to discover the syllables that make up each word.

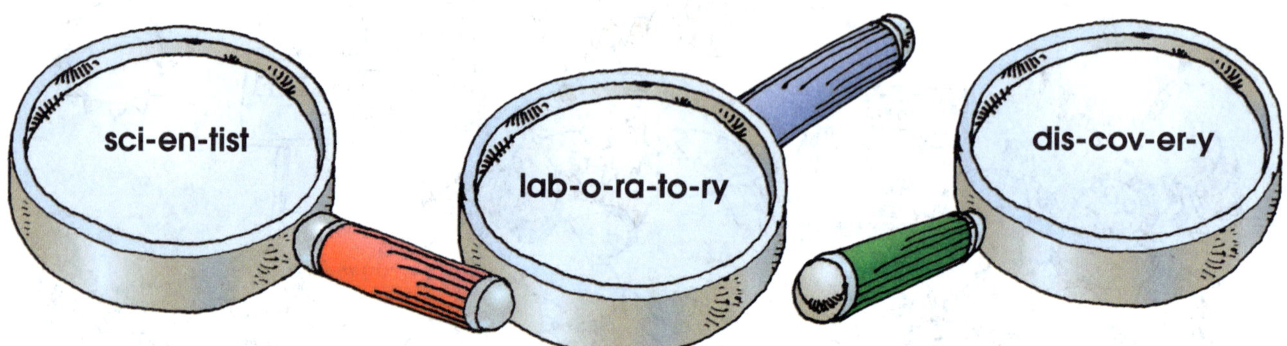

▶ Read the story below. Some of the nouns have scrambled syllables. Unscramble each noun and write it in the table.

A **tist-sci-en** and his **ther-bro** were cleaning up a spooky old **to-ra-lab-ry-o**. While they were dusting a **set-clo**, they found a **ster-mon** that was created long ago. They were excited about their **er-dis-y-cov**. They took the monster to a **mu-um-se**. The **pa-news-per** showed a **graph-to-pho** of the scientist, his brother, and the monster. They were all on the front page!

▶ List each noun you unscrambled in the correct column.

Person	Place	Thing

Write It Right!

Homophones are words that sound the same but have different spellings and meanings.

cellar
chilly
pale
beet
hoarse

▶ Read the clues.
Then write a homophone for each word.

Homophones		Clue
1. beat		a red vegetable
2. pail		light-colored
3. chili		cool in temperature
4. horse		sounding rough or husky
5. seller		room under a building

▶ Use homophone word pairs to answer each riddle.

6. What do you call a bucket that is faded? ____________________

7. What is a very tired red vegetable? ____________________

8. What is a hot food that has gotten cold? ____________________

9. What do you call a pony with a sore throat? ____________________

10. Who is a person with basements for sale? ____________________

Mind Bender
Write some homophone riddles of your own. Here are four pairs of homophones to give you ideas.

plain plane	dear deer
hare hair	bare bear

It's About Time!

▶ Read the paragraphs. Circle all of the "fashion firsts." Underline the date for each one.

Are you missing a button? Everyone was missing buttons 800 years ago. Buttons were first used as fasteners around A.D. 1200. Today, a safety pin can be handy if you lose a button. Walter Hunt invented the safety pin in 1849. Pockets were first sewn into men's clothing around 1580. Women and children had none!

Are you wearing jeans? Levi Strauss made the first jeans in 1873 for gold miners. Did you know that zippers were first used to fasten shoes in 1893? It wasn't until the 1930s that zippers appeared on clothing. Are you wearing a T-shirt with a message on it? They became popular in the 1960s. Fashions come and go and then come back again!

It's a Fact!
In the Middle East, heels were added to shoes to lift the foot from the hot sand. In the Old West, boot heels helped people keep their feet in the stirrups of horse saddles.

▶ Write the years in sequential order on the timeline. Then write the fashion first for that year.

buttons

AD 1200

▶ Use the code to find each answer.

1. N	4. C	7. G	10. A	13. Y
2. V	5. P	8. W	11. R	14. H
3. I	6. O	9. E	12. S	15. L

1. This trademark name is for a fastening device made of tiny hooks and loops.

☐ ☐ ☐ ☐ ☐ ☐
2 9 15 4 11 6

2. This tool was first used in the 1200s to twist fibers into threads.

☐ ☐ ☐ ☐ ☐ ☐ ☐ ☐   ☐ ☐ ☐ ☐ ☐
12 5 3 1 1 3 1 7   8 14 9 9 15

3. A French chemist invented the first artificial fabric and called it artificial silk.

☐ ☐ ☐ ☐ ☐
11 10 13 6 1

4. This is the main animal fiber used for textiles.

☐ ☐ ☐ ☐
8 6 6 15

Wool comes from the fine, soft hair of sheep and other animals.

Mind Bender
Check the labels of your own clothes. What are they made from? Does your wardrobe include items from the time line?

Proud Pronouns

Pronouns are words that replace nouns.

She, *he*, and *it* mean "one person."
They means "more than one person."

It's a Fact!

The White House has had some unusual pets. President Jefferson had a trained mockingbird. President John Q. Adams had a pet alligator. President Lincoln had a pet turkey named Jack.

▶ Use this mark ⸻ℓ to take out an overused noun in each sentence. Then write the correct pronoun above it.

1. Theodore Roosevelt was President from 1901 to 1909, and President Roosevelt lived at 1600 Pennsylvania Avenue.

2. When President Roosevelt lived in the White House, the White House was home for six fun-loving children.

3. The children had lots of room to play, and the children thought of new things to do each day.

4. Visitors knew about the mischief in the White House, and the visitors were always curious to see what would happen.

5. When no one was watching, the children slid down the stairs on trays, and the children roller-skated in the halls.

6. The President liked pets, so the President let the children have dogs, cats, birds, rabbits, rats, guinea pigs, raccoons, a snake, and a pony.

7. One day, the children put the pony in the elevator so the children could ride the pony upstairs.

8. Since the children often played together, the children were called "The White House Gang."

We're Even

Randy and Keisha split the money they earned by raking leaves for their neighbors.

▶ Write the amounts in each box.
Draw a line to divide the money into two equal amounts.

Family Reunion

The Longer and Shorter families are having a family reunion. They need several tables to hold all of the food.

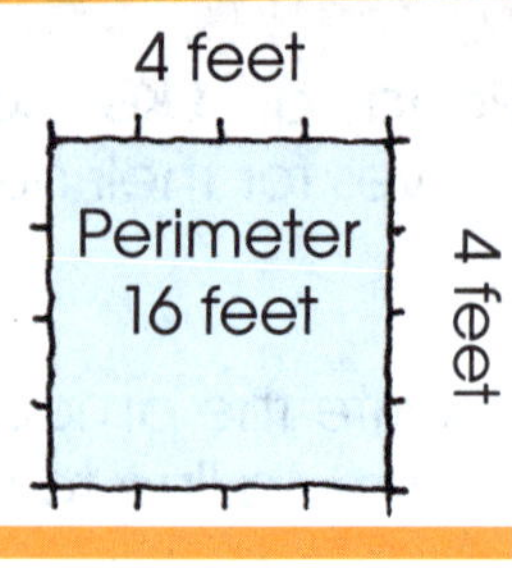

Perimeter is a measurement that tells the distance around a shape. To find the perimeter of each table, add the lengths of all four sides.

▶ Write the perimeter of each table.

1 foot

Dishes
Perimeter = ____

Drinks
Perimeter =
____

Salads
Perimeter = ____

Main Dishes
Perimeter = ____

Vegetables
Perimeter = ____

Fruits
Perimeter =
____

Breads
Perimeter =
____

Desserts
Perimeter = ____

▶ Use the tables to answer the questions.

1. Which table has the greatest perimeter?

____

2. Which table has the least perimeter?

____

3. Which two tables have the same perimeters?

____

4. Which table has the greatest perimeter, salads or breads? By how much?

____

5. Which table has the greatest perimeter, desserts or vegetables? By how much?

____

6. Can two tables have the same perimeters but different shapes? How do you know?

____

____

____

____

____

Mind Bender

Who came to the Brainy family reunion? There were 36 members of one family. There were twice as many adults as children. There were four more women than men. There were two more boys than girls. How many men, women, boys, and girls were at this reunion?

Backyard Circus

Synonyms are words that have similar meanings.

▶ Read the sentences.
Underline each synonym word pair.

1. Ask friends to be in your circus and invite them to help make posters.
2. Practice introducing the acts, and then start to rehearse.
3. Choose a ringmaster with a booming voice who will be loud enough to introduce each act.
4. Your backyard is the perfect place to perform, and blankets make ideal seats for your audience.
5. Greet each guest with a cheerful welcome.
6. Drumrolls or cymbals are important because they can draw attention to eventful moments.
7. Someone who has the ability to do cartwheels or the talent to juggle would make a great performer.
8. Clowns can wear bright costumes and colorful makeup.
9. Each clown must have a unique personality and a special act.
10. Ask young kids to be wild animals and have them growl at the trainer like ferocious beasts.

Mind Bender
Antonyms are words that mean the opposite. The words **big** and **little** are antonyms. Think of antonyms for the words **bright**, **best**, and **loud**. Would you use these new words to describe a circus?

Sentence Mix-Up

A sentence has two parts, a subject and a predicate. The **subject** tells who or what the sentence is about. The **predicate** tells what the subject does. The predicate always contains a verb.

subject **predicate**
The chef makes a terrific ravioli.

▶ Draw a line to match each subject to its predicate to make a logical sentence.

1. Hundreds of ducks	holds a gallon of water.
2. Melanie's cat	is about pirates.
3. The wooden bucket	flew over the pond.
4. Fred's car	chased the ball of yarn.
5. Hot dogs	had a flat tire.
6. My book	are Myron's favorite food.

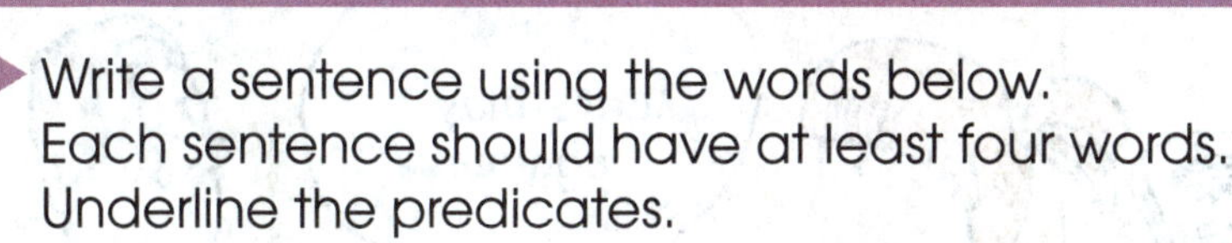

▶ Write a sentence using the words below. Each sentence should have at least four words. Underline the predicates.

7. subject: dog verb: barked

____

8. subject: tulips verb: grew

____

9. subject: monster verb: lives

____

10. subject: I verb: wrote

____

You Can Say That Again!

When you write what people have said, you must use **quotation marks**. Cartoon speech bubbles can help you remember where to write them. Everything in the balloon goes inside quotation marks.

A comma separates the speaker's name from what he or she is saying.

▶ Write each kid's comment as a sentence with quotation marks. The first one is done for you.

1. Kyle grumbled, "I want a machine to do my chores."

2. ______________________________

3. ______________________________

4. ______________________________

5. ______________________________

6. ______________________________

7. ______________________________

8. ______________________________

How Many?

Write a fraction to answer each question. The top number of a fraction, called the **numerator**, tells how many parts are being used. The bottom number, called the **denominator**, tells how many equal parts are in a whole.

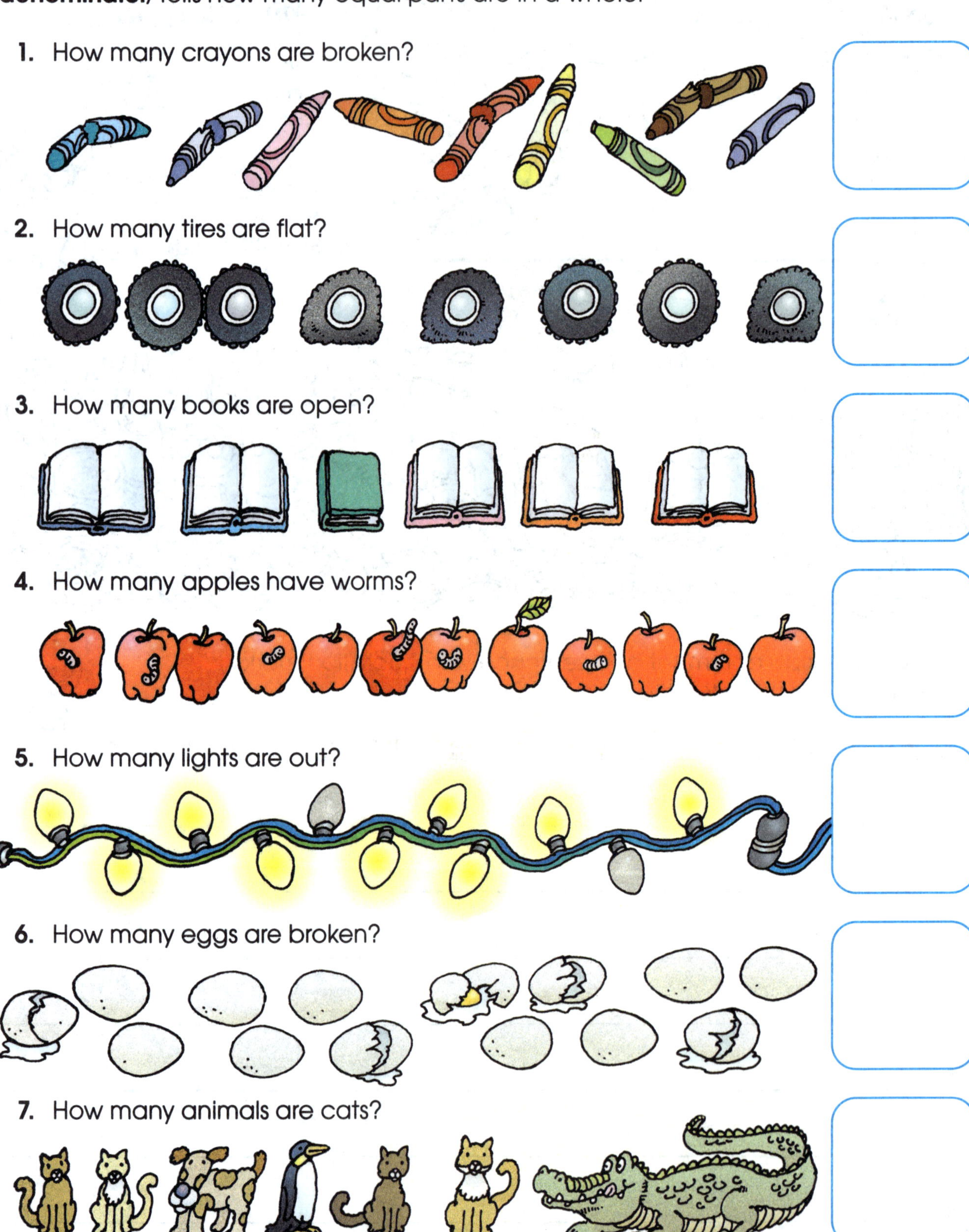

1. How many crayons are broken?
2. How many tires are flat?
3. How many books are open?
4. How many apples have worms?
5. How many lights are out?
6. How many eggs are broken?
7. How many animals are cats?

Take A Chance

▶ Pick a factor that you think will make the number sentence true. Then solve the problem to see if you were correct.

1. 88 x 3 is between 250 and 300.	2 (3) 4	88 x 3 = 264
2. 61 x ____ is between 300 and 350.	4 5 6	
3. 53 x ____ is between 450 and 500.	7 8 9	
4. 82 x ____ is between 300 and 350.	4 5 6	
5. 95 x ____ is between 750 and 800.	7 8 9	
6. 49 x ____ is between 350 and 400.	6 7 8	

What's the Problem?

These word problems have two steps. Read each word problem, and then solve it. The first one is done for you.

1. Fran and Dan played several games of checkers. Dan won 6 games. Fran won twice as many games as Dan. How many games did they play in all?

   How many did Fran win? 2 x 6 = 12 How many in all? 6 + 12 = 18 Fran and Dan played 18 games.

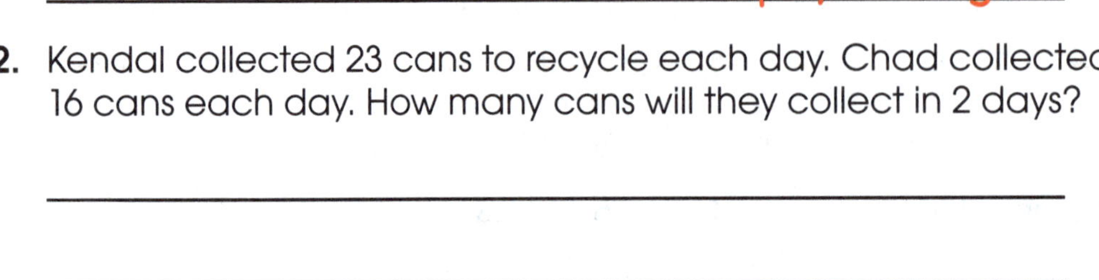

2. Kendal collected 23 cans to recycle each day. Chad collected 16 cans each day. How many cans will they collect in 2 days?

   ____

   ____

3. Mateo bought 15 flowers for his mother. Six were roses. Seven were carnations. The rest were daisies. How many flowers were daisies?

   ____

   ____

4. Sarah has 6 white marbles and 3 blue marbles. Kate has twice as many marbles as Sarah. How many marbles does Kate have?

   ____

   ____

5. Lynn baked 36 cookies. She gave 9 cookies to her brother, and 7 to her sister. How many cookies does she have left?

   ____

   ____

6. Tyrone had 42 baseball cards. He lost 7 cards. Then he got 4 more cards for his birthday. How many cards does he have now?

   ____

   ____

Happily Ever After

A complete story must have all of its parts. The **characters** do the action. The **setting** tells about where and when the story happens. The **problem** is what the characters must overcome. The **events** are the things that happen. The **outcome** is the solution to the problem.

Mind Bender
Write a story that teaches a lesson. You can use something that has happened to you in the past, or you can make up a new story. Add pictures. They can help tell your story.

▶ Here are two story plans.
Use your ideas to fill in the second one.

Characters

Chatterbox Turtle
Glenda and Gilda Goose
Sebastian Snake

Setting

Near the pond

Problem

Chatterbox Turtle never stops talking.

Events

Sebastian asks Chatterbox nicely to be quiet. But Chatterbox keeps talking. Then Glenda has an idea. She makes peanut butter sandwiches for her friends.

Outcome

The peanut butter makes Chatterbox's mouth stick shut. Sebastian, Glenda, and Gilda enjoy the peace and quiet.

Characters

Setting

Problem

Events

Outcome

Shifty Shapes

You can shift a figure three ways.

You can **slide** it.
You can **flip** it.
You can **turn** it.

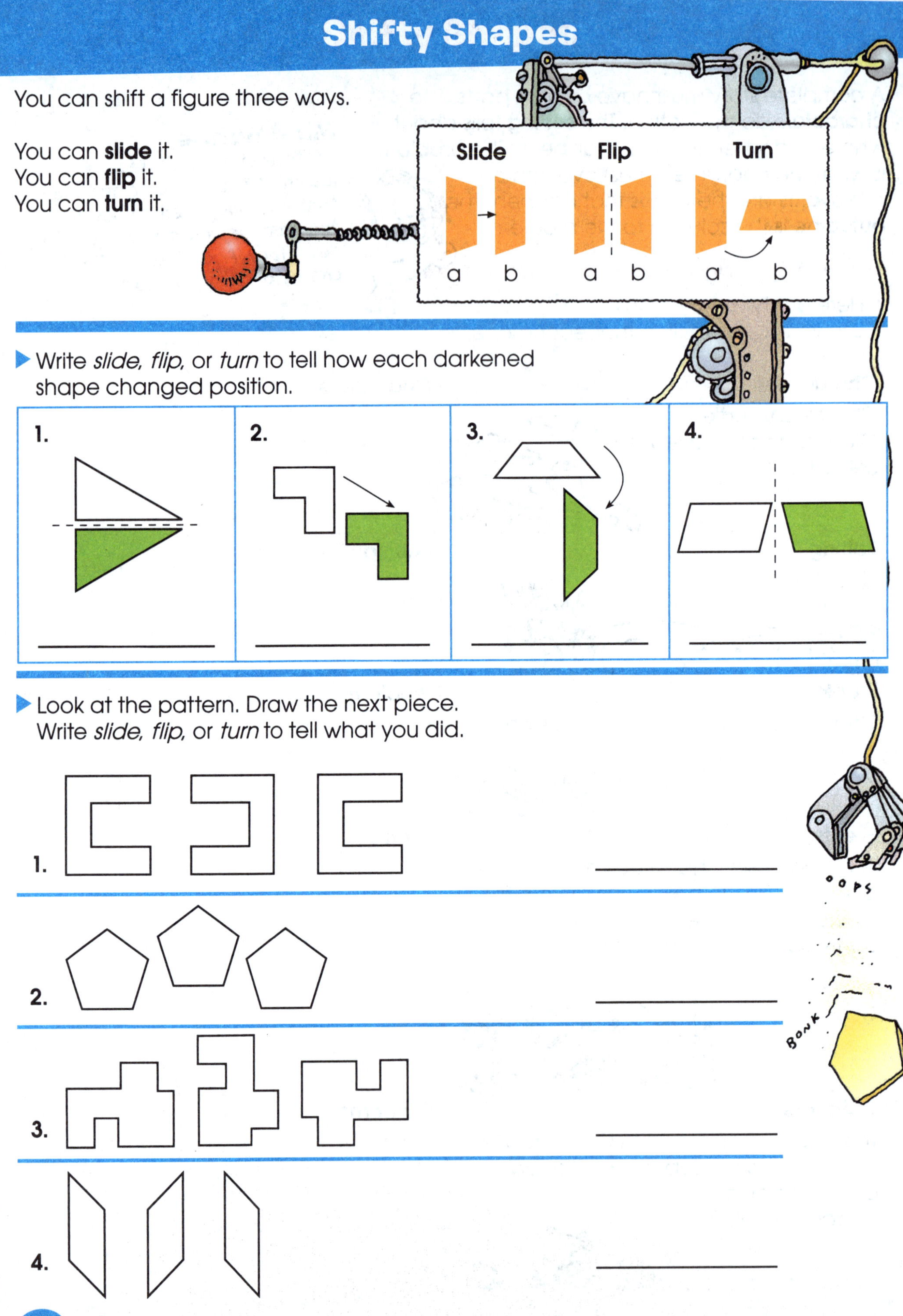

▶ Write *slide, flip,* or *turn* to tell how each darkened shape changed position.

1. ______ 2. ______ 3. ______ 4. ______

▶ Look at the pattern. Draw the next piece. Write *slide, flip,* or *turn* to tell what you did.

1. ______

2. ______

3. ______

4. ______

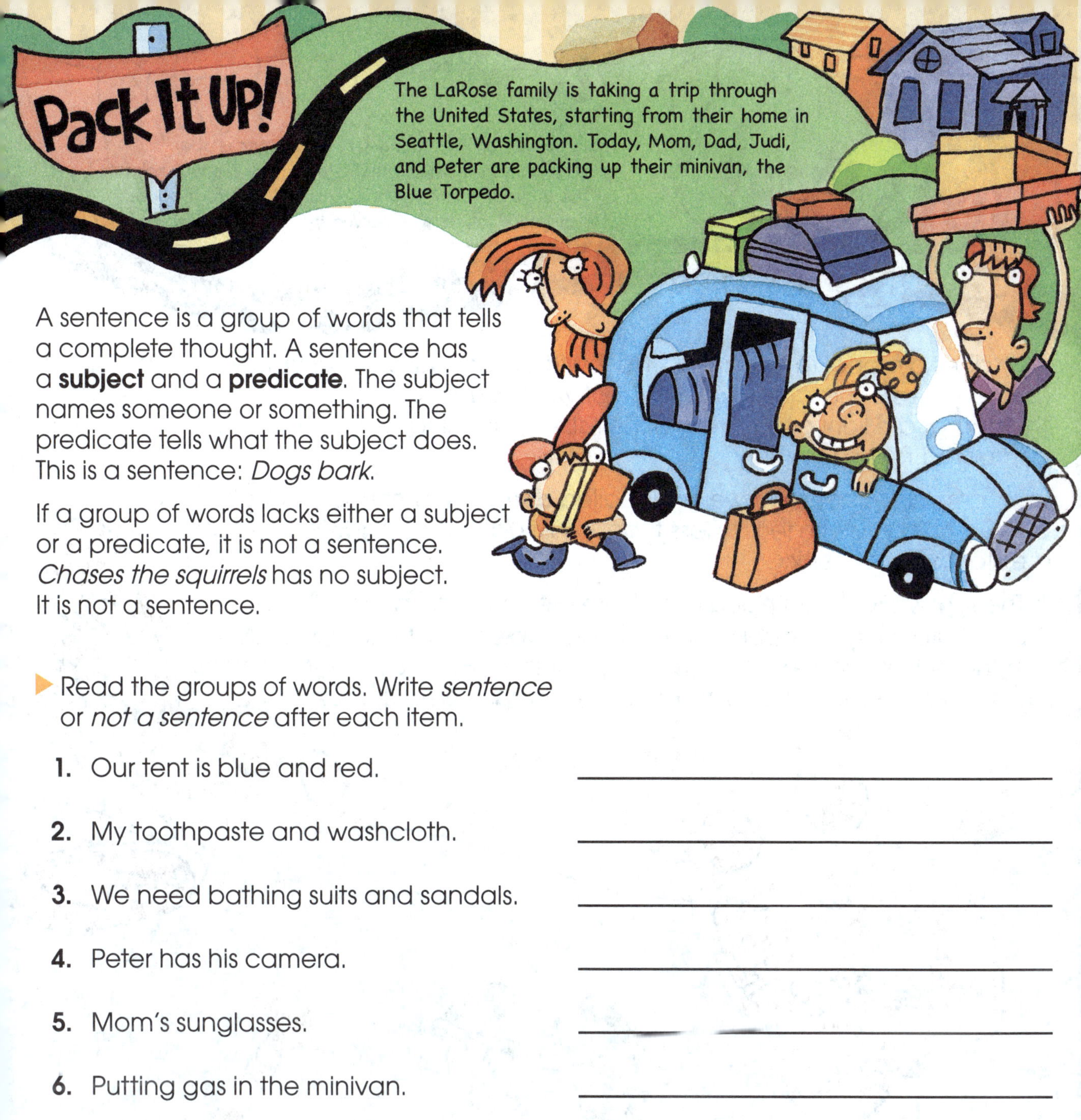

The LaRose family is taking a trip through the United States, starting from their home in Seattle, Washington. Today, Mom, Dad, Judi, and Peter are packing up their minivan, the Blue Torpedo.

A sentence is a group of words that tells a complete thought. A sentence has a **subject** and a **predicate**. The subject names someone or something. The predicate tells what the subject does. This is a sentence: *Dogs bark.*

If a group of words lacks either a subject or a predicate, it is not a sentence. *Chases the squirrels* has no subject. It is not a sentence.

▶ Read the groups of words. Write *sentence* or *not a sentence* after each item.

1. Our tent is blue and red. ____________________
2. My toothpaste and washcloth. ____________________
3. We need bathing suits and sandals. ____________________
4. Peter has his camera. ____________________
5. Mom's sunglasses. ____________________
6. Putting gas in the minivan. ____________________
7. Have to get up early in the morning. ____________________
8. The juice and crackers are in the cooler. ____________________
9. Judi packs her suitcase. ____________________
10. In the back with the sleeping bags. ____________________

Know What?

Pioneers from Illinois founded a settlement along Puget Sound in 1851. They named their new town Seattle after Chief Sealth, a Duwamish Indian who had become their friend.

Let's Float

Hells Canyon on the Idaho-Oregon border is the deepest canyon in the United States. The highest point of the edge of the canyon is almost 8,000 feet above the canyon floor. It was carved by the Snake River.

Why does a rubber raft float in a river? It floats because of **buoyancy** (**boy**-uhn-see). Buoyancy is the force of water pushing on an object. Things that are light compared to their size float. Things that are heavy compared to their size sink.

The comparison of size to weight is called **density**. Water has a density of 1. Anything with a density less than 1 will float. Anything with a density greater than 1 will sink.

▶ The family's raft has tipped over. Here are some things from their boat. Draw $\uparrow$ in the bubble next to each object that will float. Draw $\downarrow$ in the bubble near each object that will sink. (*Hint: Look at the objects' densities: < 1 means less than 1 and > 1 means greater than 1.*)

▶ Fill in the blanks.

Dad's sunglasses ______________________ because their density

is ______________________ than the density of water.

Go For It!

Plan a rafting trip. Draw a map of a river and show your route. Put in people, animals, trees, and other things you might see.

Know What?

Daredevil rider Evel Knievel tried to jump the Snake River Canyon on a rocket-powered motorcycle in 1974. He did not make it to the other side. His parachute opened too early, and he floated safely to the ground.

Montana is the fourth largest state in the United States. Western Montana has tall, rugged mountains with forests and mines. Eastern Montana, with its open plains, has the nickname "Big Sky Country."

The LaRose family is driving through Montana. They notice on the map that the distance from Missoula to Montana's capital, Helena, is about 113 miles. You can write 113 in expanded notation: 113 = 100 + 10 + 3.

▶ Write these distances in Montana in expanded notation.

1. 48 = ____________________ **2.** 120 = ____________________

3. 125 = ____________________ **4.** 236 = ____________________

5. 79 = ____________________ **6.** 261 = ____________________

7. 435 = ____________________ **8.** 372 = ____________________

9. 303 = ____________________ **10.** 197 = ____________________

Go For It!

Write the numbers above in expanded notation, but use words instead of numerals. For example: 113 = one hundred + ten + three.

Know What?

Montana's Glacier National Park is on the Continental Divide. The rivers on the west side flow to the Pacific Ocean. The rivers on the east side flow to the Atlantic Ocean and the Gulf of Mexico.

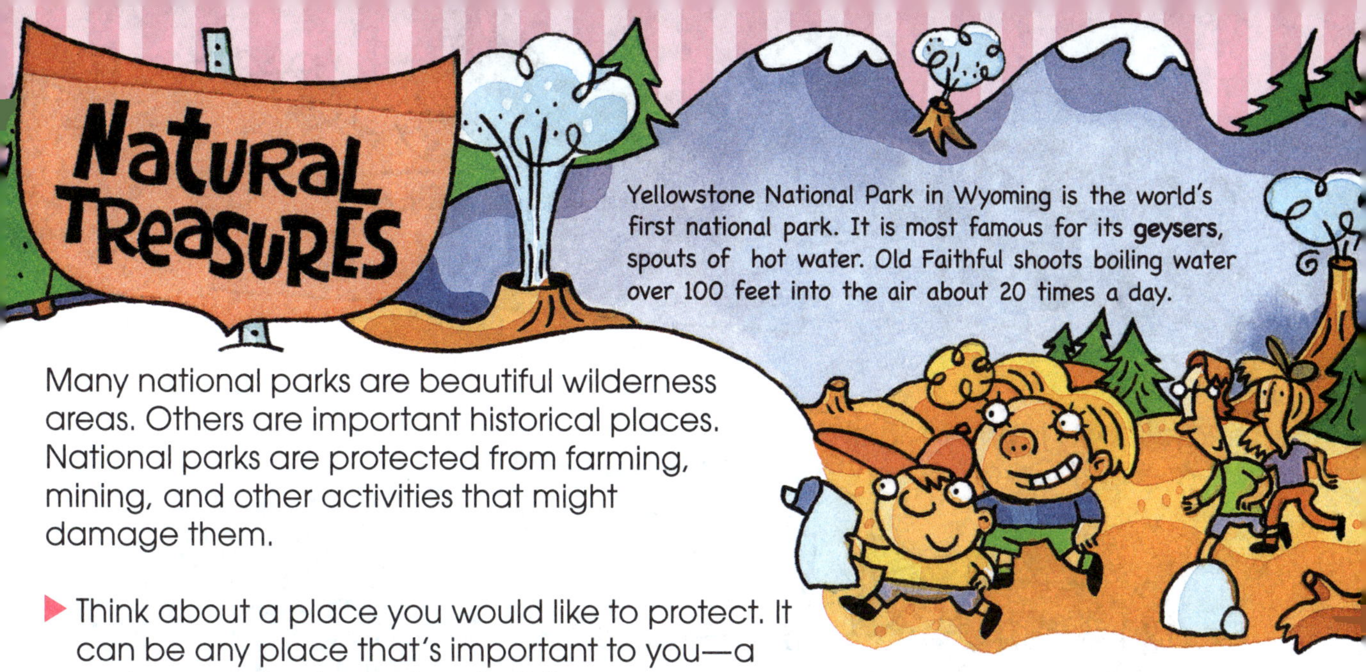

Natural Treasures

Yellowstone National Park in Wyoming is the world's first national park. It is most famous for its **geysers**, spouts of hot water. Old Faithful shoots boiling water over 100 feet into the air about 20 times a day.

Many national parks are beautiful wilderness areas. Others are important historical places. National parks are protected from farming, mining, and other activities that might damage them.

▶ Think about a place you would like to protect. It can be any place that's important to you—a park, a patch of woods, a building, or even a vacant lot.

What and where is your place? ______________________________

____

Describe it. ______________________________

____

____

____

____

Why do you want to protect the place? Give at least three reasons.

____

____

____

____

____

Go For It!

Choose a national park you would like to visit. Write to the park to ask for information about it.

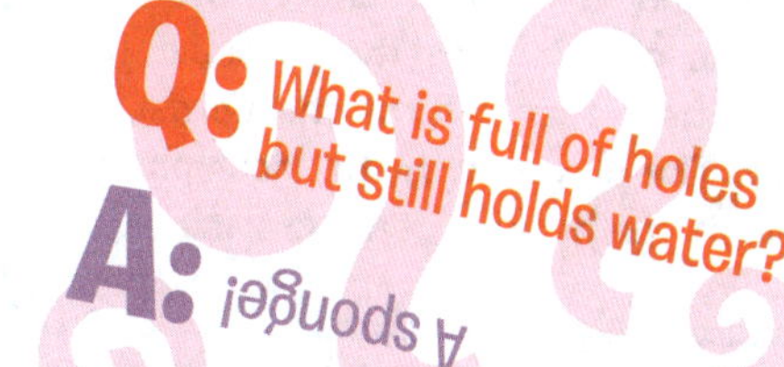

Dakota Addition

In South Dakota, farms and ranches cover much of the land. There are lots of corn, soybean, and wheat fields and huge herds of cattle.

The LaRose family is visiting South Dakota's best-known attraction.

SUM
The answer to an addition problem.

Know What?

The Homestake Mine, opened in 1876, was the oldest continuously operating gold mine in the world. Located in the town of Lead in the Black Hills, the mine closed in 2002.

▶ Write the sums. Then write the letter next to each sum to decode the message.

O	U	T	S	R
33 + 4	25 + 16	99 + 2 + 3	49 + 5 + 60	10 + 15 + 11

E	N	H	M
34 + 28 + 17	72 + 9 + 8	10 + 0 + 7	12 + 25 + 29

Where are Judi and Peter?

___ ___ ___ ___ ___   ___ ___ ___ ___ ___ ___ ___ ___

66 37 41 89 104   36 41 114 17 66 37 36 79

Go For It!

Play this addition game with a friend. Make a deck of 40 cards using the numbers 0 to 19 twice. Mix the cards up and place them facedown. Take turns drawing any two cards and saying the sum. If the sum is right, the player takes the cards. If it is wrong, the player returns the cards to the deck. The player with the most pairs of cards when the deck is used up wins.

Mega Mall

The Mall of America in Bloomington, Minnesota, is one of the biggest shopping malls in the world. It has more than 500 stores, an indoor amusement park, and an aquarium complete with sharks.

Parts of speech are words that do jobs in sentences. Nouns name people, places, or things. Verbs tell what nouns do. Adjectives tell more about nouns, and adverbs describe verbs and adjectives. Adverbs often end in *-ly*.

The thirsty shoppers slurped their smoothies sloppily.

thirsty — adjective; shoppers — noun; slurped — verb; smoothies — noun; sloppily — adverb

▶ Read the paragraph. Identify the part of speech for each underlined word. Write the verbs in Mom's shopping bag, the adjectives in Dad's, the adverbs in Judi's, and the nouns in Peter's.

Nickelodeon Universe in the Mall of America is a <u>big</u> theme <u>park</u>. Though it is indoors, the park looks like it is outdoors. The <u>sun</u> <u>shines</u> <u>brightly</u> through skylights. Many <u>tall</u> <u>trees</u> and plants <u>grow</u> in the park. Sometimes, insects <u>attack</u> these plants. So gardeners have let <u>ladybugs</u> loose in the park. The hungry ladybugs <u>quickly</u> <u>gobble</u> up the <u>harmful</u> insects.

Verbs

______

______

______

______

Go For It!

Choose an interesting article from an old newspaper. After you read it, circle the nouns. Underline the verbs. Draw a box around the adjectives. Draw a line through the adverbs. Which parts of speech did you notice most? Why do you think that is?

Know What?

Workers brought in many semi-truckloads of black dirt so that the plants and trees in Nickelodeon Universe could grow.

Lake Superior is the world's largest freshwater lake in terms of surface area. It is the largest, deepest, and cleanest of the five Great Lakes that share part of the border between the United States and Canada.

▶ The LaRose family is traveling around Lake Superior. Find each difference, and write it in the blank. Then write the differences next to the cities near Lake Superior. You will see which way the LaRoses went.

1. 27 – 18 = ______ Ironwood
2. 136 – 119 = ______ Ashland
3. 285 – 283 = ______ Sault Ste. Marie (U.S.)
4. 276 – 190 = ______ Thunder Bay
5. 179 – 21 = ______ Nipigon
6. 158 – 39 = ______ Sault Ste. Marie (Canada)
7. 81 – 27 = ______ Superior
8. 91 – 83 = ______ Copper Harbor
9. 52 – 49 = ______ Marquette

COOL WORD

DIFFERENCE
The answer to a subtraction problem.

Nipigon
Thunder Bay
Canada
U.S.A.
Lake Superior
Sault Ste. Marie
Copper Harbor
Sault Ste. Marie
Marquette
Superior
Ashland
Ironwood

Go For It!

Write two word problems using subtraction facts. Write a "take-away" story and a story comparing two different things.

Know What?

Whitefish Bay is known as a graveyard for ships. In 1975, the *Edmund Fitzgerald*, a 729-foot supership, along with its 29-man crew, sank without a trace. The wreck was found off Whitefish Point. Some people believe that the pressure on the ship from huge swells of water made it break in half.

Eat Write!

Wisconsin is nicknamed "America's Dairyland" because its farms produce so much milk, butter, and cheese. Wisconsin farms also produce many other foods, such as beef, pork, chicken, and eggs.

The food we eat gives us the nutrients (**noo**-tree-uhnts) we need to grow and be healthy. We need starch from rice, bread, and pasta for energy. Fat from nuts, vegetable oils, and butter helps our cells grow. Protein from lean meat, cheese, eggs, beans, and fish builds and repairs cells. Fiber from fruits and vegetables helps our digestive systems work smoothly.

▶ Sit down to a yummy picnic of healthful foods from a Wisconsin farm. For each of the foods pictured, write whether it contains mainly starch, fat, protein, or fiber.

1. ____________ 2. ____________ 3. ____________

4. ____________ 5. ____________ 6. ____________

1 2 3 4 5 6

Go For It!

Make a food group poster. Cut out pictures of foods from grocery store advertisements. Write *Starches*, *Proteins*, *Fats*, and *Fiber* as headings on a large sheet of paper. Paste the pictures in the correct columns. Hang your poster in the kitchen.

We use four main types of sentences.

A **statement** tells something. *Chicago's nickname is the "Windy City."*
A **question** asks something. *What is on the menu at your favorite restaurant?*
A **command** gives an order. *Don't forget to buy tickets.*
An **exclamation** expresses a strong feeling. *Everything is expensive!*

▶ Identify the sentences in the picture. Write *s* in the box if the sentence is a statement. Write *q* if the sentence is a question. Write *c* if the sentence is a command. Write *e* if the sentence is an exclamation.

Go For It!

Write a command, a statement, an exclamation, and a question. Use a different word below in each sentence.

drive skyscraper basketball buy

Know What?

The Chicago River is known as the river that flows backward. In 1900, engineers made the river flow away from Lake Michigan instead of into it. They did this to prevent the dirty water in the river from polluting the lake.

Let's Race!

Indiana has a mix of industrial areas and rolling farmland. Indianapolis, its capital and largest city, is known for the Indy 500 automobile race, which is held on Memorial Day.

▶ Speed around the racetrack as you find each sum.

Cool Word

ADDENDS are the numbers to be added. In 43 + 57 = 100 43 and 57 are the addends.

Start

1. $43 + 56$
2. $29 + 15$
3. $150 + 28$
4. $46 + 29$
5. $373 + 218$
6. $340 + 420$
7. $183 + 671$
8. $406 + 35$
9. $346 + 713 + 187$
10. $298 + 429 + 409$

Pit

Go For It!

There are many different addition problems that have a sum of 100. Think of at least 10 addition problems with two-digit addends that add up to 100.

Know What?

The first long-distance automobile race on a track in the United States took place on May 30, 1911, at the Indianapolis Motor Speedway. Ray Harroun won the 500-mile race, averaging a speed of about 75 miles per hour.

A **common noun** names any person, place, or thing. A **proper noun** names a particular person, place, or thing. Proper nouns begin with uppercase letters.

Common Nouns	**Proper Nouns**
person	Judi
month	April
place	Beech Street
state	Ohio

▶ The paragraph below has several mistakes. Draw this mark ≡ under letters that should be uppercase. Draw this mark / through letters that should not be uppercase. *Hint: remember that sentences begin with uppercase letters.*

Example: judi and Peter went to the football Game.

The Stars of football shine at the Pro Football Hall of Fame in canton, ohio. the Hall of Fame opened on september 7, 1963. Every year, the league names a few of its Best players to the Hall of Fame. there, visitors can See pictures of these players, their Uniforms, and their equipment.

Go For It!

Write the name of your favorite athlete. If the athlete plays for a team, write the name of the team and the team's home city. Make sure you use uppercase letters in the right places.

Niagara Falls, one of North America's most famous attractions, lies on the Niagara River between Lake Erie and Lake Ontario. Part of the falls lies in the United States and part lies in Canada. Horseshoe Falls is in Canada. American Falls is in the U.S.

A map is a special kind of picture. Maps give information about an area using lines, colors, shapes, and other symbols. These symbols show where roads, cities, rivers, lakes, and many other things are located. The part of a map that tells what the symbols mean is called the **key** or **legend**.

▶ Use the map and key to answer the questions.

1. How many power plants are shown on the map? ______________________
2. What is the name of the big island? ______________________
3. About how many miles wide is it? ______________________
4. What does this symbol [city symbol] mean? ______________________
5. How many lakes are shown on the map? ______________________
6. What are their names? ______________________

Go For It!

Hide a treat somewhere around your house. Draw a map showing where the treat is hidden. Use symbols and include a legend to explain what your symbols mean. Ask a friend to use your map to find the treat.

Verbs have different forms, or **tenses**, to tell what happened, what's happening now, or what will happen. To make many verbs past tense, add the letters *-ed* to the end of the verb. *The river flow**ed** to the sea.* To make a verb future tense, add *will* before the verb. *I **will** see you on the boat tomorrow.*

▶ Write the correct tense of the word in parentheses in each blank.

1. The Seaway ______________________ (open) in 1959.
2. Today, ships from many countries ______________________ (use) the Seaway.
3. The Seaway ______________________ (close) every winter because of ice.
4. Improvements to the St. Lawrence Seaway ______________________ (continue).
5. The French ______________________ (construct) a canal around the St. Lawrence River in 1680.
6. Peter ______________________ (read) more about the St. Lawrence Seaway when he gets home.

Go For It!

Write a sentence about something you did yesterday. Then rewrite that sentence using present and future tenses.

What Flowers Are for

The Adirondack Mountains are in northeastern New York. More than 40 of the peaks in the Adirondacks rise more than 4,000 feet. The mountains are famous for their forests and hundreds of beautiful lakes.

All the parts of a flower do a different job in making seeds.

- The male parts of a flower, the **stamens**, make pollen. Most plants have several stamens. The stamens are often tan.
- The female parts of the flower, the **pistil**, make ovules (**ohv**-yools). Most pistils are green.
- The colorful **corolla** is made of petals that attract birds and insects. These animals spread the pollen from one flower to the ovules of another flower so seeds can begin to form.
- The **calyx** is the outer part of the flower. It has little leaves.

▶ Label the parts of the flower.

▶ Why do most plants need seeds?

____

____

Go For It!

Make a notebook of pressed flowers. Collect some wildflowers. Put them in an old phone book or under a heavy weight. When the flowers are dry, tape them into a notebook. Look up their names and write labels to identify the flowers.

Tea Time

Many important events in America's fight for independence from England happened in Boston. The Boston Tea Party was one of them.

Writers often use words like *first, next, then, after,* and *later* to help readers understand the order that things happen in a story.

▶ These sentences are out of order. Number them in the correct order. The first one is done for you.

_____ Next, they sneaked onto the British ships.

__1__ A group of British ships carrying tea arrived in Boston.

_____ However, the governor said no.

_____ When the colonists saw the ships, they asked the governor to send them back.

_____ First, some of the colonists dressed up as Native Americans.

_____ After that, a group of colonists decided to take action.

_____ Once on the ship, they dumped the tea into the water.

Know What?

English Puritans founded Boston in 1630. They named the city after Boston, England, where they used to live.

Go For It!

Write about an interesting day in your life. You can write a true story or a made-up story. Use words such as *first, next, then,* and *finally* to make the order that things happen in your story clear.

There are many tall buildings in New York City.

▶ Number the buildings from 1 to 4 to show the order of the buildings from tallest to shortest. (1 = tallest)

______ Chrysler Building, 1,046 feet

______ Citigroup Center, 915 feet

______ Empire State Building, 1,250 feet

______ GE Building, 850 feet

Know What?
The Empire State Building has 102 floors, 1,860 steps, 73 elevators, 70 miles of pipes, and 6,500 windows.

▶ How much taller is the tallest building than the shortest building?

____

____

New York City is made up of five parts called **boroughs**: the Bronx, Brooklyn, Manhattan, Queens, and Staten Island. Many bridges and tunnels connect the boroughs.

Bridge	Connects
Brooklyn	Manhattan and Brooklyn
George Washington	Manhattan and New Jersey
Queensboro	Manhattan and Queens
Verrazano-Narrows	Staten Island and Brooklyn
Williamsburg	Manhattan and Brooklyn

▶ Write the name or names of the bridge or bridges.

1. Which bridges connect Brooklyn and Manhattan?

____

2. Which bridge connects Staten Island and Brooklyn?

____

3. Which bridge connects Queens and Manhattan?

____

4. Which bridge connects Manhattan and New Jersey?

____

Go For It!

Arrange five objects from longest to shortest or from tallest to shortest. (You may want to measure with a ruler.) Record your results in a chart or graph.

The Declaration of Independence was signed in Philadelphia. Philadelphia is also the country's pretzel capital. People in Philadelphia eat about 12 times more pretzels than people anywhere else in the country.

Periods are one of the most useful punctuation marks. Here are some ways periods are used:

- at the end of sentences that are statements or commands:
  You can visit a pretzel factory in Philadelphia.
- after the letters *a.m.* and *p.m.* in times: 7:00 *a.m.*
- after abbreviations, words that are shortened: *Tues., Dec., Calif.*
- after a person's abbreviated title: *Dr. Johnson, Mrs. Minniver*

▶ The LaRose family is learning a lot about Philadelphia. Read about their discoveries as you practice using periods. Put periods where they belong in the sentences.

1. Philadelphia is nicknamed "Philly" and "The City of Brotherly Love "
2. Independence Hall, where the Declaration of Independence was adopted, is located in Philadelphia , Penn , and is open for tours
3. America's first pretzel bakery opened in Lititz, Penn , in 1861
4. Mr LaRose ate six pretzels on their visit to Philadelphia
5. They bought a box of pretzels for their friend, Dr Banks
6. The LaRose family is leaving Philadelphia, Penn , tomorrow at 9:00 a m

Go For It!

Periods have more uses than those listed on this page. The next time you read a book, magazine, or newspaper, pay attention to the periods. Try to find some other ways periods are used.

Know What?

Pretzels were first baked over 1,000 years ago to reward children who learned their prayers. The shape of these salty treats was meant to look like arms crossed in prayer.

Make a Timeline

Baltimore is Maryland's largest city. It lies on Chesapeake Bay. Ships from all over the world come to Baltimore to load and unload goods.

A timeline is one good way to show the order of events.

▶ Use the information in the paragraph below to fill in the blanks in this timeline.

The Port of Baltimore was founded in 1706. In 1729, Baltimore Town was founded. Eighty-five years later, Francis Scott Key wrote "The Star-Spangled Banner" after he watched the British attack the city. Most of the downtown area of Baltimore burned to the ground in the Great Baltimore Fire of 1904. Eighty-eight years after that, the Baltimore Orioles baseball team got a new stadium.

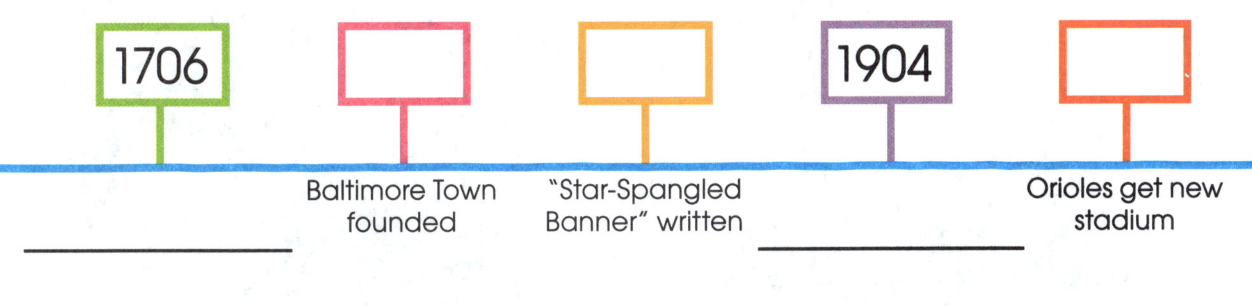

1706	____	____	1904	____
________ ________ ________	Baltimore Town founded	"Star-Spangled Banner" written	________ ________ ________	Orioles get new stadium

Go For It!

Make a timeline of your life. Start when you were born and put in the most important things that have happened to you. If you like, draw a small picture showing each event.

Know What?

Cal Ripken, Jr., of the Orioles made baseball history on September 6, 1995, in Baltimore. That's when he played his 2,131st game in a row to break Lou Gehrig's record.

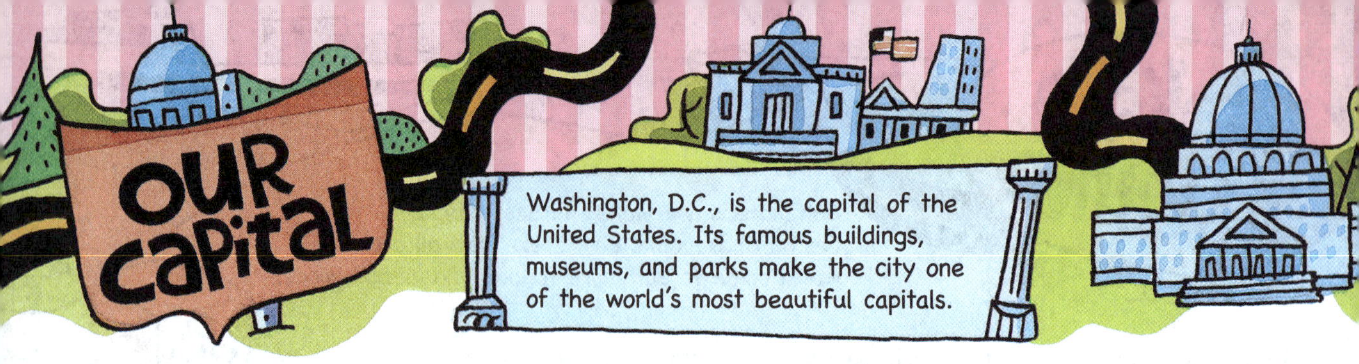

Words that have opposite meanings are called **antonyms**. Words that have about the same meaning are called **synonyms**. Words that sound alike but have different spellings and meanings are called **homophones**.

▶ Look at the words in the picture. On the line near each word pair, write *antonyms, synonyms,* or *homophones.*

1. ______________________________

2. ______________________________

3. ______________________________

4. ______________________________

5. ______________________

6. 

7. ______________________

8. ______________________

9. ______________________

10. ______________________

Go For It!

Play a synonym game with a friend or two. Write some common words on slips of paper. Choose a slip. See how many synonyms you can write in one minute.

Know What?

The city of Washington, D.C., was designed by a French engineer, Pierre Charles L'Enfant. It's one of the few cities in the world that was designed before it was built.

Go For It!

Check your answers using addition.

Example: $\begin{array}{r} 75 \\ -\ 29 \\ \hline 46 \end{array}$ Check: $\begin{array}{r} 46 \\ +\ 29 \\ \hline 75 \end{array}$

Know What?

Virginia is called the "Mother of Presidents" because eight U.S. presidents were born there. They include four of the first five presidents. Can you name them? If you can't, how can you find their names?

Going Caving

Mammoth Cave in Kentucky, the longest known cave system in the world, has more than 300 miles of passageways. Underground rivers flow into dark lakes where blind fish and shrimp live.

Caves are formed when water drips through the earth and eats away a hollow in the rock underground. When the water flows away, a cave remains. Here are some parts of a cave:

- **chamber**—a large "room" in a cave
- **stalagmite**—a pointy pillar that rises from the cave's floor
- **stalactite**—a pointy "icicle" that hangs from the cave's ceiling
- **column**—a pillar formed when a stalactite and stalagmite join

▶ Write the names of the cave parts on the lines.

Go For It!

Use modeling clay of various colors and a cardboard box to build a model of a cave. Make chambers, stalagmites, stalactites, and columns.

Missouri used to be called the "Gateway to the West." St. Joseph was the eastern starting point of the Pony Express. The Oregon Trail began in Independence.

Judi and Peter are using ordered pairs to find Springfield on the map. First they find the 4, and then they go up to B. Springfield is at (4,B).

▶ Write the city for each ordered pair.

1. (4,A) ____________________

2. (2,B) ____________________

3. (8,F) ____________________

4. (10,A) ____________________

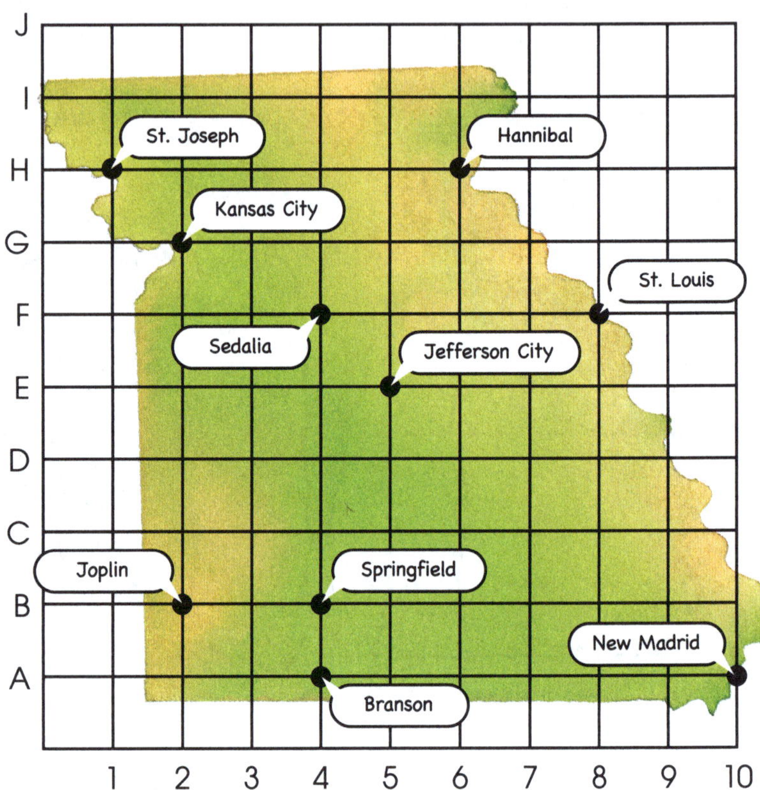

▶ Give the ordered pairs for these cities.

5. Jefferson City: (____, ____)

6. Sedalia: (____, ____)

7. Hannibal: (____, ____)

8. St. Joseph: (____, ____)

Go For It!

Look at a map of a city or state. Find five places on the map. Then write ordered pairs for their locations.

Know What?

The Gateway Arch in St. Louis was built to honor the 19th-century pioneers who traveled west. The Arch is 630 feet tall, 75 feet higher than the Washington Monument. Approximately 900 tons of stainless steel were needed to build the Arch.

Graceland, in Memphis, Tennessee, was the home of the singer Elvis Presley. His home looks much like it did when Elvis lived there. You can see Elvis's cars, music awards, and grave site.

If you want to convince someone to do or believe something, you have to give them good reasons. For example, you might think peanut butter and jelly sandwiches make the best lunch in the world. To convince someone, you could tell them that peanut butter and jelly sandwiches give you energy, fill you up, and taste delicious.

▶ Write a paragraph to persuade people that Elvis Presley was the greatest musical performer of all time. Include three of the facts below that support that opinion. Add ideas of your own.

- Elvis is one of the best-selling artists in the history of pop music.
- Elvis appeared in over 30 movies.
- Thousands of people visit Graceland every year.
- The Jungle Room at Graceland has furry furniture and statues of monkeys.
- Many people enjoy watching performers who dress up like Elvis and sing his songs.
- Many famous musicians copied Elvis's style.
- Elvis died in 1977, but some people believe he is still alive.
- Elvis's nickname is "The King."

Go For It!

Choose a favorite musician or actor. Write a paragraph to convince someone that this person is the best in the world. Support your opinion with good reasons.

The Great Smoky Mountains National Park covers more than 520,000 acres and is about evenly divided between Tennessee and North Carolina.

The LaRoses are planning a route from Memphis to the Great Smoky Mountains National Park. The park has entrances at Gatlinburg, Tennessee and Cherokee, North Carolina.

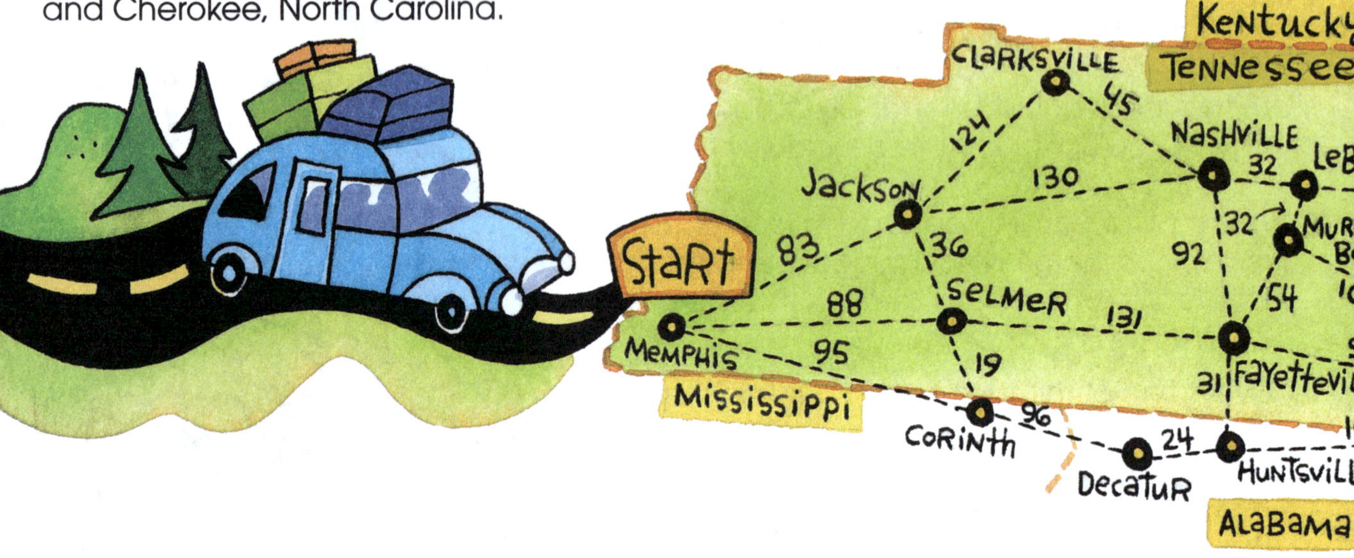

▶ Follow each route from Memphis to the park. Write the number of miles between each pair of cities. Then calculate the total number of miles.

Memphis → Jackson → Nashville → Lebanon → Knoxville → Gatlinburg

______ + ______ + ______ + ______ + ______ = ______

Memphis → Selmer → Fayetteville → Chattanooga → Cleveland → Cherokee

______ + ______ + ______ + ______ + ______ = ______

Memphis → Selmer → Fayetteville → Nashville → Lebanon → Knoxville → Gatlinburg

______ + ______ + ______ + ______ + ______ + ______ = ______

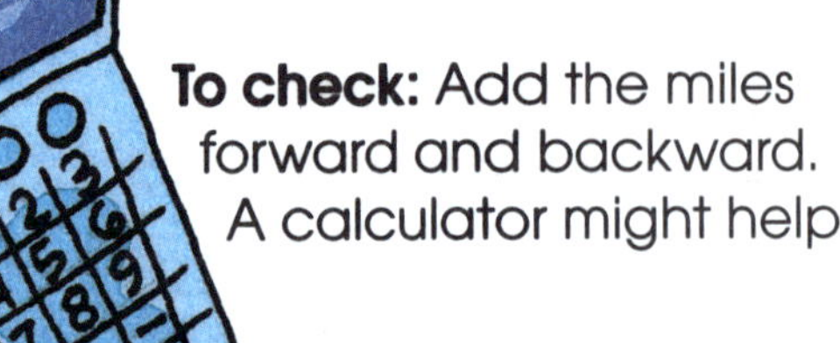

To check: Add the miles forward and backward. A calculator might help!

Know What?

The Great Smoky Mountains got their name from the smokelike fog that often hangs over the peaks. Due to the heights of the Great Smoky Mountains, the area receives heavy amounts of precipitation, which supports the growth of many kinds of trees, plants, and shrubs in the Great Smoky Mountains.

▶ Find one way to get from Memphis to the park going through Murfreesboro and traveling only in Tennessee. Name the cities through which you would travel, and calculate the total number of miles.

____

____

▶ Find a way to get from Memphis to the park traveling through more than two states. Name the cities through which you would travel, and calculate the total number of miles.

____

____

Go For It!

Make a map of a room in your house. Draw five or six objects in the room. Count the number of steps to get from one object to another. Then plan a way to touch at least three of the objects in the room, and calculate the total number of steps.

Who's there?
Shelby.
Shelby who?
Shelby comin' around the mountain when she comes...

Dahlonega, Georgia, is located on top of the largest gold deposits found east of the Mississippi River. Visitors can tour old gold mines and rent equipment to search for gold. They get to keep all the gold they find!

The past tense of most verbs is made by adding the letters *-ed* to the present tense of the verb. But irregular verbs break that rule. How do you learn irregular verbs? You memorize them.

▶ Mr. LaRose, Mrs. LaRose, Peter, and Judy are panning for gold. On each nugget, write the past tense of the verb.

▶ Now that you have written all the past tenses, color the nuggets with irregular verbs yellow.

Which person has the most gold? ____________________

Go For It!

You can play Go Fish with irregular verbs. Use index cards to make your own deck. Write 26 irregular verbs and their past tense forms on separate cards. Match each verb with its past tense form to play.

Parts of the North Carolina coastline are protected in two national seashores—Cape Hatteras and Cape Lookout. Cape Hatteras has dangerous currents and shallow waters that have caused many shipwrecks. Cape Lookout has a famous lighthouse.

The coast is the place where sea and land meet. Lighthouses let ships know where the land begins. The ocean rises at high tide and withdraws at low tide. Sand piles high on shore to form dunes and creates shallow places in the water called sandbars. Marshy areas often run along a coast.

▶ Look at the picture.
Color the different parts of the coastline this way:

dunes—yellow
sandbars—tan
ocean—blue
lighthouse—red
the area between low tide and high tide—brown

Go For It!

Lighthouses flash their lights in special patterns to give ships information. Write a code using patterns of flashing colors. For example, red, red, long white, short white might mean "Come over and play." Share your code with a friend.

Know What?

Ocracoke Island, off the coast of North Carolina, was a hideout of the pirate Blackbeard.

The Florida Keys are a group of small islands that stretch in a curve from the southeastern tip of the Florida peninsula into the Gulf of Mexico. The coral reefs and sport fishing attract lots of tourists.

COOL WORD

PRODUCT the answer to a multiplication problem

▶ Write the product for each multiplication fact. Then write the products on the map to act as mile marker (MM) addresses on the islands.

Big Pine Key	7 x 5 = ____	Long Key	8 x 7 = ____
Grassy Key	6 x 9 = ____	Seven Mile Bridge	6 x 7 = ____
Indian Key	8 x 8 = ____	Stock Island	3 x 4 = ____
Key Largo	9 x 9 = ____	Summerland Key	8 x 2 = ____
Key West	7 x 0 = ____	Windley Key	8 x 9 = ____

Go For It!

Practice the multiplication facts with a friend. See how fast you can say the 6 facts, 7 facts, 8 facts, and 9 facts.

Know What?

The only address many people have in the Florida Keys is a mile marker (MM) number. The markers are small, green and white, rectangular signs along the sides of the highway. The numbers begin with MM 126 on the Florida coast and end with MM 0 in Key West.

At the Kennedy Space Center in Florida, you can learn all about the space program. You can go on a simulated ride into space, look at rockets, see movies on a screen that's five stories tall, and even watch a real space shuttle launch.

Scientists learn about space by sending space probes to fly through space or land on planets. Space probes send information back to Earth. Rovers ride around on the surface of a planet. Satellites travel around and around, or **orbit**, Earth. They are used for communication, navigation, weather forecasting, scientific research, and even spying. People ride into space on a space shuttle, where they do experiments. A space station orbits Earth. Astronauts may live on a space station for months at a time.

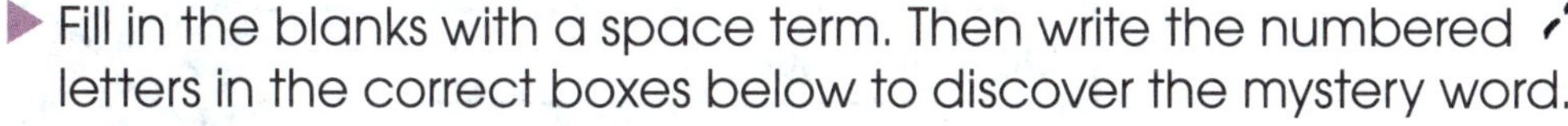

▶ Fill in the blanks with a space term. Then write the numbered letters in the correct boxes below to discover the mystery word.

1. A space ____ ____ ____ ____ ____ may land on a planet.
   (1 under the 2nd blank)
2. A ____ ____ ____ ____ ____ ____ ____ ____ ____ travels around Earth.
   (2 under the 4th blank)
3. Astronauts can live on a space ____ ____ ____ ____ ____ ____ ____.
   (3 under the 1st blank; 4 under the 7th blank)
4. Astronauts ride into space and back on a space ____ ____ ____ ____ ____ ____ ____.
   (5 under the 3rd blank)
5. To ____ ____ ____ ____ ____ means to travel around a planet.
   (6 under the 4th blank)
6. A ____ ____ ____ ____ ____ can ride around on a planet's surface.
   (7 under the 3rd blank; 8 under the 4th blank)

5	4	6	7	8	1	3	2

Go For It!

Venus is hotter than an oven, and its air is mostly poisonous gases. What if a creature could live there? Think about what that creature might look like, and then draw it.

Tourists love to visit Florida's many animal parks, including SeaWorld, Discovery Cove, Disney's Animal Kingdom, Busch Gardens, Lion Country Safari, and Jungle Island.

▶ Use logic to solve these story problems about animals the LaRoses see in Florida. Read the clues. Then fill in the chart to solve the problems. Here is an example.

Peter, Judi, and Dad are watching **different** animals. Who is watching each animal?

Dad is not watching the panther.

	panther	pelican	deer
Judi			
Peter			
Dad	No		

Judi is not watching the panther either. Peter must be watching the panther.

	panther	pelican	deer
Judi	No		
Peter	Yes		
Dad	No		

Dad is not watching the pelican. Dad must be watching the deer. Judi must be watching the pelican.

	panther	pelican	deer
Judi	No	Yes	No
Peter	Yes	No	No
Dad	No	No	Yes

1. Write the animal each person is watching.

Judi ______________ Peter ______________ Dad ______________

Go For It!

Make up a logic problem. Challenge a friend to solve your logic problem.

Know What?

Marineland of Florida is known as the world's first oceanarium. It was built in 1937 on Florida's Atlantic coast south of St. Augustine.

Dad, Mom, Judi, and Peter each have a **different** favorite Florida animal. Which animal is each person's favorite? Fill in the chart completely to find out.

Judi's favorite animal is not the alligator.

Judi's favorite animal is not the manatee.

Dad's favorite animal is not the alligator or the anhinga.

Judi's favorite animal is not the anhinga.

Peter's favorite animal is not the anhinga.

	turtle	alligator	manatee	anhinga
Judi				
Dad				
Peter				
Mom				

2. Write each person's favorite animal.

Judi ____________________ Dad ____________________

Peter ____________________ Mom ____________________

The Everglades are wetlands located at the southern tip of Florida. The area is home to unusual plants, such as a kind of tall grass called sawgrass, and animals, including panthers, manatees, alligators, and anhingas.

The words *a, an,* and *the* are special adjectives called **articles**. *A* and *an* are used before nouns that aren't specific. For example, **a** book. It could be any book. *A* comes before nouns that begin with a consonant sound. *An* is used before nouns that begin with a vowel sound. *The* refers to a specific object and is used both before nouns that name one and nouns that name more than one. For example, **the** book. It refers to a specific book.

▶ Help Judi and Peter find their way out of the Everglades maze. If you run into a picture that shows a noun that goes with *an,* your path is blocked. But if you run into a picture of a noun that goes with *a,* you can continue.

Go For It!

Play a guessing game with a friend. Take turns giving wordless clues for the nouns in the maze. See who can come up with the best clues.

Who's there?
Everglade.
Everglade who?
Am I Everglade to see you!

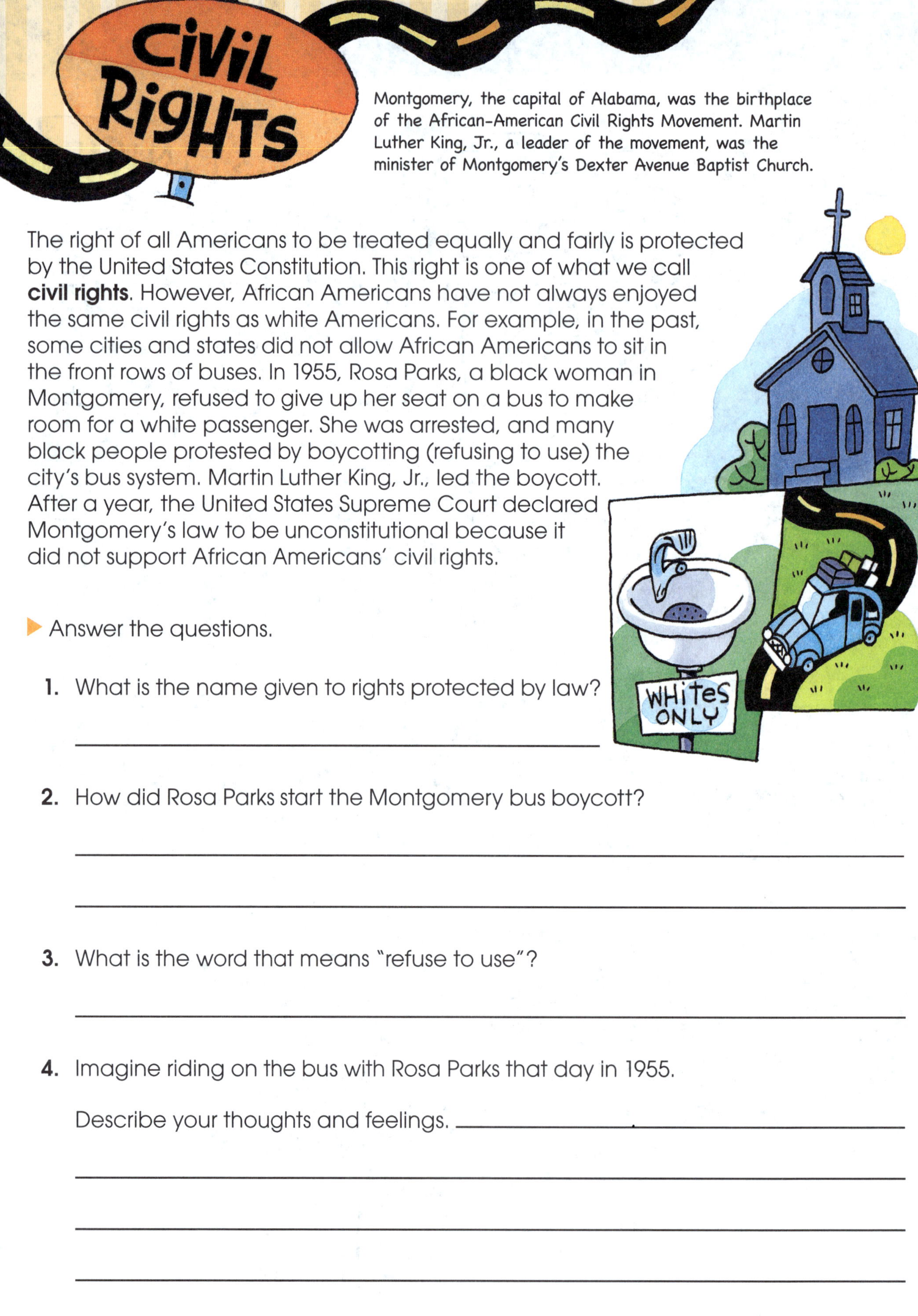

Civil Rights

Montgomery, the capital of Alabama, was the birthplace of the African-American Civil Rights Movement. Martin Luther King, Jr., a leader of the movement, was the minister of Montgomery's Dexter Avenue Baptist Church.

The right of all Americans to be treated equally and fairly is protected by the United States Constitution. This right is one of what we call **civil rights**. However, African Americans have not always enjoyed the same civil rights as white Americans. For example, in the past, some cities and states did not allow African Americans to sit in the front rows of buses. In 1955, Rosa Parks, a black woman in Montgomery, refused to give up her seat on a bus to make room for a white passenger. She was arrested, and many black people protested by boycotting (refusing to use) the city's bus system. Martin Luther King, Jr., led the boycott. After a year, the United States Supreme Court declared Montgomery's law to be unconstitutional because it did not support African Americans' civil rights.

▶ Answer the questions.

1. What is the name given to rights protected by law?

   ____

2. How did Rosa Parks start the Montgomery bus boycott?

   ____

   ____

3. What is the word that means "refuse to use"?

   ____

4. Imagine riding on the bus with Rosa Parks that day in 1955.

   Describe your thoughts and feelings. ______________________________

   ____

   ____

   ____

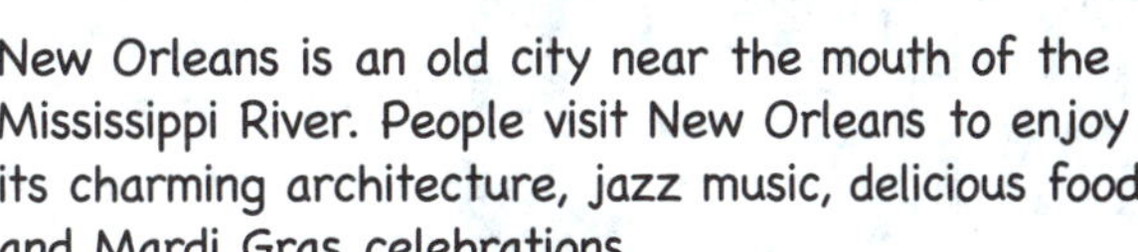

New Orleans is an old city near the mouth of the Mississippi River. People visit New Orleans to enjoy its charming architecture, jazz music, delicious food, and Mardi Gras celebrations.

Commas separate the parts of a sentence and help make the meaning clear. Commas are used in the following ways:

- to separate three or more items in a list: *We ate gumbo, shrimp, and hush puppies.*
- between the day and the year in a date: *February 16, 2010*
- between the city and state or city and country: *New Orleans, Louisiana, is on the Mississippi.*
- when connecting two complete sentences into one sentence using *and, or, for, nor, but, so,* or *yet*: *We went to the parade, and we saw colorful dancers.*

Know What?

Mardi Gras means "fat Tuesday" in French. A long time ago, people used to parade a fat ox through French villages during Mardi Gras celebrations.

▶ Add commas where they belong in the sentences.

1. Mardi Gras is an ancient festival but people still enjoy it.
2. New Orleans Louisiana has a big Mardi Gras celebration.
3. People celebrate with food music parties and parades.
4. Musicians play and colorful floats roll down the street.
5. Riders on the floats throw coins necklaces and toys.
6. The LaRose family met some people from Berlin Germany at Mardi Gras.
7. The people from Berlin spoke English so the two families enjoyed the parade together.
8. Then they went to a restaurant where they ate crayfish gumbo and jambalaya.

Go For It!

Play pin the comma on the sentence. Cut big commas from black construction paper. Write a sentence that needs commas on a large sheet of paper—but leave the commas off. Blindfold a friend and see whether your friend can put a comma in the right place.

Padre Island National Seashore is a sand-dune-covered barrier island that parallels the Texas coast between Port Isabel and Corpus Christi on the Gulf of Mexico.

▶ Write the quotient for each division fact.

1. 24 ÷ 8 = ____
2. 63 ÷ 9 = ____
3. 42 ÷ 7 = ____
4. 48 ÷ 6 = ____
5. 45 ÷ 5 = ____
6. 54 ÷ 6 = ____
7. 36 ÷ 4 = ____
8. 81 ÷ 9 = ____
9. 56 ÷ 8 = ____
10. 64 ÷ 8 = ____
11. 27 ÷ 3 = ____
12. 72 ÷ 9 = ____

Go For It!

Write the division facts another way.
For example, 35 ÷ 5 = 7 can be written as $5\overline{)35}$ with 7 above.

Know What?
Padre Island is the longest barrier island in the world.

The Mississippi River is sometimes called "Old Man River." It flows from Lake Itasca in Minnesota over 2,000 miles to the Gulf of Mexico.

What should you do when you're reading and come across words you don't understand? One thing you can do is keep reading. The words around the unknown word, or the **context**, can help you. You can also get meaning clues from illustrations.

▶ Read the paragraph and figure out what the underlined words mean. Then draw a line to match each word to its meaning.

The Mississippi River grows as it travels south! Tributaries, such as the Arkansas River, just keep adding to its amount of water. There, the river twists and winds around in loops, forming oxbow lakes. The river also deposits soil on the shore to create natural levees. The southern Mississippi River is especially important for shipping cargo. Agricultural products, such as corn and wheat, travel on barges pushed by tugboats.

1. tributary	goods moved by boat, airplane, or vehicle
2. oxbow lake	to dump or place
3. deposit	a high mound along the bank of a river
4. levee	a horseshoe-shaped body of water
5. cargo	a large, flat boat
6. agricultural	a smaller river that flows into a larger one
7. barge	made or grown on a farm

ARKANSAS RIVER

Mississippi River

Here's a dictionary game to play with a group. Have one player find a hard word in a dictionary and write its definition. Everyone else writes made-up definitions for the word. The person who chose the word reads the actual definition and the made-up ones. Players guess which definition is real. Whoever wrote the definition that fooled the most people gets to choose the next word.

Are You My Mom?

San Antonio, Texas, is an important city in United States history. It is the home of a former mission, now a museum, called the Alamo. A famous battle was fought there during Texas' fight for independence from Mexico.

Some animal babies look a lot like their parents. Young monkeys look like grown-up monkeys. Elephant babies do not look that different from grown-up elephants. But some animal babies don't look at all like their parents. Young butterflies and moths are caterpillars. Young frogs are tadpoles. Young mosquitoes are little, wiggly things that live in water. These animals change shape completely as they grow into adults. This change is called **metamorphosis** (meh-tuh-**morf**-uh-sihs).

▶ Take a stroll around the San Antonio Zoo. Write the names of the adult animals and their babies. Write *m* in the boxes by the animals that change by metamorphosis.

☐ ______ ______

☐ ______ ______

☐ ______ ______

☐ ______ ______

☐ ______ ______

Go For It!

Frogs go through several steps as they grow. Find out what these steps are. Draw frogs in their various stages on pieces of paper, and color your drawings with bright colors. Label the steps.

El Paso is in the far western part of Texas. It's so far west that it's in a different time zone from most other Texas cities!

To find what time it will be in the future, add hours or minutes.

The time is 7:25.

In 2 hours, it will be 9:25.

In 10 minutes it will be 7:35.

▶ What time will it be in 3 hours?

1. ____________________ **2.** ____________________ **3.** ____________________

▶ What time will it be in 20 minutes?

4. ____________________ **5.** ____________________ **6.** ____________________

▶ What time will it be

in 4 hours?

in 25 minutes?

in 40 minutes?

7. ____________________ **8.** ____________________ **9.** ____________________

White Sands National Monument is an area of pure-white sand dunes in southern New Mexico. The dunes are made of a mineral called gypsum.

A possessive noun shows that a person or thing owns something. Add *'s* to most singular nouns to show possession: *dog's bowl, Judi's hat.* Add *'* to most plural nouns to show possession: *parents' maps, dunes' shapes.*

▶ Write a sentence to describe each scene from the LaRose family's day at White Sands. Use the possessive form of a noun in each sentence.

1.

____

____

____

2.

____

____

____

3.

____

____

____

4.

____

____

____

Go For It!

On a separate piece of paper, rewrite your sentences. Keep the same meaning, but don't use any possessive nouns. Can you do it?

Know What?

The state bird of New Mexico, the roadrunner, can run at speeds of up to 20 miles per hour.

Carlsbad Caverns National Park is a series of huge caves in southeastern New Mexico. Lighted trails display fantastic rock formations. The Caverns provide a home for thousands of Mexican Free-tailed Bats.

Figures are **symmetric** when one side matches the other side. Symmetric figures have at least one line of symmetry.

1 line of symmetry

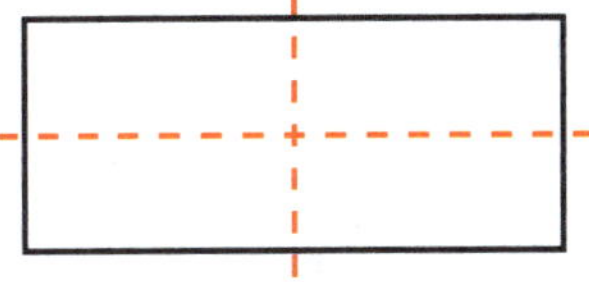

2 lines of symmetry

▶ Name each figure. Use the words in the box if you need help. Then draw lines of symmetry.

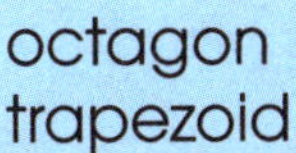

octagon	circle	parallelogram	square
trapezoid	triangle	rectangle	pentagon

1. ____________________

2. ____________________

3. ____________________

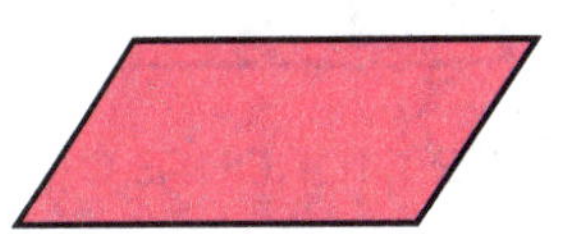

4. ____________________

5. ____________________

6. ____________________

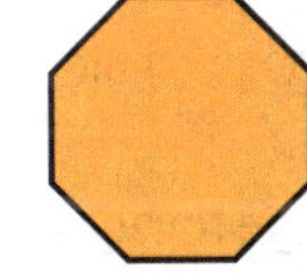

7. ____________________

8. ____________________

▶ Draw these as symmetric figures.

9. a cave entrance

10. a lightbulb

West Texas

West Texas is a region of dry, treeless plains and rugged mountains. It is one of the most important oil-drilling areas in the U.S. Cowboys drove their herds of cattle from Texas to be shipped by rail to markets in the East.

Pronouns take the place of nouns.

Suzy lives in West Texas. *She lives in West Texas.*

The word *she* is a pronoun. *I, he, they, it, them,* and *you* are some other pronouns.

Possessive pronouns take the place of possessive nouns.

Suzy's ten-gallon hat *her ten-gallon hat*

Her is a possessive pronoun. *My, his, its, our, their,* and *your* are some other possessive pronouns.

▶ Write pronouns and possessive pronouns to take the place of the underlined words.

1. Young Pecos Bill fell from his parents' wagon. ______________________
2. Pecos Bill's life changed forever. ______________________
3. From then on, he was the coyotes' child. ______________________
4. The storm cloud's flood dug the Grand Canyon. ______________________
5. Pecos Bill's fall made a dent called Death Valley. ______________________
6. Pecos Bill's sweetheart was Slue-Foot Sue. ______________________
7. Sue's adventures were astonishing, too. ______________________
8. Mary's favorite stories are tall tales. ______________________

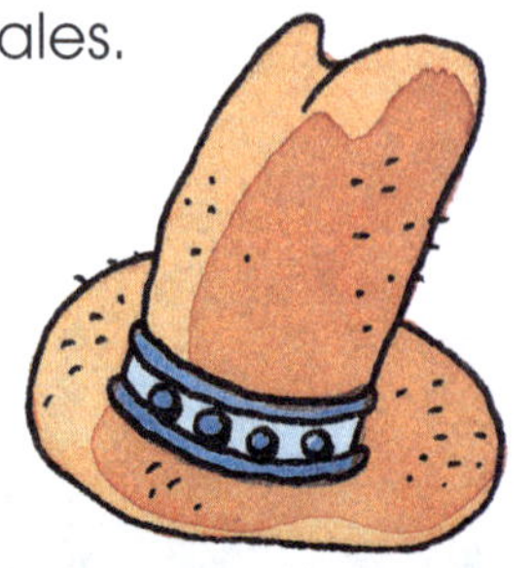

Santa Fe is the capital of New Mexico. The city is arranged around a city square called the "Plaza." The Plaza has been an important center of commerce, festivals, and history for hundreds of years.

A figure can be moved in many ways. You can make interesting geometric patterns with shapes and moves. Lots of Native American art has patterns made by using this method.

slide

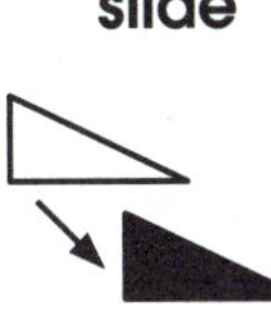

flip

turn

▶ Write the word *slide, flip,* or *turn* to explain how to get each dark figure.

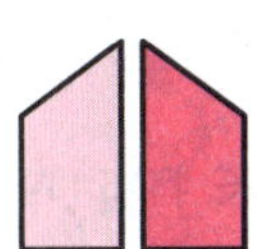

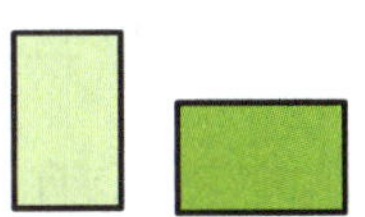

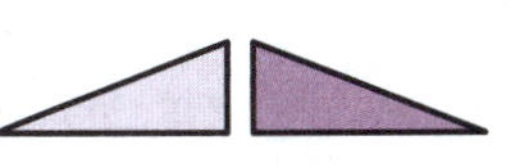

1. ______________ 2. ______________ 3. ______________ 4. ______________

▶ Look at each pattern. Draw and color the next figure.
Write *slide, flip,* or *turn* in the blank to explain what you did.

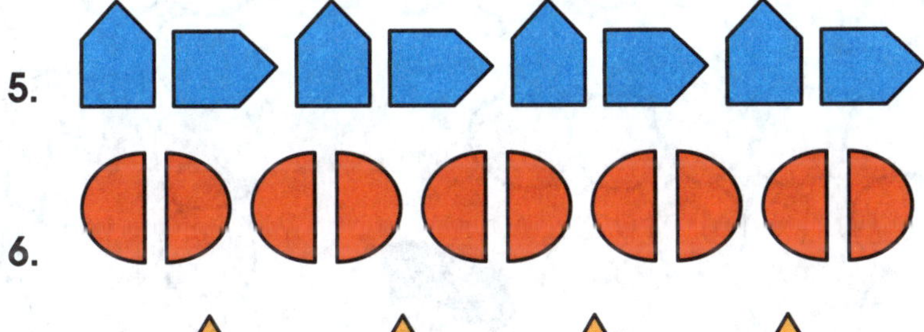

5. ______________

6. ______________

7. ______________

8. ______________

Go For It!

Design a T-shirt with a pattern. Use a geometric shape with slides, turns, or flips. Color your design.

Know What?

The state capitol of New Mexico has a round design that resembles the Zia Sun Symbol, the official emblem of the state.

You can see ruins of cliff dwellings in Mesa Verde National Park in southern Colorado. Ancient Indians built these dwellings on ledges of high cliffs. Over 600 different dwellings have been documented. Some are like apartment buildings with many different rooms.

Some Pueblo Indians live in villages called **pueblos** (**pweb**-lohz) in New Mexico and Arizona. Many of their houses are similar to the cliff dwellings at Mesa Verde. Many pueblo dwellers follow their old ways of life and religion. They hold religious ceremonies in underground rooms called **kivas** (**kee**-vuhz). The Pueblo people make beautiful pottery and baskets.

▶ Use the clues to fill in the words in the puzzle.

Across

1. Pueblo Indians make beautiful ____.
4. A ____ is an underground room.
5. A flat-topped hill is called a ____.
7. Many Pueblos are in New ____.

Down

1. Another name for a village is ____.
2. Some cliff dwellings have many ____.
3. *Mesa* is the Spanish word for ____.
6. Ancient Indians built ____ dwellings.

Go For It!

Dancing is important to many Native Americans. Make up a dance to express something about yourself or how you feel. Perform the dance for someone.

Know What?

Mesa means "table" in Spanish, and *verde* means "green." Spanish-speaking people named the flat-topped hills of the Southwestern United States *mesas* because they look like giant tables. Why do you think they called the hills *verde*?

Desert Crawlers

In southern Utah, winds and rains have carved sandstone into wondrous towers, arches, canyons, and bluffs. The water in the Great Salt Lake in northern Utah is saltier than the ocean.

The desert is a harsh place, but many insects and spiders are right at home there.

- The thistledown velvet ant is actually a wingless wasp that lives in the sand. Its body is covered with hairs, so it looks like a cotton ball. It feeds on nectar.
- Wind scorpions are yellowish-brown and about an inch long. They catch insects, lizards, and other small animals with their large pincers.
- The trapdoor spider digs a burrow with a trap door made of dirt, vegetation, and silk. It lies in wait in its burrow and grabs passing insects.
- The black cactus longhorn beetle is shiny and black with long feelers. It eats cactus.

▶ Below are drawings of parts of the creatures described. Figure out which bug each part belongs to. Write the names of the creatures on the lines.

1. 

____

2. 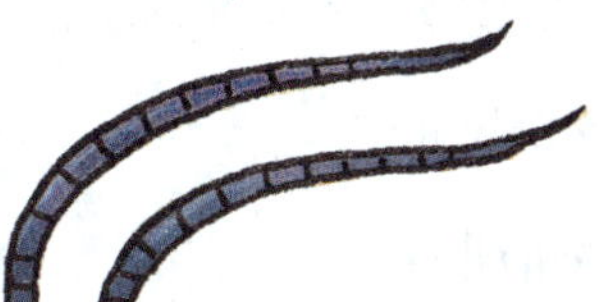

____

3. 

____

4. 

____

5. 

____

6. 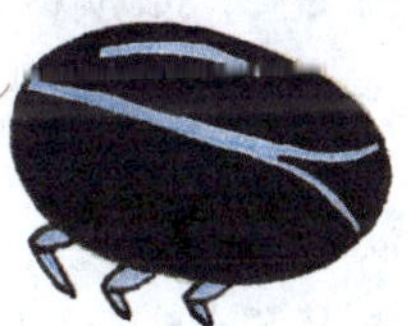

____

Go For It!

Insects are everywhere. If it's the right time of year, find an insect or spider to observe. It could be an ant gathering food, a spider spinning a web, or a bee visiting flowers. Write or draw your observations.

Know What?

Tarantulas got their name from a type of spider found near Taranto, Italy. People used to believe that doing a dance called the Tarantella cured the sickness caused by this spider's bite.

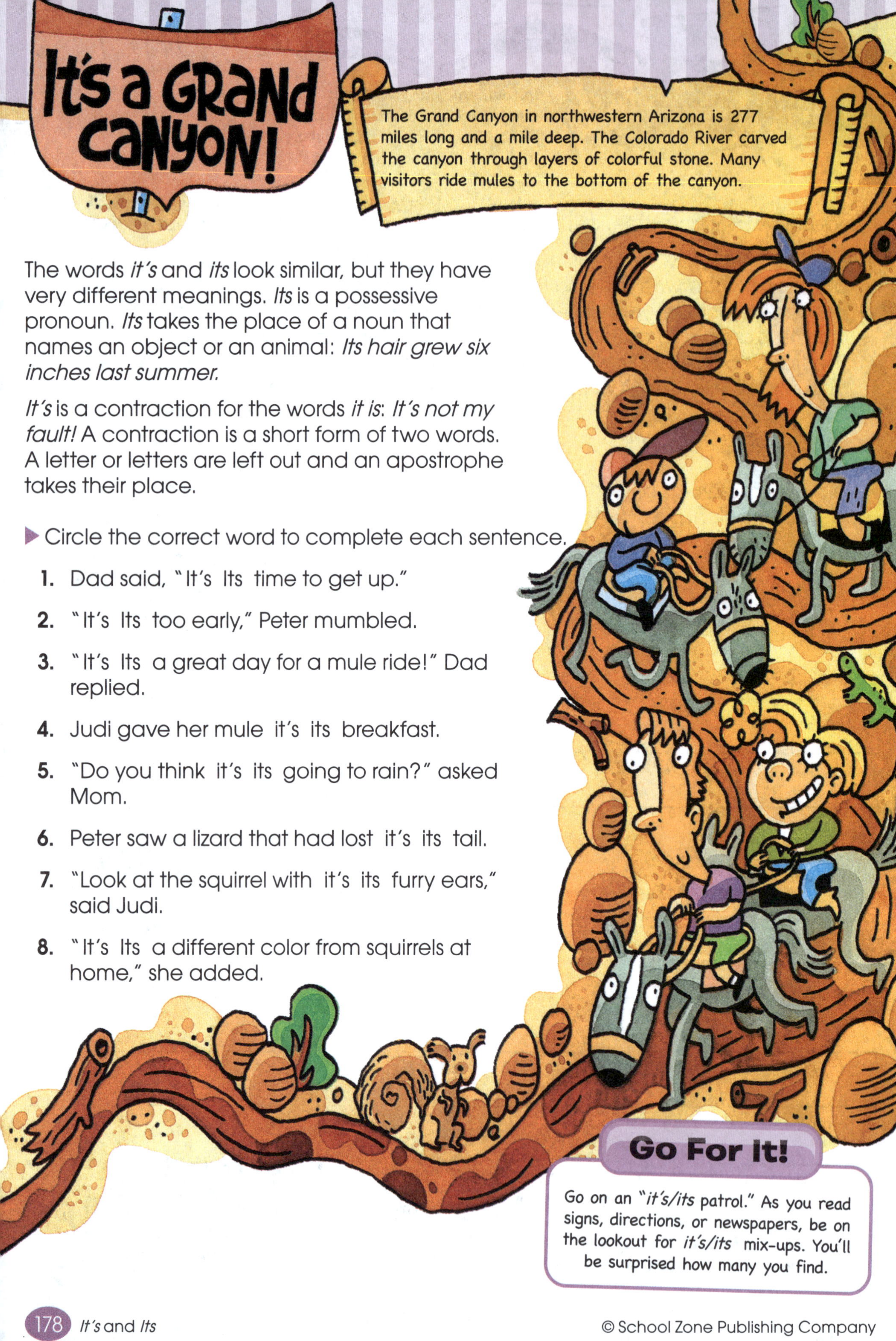

It's a Grand Canyon!

The Grand Canyon in northwestern Arizona is 277 miles long and a mile deep. The Colorado River carved the canyon through layers of colorful stone. Many visitors ride mules to the bottom of the canyon.

The words *it's* and *its* look similar, but they have very different meanings. *Its* is a possessive pronoun. *Its* takes the place of a noun that names an object or an animal: *Its hair grew six inches last summer.*

It's is a contraction for the words *it is*: *It's not my fault!* A contraction is a short form of two words. A letter or letters are left out and an apostrophe takes their place.

▶ Circle the correct word to complete each sentence.

1. Dad said, "It's Its time to get up."
2. "It's Its too early," Peter mumbled.
3. "It's Its a great day for a mule ride!" Dad replied.
4. Judi gave her mule it's its breakfast.
5. "Do you think it's its going to rain?" asked Mom.
6. Peter saw a lizard that had lost it's its tail.
7. "Look at the squirrel with it's its furry ears," said Judi.
8. "It's Its a different color from squirrels at home," she added.

Go For It!

Go on an "*it's/its* patrol." As you read signs, directions, or newspapers, be on the lookout for *it's/its* mix-ups. You'll be surprised how many you find.

Death Valley is a desert trough in east-central California. The lowest part, 282 feet below sea level, is near the city of Badwater. The highest temperature ever recorded in the United States, 134°F, was reported there in 1913.

You can use a Fahrenheit thermometer to measure the temperature. The one at the right shows some temperatures to remember.

▶ Write the temperatures in degrees Fahrenheit.

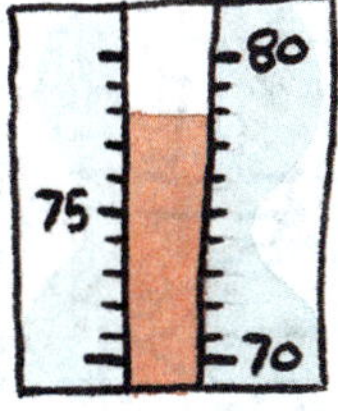

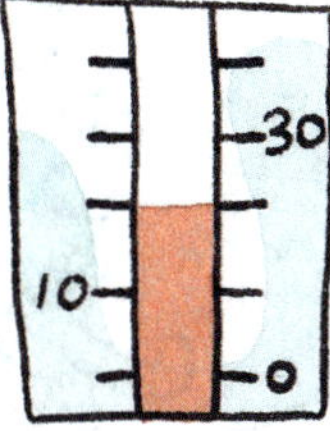

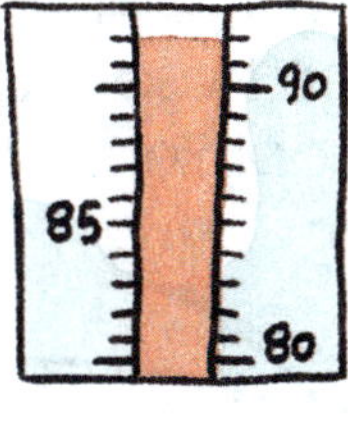

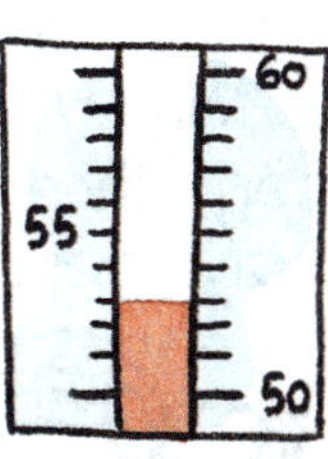

1. ______ 2. ______ 3. ______ 4. ______

▶ Look at the temperatures. Which is the most reasonable for each picture? Write the temperature under each picture.

18° F	59° F
80° F	101° F

5. ______ 6. ______ 7. ______ 8. ______

Go For It!

Write a letter to someone who lives in a different climate from yours. Discuss the seasons: what the weather is like, what clothing you need, which activities are fun.

Know What?

The average rainfall on the floor of Death Valley is less than 2 inches per year!

San Francisco's many attractions include Golden Gate Park, Chinatown, and Fisherman's Wharf. Visitors enjoy views of twinkling ocean waters from atop tall hills. They love the cable cars that chug up and down steep, narrow streets.

When we read, we often come across statements that are facts. Facts can be proved: *San Francisco is in California.*

We also read opinions: *San Francisco is the most beautiful city in California.* Opinions can't be proved.

▶ Tour the city with the LaRose family. They'll hear some information from the tour guide. Write *f* under those that are facts. Write *o* under the statements that are opinions. Write *f* + *o* under those that contain facts and opinions.

1. The best seafood restaurant is Wing Chun, which is in Chinatown. ________

2. Chinatown is in the northeast corner of the city. ________

3. Wing Chun is owned by my uncle. ________

4. You will be disappointed if you do not eat at Wing Chun. ________

5. Wing Chun has a team of master chefs trained in China. ________

6. At Wing Chun, you have a choice of hot or mild sauce, but the hot sauce is the tastiest. ________

7. Wing Chun serves forty-two types of shrimp dumplings. ________

8. No dish on the menu costs more than $8.95. ________

9. My cousin will offer you a mint as you leave. ________

10. Wing Chun is a real bargain! ________

Go For It!

In your opinion, did the LaRose family learn much about Chinatown on their tour? On a separate piece of paper, explain why or why not.

Know What?

Lombard Street in San Francisco is called the most crooked street in the world. In just one steep block, Lombard makes eight sharp turns.

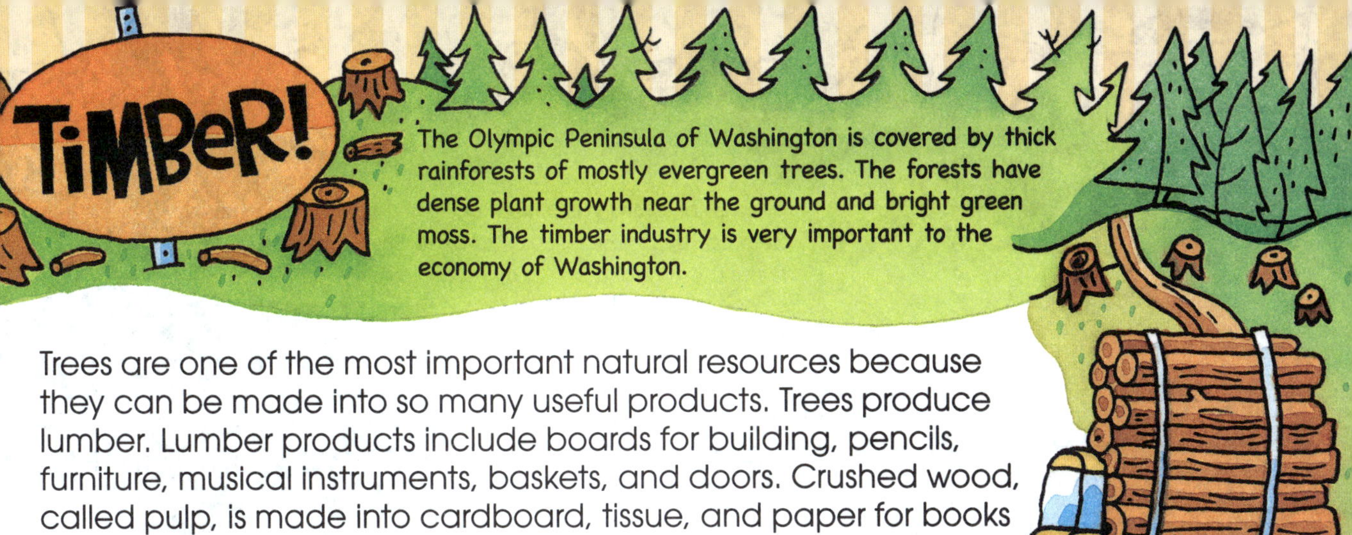

The Olympic Peninsula of Washington is covered by thick rainforests of mostly evergreen trees. The forests have dense plant growth near the ground and bright green moss. The timber industry is very important to the economy of Washington.

Trees are one of the most important natural resources because they can be made into so many useful products. Trees produce lumber. Lumber products include boards for building, pencils, furniture, musical instruments, baskets, and doors. Crushed wood, called pulp, is made into cardboard, tissue, and paper for books and newspapers. The chemicals in wood make cellophane, plastic, ink, paint, dye, cloth, and cement.

▶ Below are some products made from trees.
Write the name of each product in the correct row.

Lumber					
Pulp					
Chemicals					

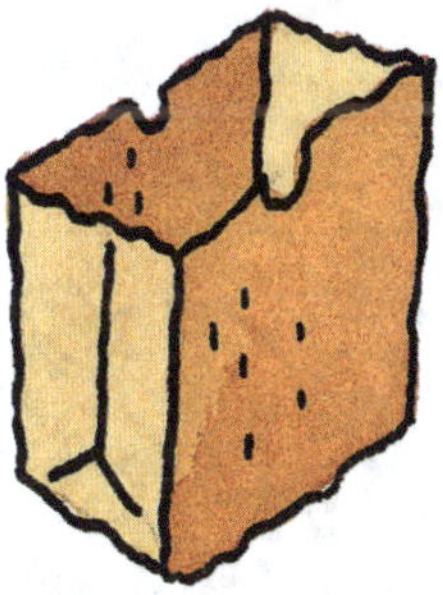

Go For It!

Think of a product or service you could offer people. What would you call your business? How much would you charge? How would you let people know about your business? Write your ideas.

Write on Home

The LaRose family is finally back at home in Seattle after their vacation. Have you learned a lot and enjoyed the trip as much as they have?

A **paragraph** is a group of sentences about one idea. Often, the first sentence is a **topic sentence** that tells what the paragraph is about. The first sentence is indented. **Supporting sentences** give more information about, or support, the topic sentence. Often, a **conclusion** sums up the paragraph.

▶ Write a paragraph about home. It can be about your town, your house, your family, or a place you would like to live. Make sure the paragraph has the three parts described above.

____

____

____

____

____

____

____

____

____

____

____

Go For It!

Did you smile at the knock knock jokes in the book? Try writing some knock knock jokes of your own—the sillier the better!

Count by Tens, Fives, and Twos

▶ Connect the dots.

Start at the ▲ and count by tens to 100.

Start at the ● and count by fives to 100.

Start at the ■ and count by twos from 50 to 100.

Greater or Less

35  32

Greater means more than.
Less means not as many.

The symbol points to the number that is less.

35 is **greater** than 32.
35 > 32
or
32 is **less** than 35.
32 < 35

▶ Write the number for each group. Compare the numbers. Then write < or > in the ☐.

1. 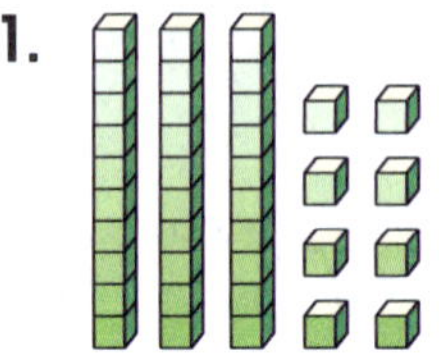 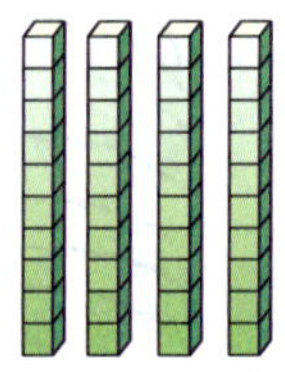

____ ☐ ____

2. 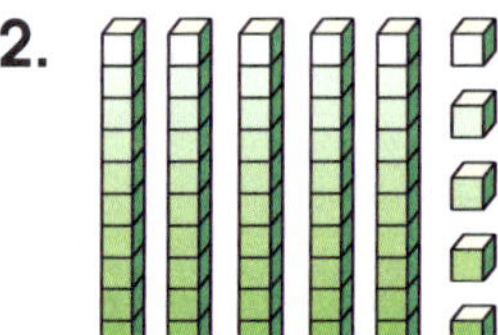 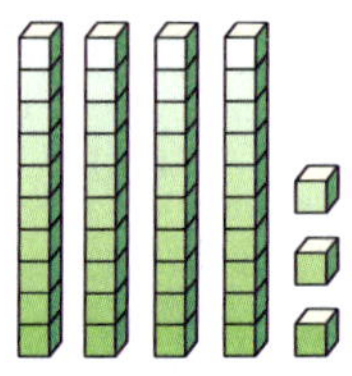

____ ☐ ____

3. 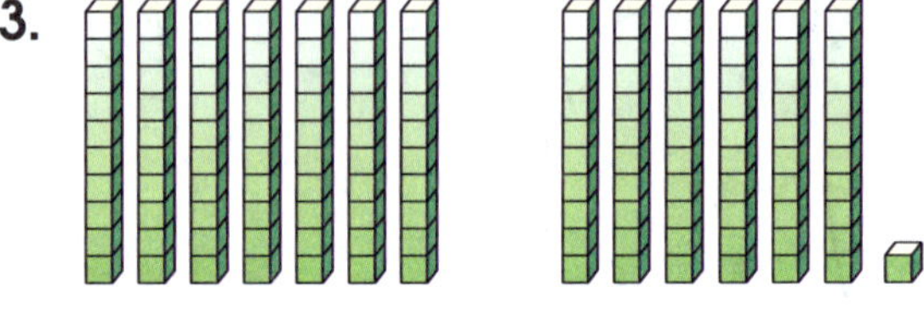

____ ☐ ____

4. 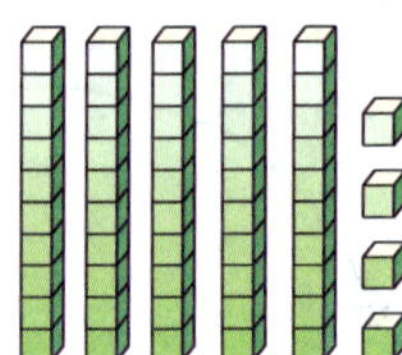

____ ☐ ____

▶ Compare the numbers. Then write < or > in the ☐.

5. 48  58

6. 72  27

7. 70  67

8. 77  69

9. 39  93

10. 57  51

Numbers in Order

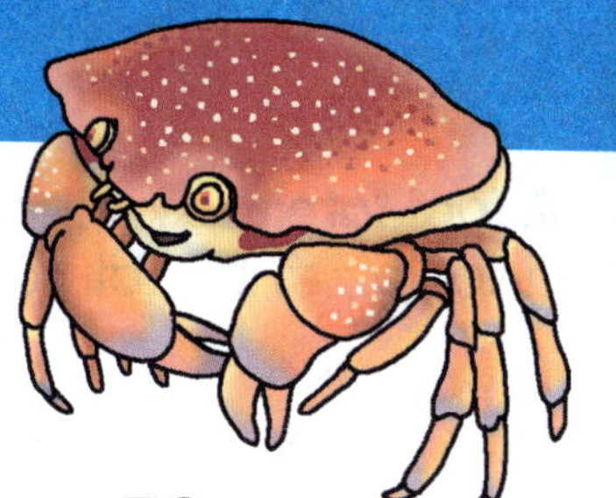

▶ Write the missing numbers.

1. 41, 42, ____, 44, ____, ____, 47, ____, ____, 50

2. 87, ____, 89, ____, 91, ____, ____, 94, ____, 96

3. 66, ____, ____, 69, ____, ____, 72, ____, 74, ____

4. ____, 74, ____, ____, 77, ____, 79, ____, 81, ____

5. ____, ____, 38, ____, ____, 41, ____, ____, 44, ____

▶ Write the numbers in order from least to greatest.

6. 36; 19; 47; 21 ____; ____; ____; ____

7. 76; 65; 33; 56 ____; ____; ____; ____

8. 59; 46; 32; 17 ____; ____; ____; ____

9. 89; 26; 39; 19 ____; ____; ____; ____

10. 73; 67; 37; 63 ____; ____; ____; ____

Fact Families

A **fact family** uses the same numbers in its addition and subtraction problems.

4	[3]	7	[7]
+ 3	+ 4	− 3	− 4
[7]	7	[4]	3

▶ Write the missing numbers to complete the fact family.

1.

2	5	7	☐
+ 5	+ ☐	− 2	− 5
☐	7	☐	2

2.

☐	3	9	9
+ 3	+ 6	− ☐	− ☐
9	☐	3	6

3.

4	☐	9	☐
+ 5	+ 4	− ☐	− 5
☐	9	5	4

4.

6	0	6	6
+ ☐	+ ☐	− ☐	− ☐
6	6	0	6

5.

6	☐	13	☐
+ 7	+ 6	− 7	− 6
☐	13	☐	7

6.

8	5	13	13
+ ☐	+ 8	− ☐	− 5
13	☐	5	☐

7.

7	☐	16	☐
+ 9	+ 7	− 9	− 7
☐	16	☐	9

8.

4	8	12	12
+ ☐	+ 4	− ☐	− ☐
12	☐	4	8

More Fact Families

All of the number sentences in a **fact family** use the same numbers.

3, 9, 12

3 + 9 = 12

9 + 3 = 12

12 − 3 = 9

12 − 9 = 3

▶ Write the addition and subtraction facts for the family.

1. 6, 8, 14

______
______
______
______

2. 4, 9, 13

______
______
______
______

3. 7, 8, 15

______
______
______
______

4. 5, 7, 12

______
______
______
______

5. 5, 9, 14

______
______
______
______

6. 8, 9, 17

______
______
______
______

7. 6, 9, 15

______
______
______
______

8. 9, 0, 9

______
______
______
______

9. 7, 7, 14

______
______

Round Two-Digit Numbers

To **round** a number to the **nearest ten**, look at the **ones** place.
If the digit in the ones place is **5 or more**, then **round up**.
If the digit in the ones place is **4 or less**, then **round down**.

Is 83 closer to 80 or 90? 80

Round 83 to 80.

90
89
88
87
86
85
84
83
82
81
80

▶ Look at the boldface number. To round, circle the nearest ten.

1. **32** 30 40
2. **89** 80 90
3. **19** 10 20
4. **64** 60 70
5. **55** 50 60
6. **26** 20 30
7. **41** 40 50
8. **77** 70 80
9. **28** 20 30
10. **39** 30 40
11. **62** 60 70
12. **33** 30 40

▶ Round the number to the nearest ten.

13. 64 ______
14. 86 ______
15. 22 ______
16. 49 ______
17. 31 ______
18. 43 ______
19. 35 ______
20. 67 ______
21. 18 ______
22. 13 ______
23. 89 ______
24. 76 ______

Estimate Sums and Differences

Estimate the sums and differences by **rounding** to the **nearest ten**.

The answer to an addition problem is called the **sum**. The answer to a subtraction problem is called the **difference**.

Estimate the sum.

		Estimate:
52	→	50
+ 35	→	+ 40
		90

Estimate the difference.

		Estimate:
71	→	70
− 35	→	− 40
		30

▶ Round the numbers to the nearest ten.
Write the estimate for the sum or difference.

1.

		Estimate:
17	→	______
+ 22	→	+ ______
		______

2.

		Estimate:
65	→	______
− 19	→	− ______
		______

3.

		Estimate:
75	→	______
− 47	→	− ______
		______

4.

		Estimate:
53	→	______
+ 29	→	+ ______
		______

▶ Estimate the sum or difference.

5. 46 + 38 ______

6. 81 − 29 ______

7. 46 − 38 ______

8. 43 + 25 ______

9. 83 + 12 ______

10. 83 − 12 ______

Add Two-Digit Numbers

Add the **ones**.
Regroup as needed.

$$\begin{array}{r} {}^{1} \\ 36 \\ +\ 59 \\ \hline 5 \end{array}$$

6 + 9 = **15 ones**
15 ones is
1 ten and **5 ones**.

Add the **tens**.

$$\begin{array}{r} {}^{1} \\ 36 \\ +\ 59 \\ \hline 95 \end{array}$$

1 + 3 + 5 = **9 tens**
The **sum** is **95**.

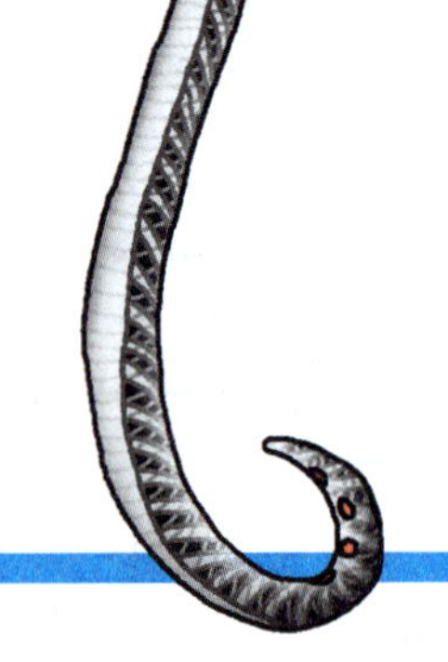

Estimate:

$$\begin{array}{r} 40 \\ +\ 60 \\ \hline 100 \end{array}$$

▶ Find the sums to fill in the puzzle.

Across

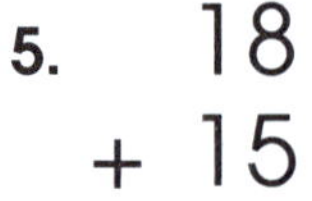

1. $\begin{array}{r} 55 \\ +\ 37 \\ \hline \end{array}$
2. $\begin{array}{r} 29 \\ +\ 46 \\ \hline \end{array}$
3. $\begin{array}{r} 47 \\ +\ 18 \\ \hline \end{array}$
5. $\begin{array}{r} 18 \\ +\ 15 \\ \hline \end{array}$
6. $\begin{array}{r} 59 \\ +\ 17 \\ \hline \end{array}$
8. $\begin{array}{r} 77 \\ +\ 15 \\ \hline \end{array}$
9. $\begin{array}{r} 25 \\ +\ 18 \\ \hline \end{array}$
10. $\begin{array}{r} 24 \\ +\ 67 \\ \hline \end{array}$
14. $\begin{array}{r} 14 \\ +\ 19 \\ \hline \end{array}$
15. $\begin{array}{r} 35 \\ +\ 16 \\ \hline \end{array}$

1.			2.			3.	4.
						5.	
	6.	7.		8.			
	9.					10.	
11.			12.		13.		
14.					15.		

Down

1. $\begin{array}{r} 28 \\ +\ 68 \\ \hline \end{array}$
2. $\begin{array}{r} 39 \\ +\ 35 \\ \hline \end{array}$
3. $\begin{array}{r} 24 \\ +\ 39 \\ \hline \end{array}$
4. $\begin{array}{r} 17 \\ +\ 36 \\ \hline \end{array}$
6. $\begin{array}{r} 28 \\ +\ 46 \\ \hline \end{array}$
7. $\begin{array}{r} 34 \\ +\ 29 \\ \hline \end{array}$
8. $\begin{array}{r} 76 \\ +\ 14 \\ \hline \end{array}$
11. $\begin{array}{r} 45 \\ +\ 38 \\ \hline \end{array}$
12. $\begin{array}{r} 37 \\ +\ 58 \\ \hline \end{array}$
13. $\begin{array}{r} 29 \\ +\ 36 \\ \hline \end{array}$

Add Three or More Numbers

Add: 32 + 8 + 14
Add the **ones**.
Regroup as needed.

$$\begin{array}{r} {}^{1}\\ 32 \\ 8 \\ +\ 14 \\ \hline 4 \end{array}$$

2 + 8 + 4 = **14 ones**
14 ones is
1 ten and **4 ones.**

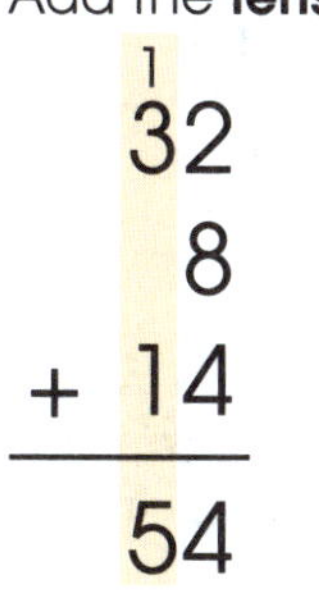

Add the **tens**.

$$\begin{array}{r} {}^{1}\\ 32 \\ 8 \\ +\ 14 \\ \hline 54 \end{array}$$

1 + 3 + 1 = **5 tens**
The **sum** is **54**.

Estimate:

$$\begin{array}{r} 30 \\ 10 \\ +\ 10 \\ \hline 50 \end{array}$$

▶ Find the sum.

1. $\begin{array}{r} 32 \\ 7 \\ +\ 20 \\ \hline \end{array}$

2. $\begin{array}{r} 18 \\ 1 \\ +\ 36 \\ \hline \end{array}$

3. $\begin{array}{r} 21 \\ 0 \\ +\ 3 \\ \hline \end{array}$

4. $\begin{array}{r} 76 \\ 2 \\ +\ 11 \\ \hline \end{array}$

5. $\begin{array}{r} 2 \\ 18 \\ +\ 5 \\ \hline \end{array}$

6. $\begin{array}{r} 51 \\ 5 \\ +\ 2 \\ \hline \end{array}$

7. $\begin{array}{r} 8 \\ 27 \\ +\ 9 \\ \hline \end{array}$

8. $\begin{array}{r} 32 \\ 22 \\ +\ 5 \\ \hline \end{array}$

9. $\begin{array}{r} 56 \\ 33 \\ +\ 10 \\ \hline \end{array}$

10. $\begin{array}{r} 35 \\ 42 \\ +\ 5 \\ \hline \end{array}$

11. $\begin{array}{r} 25 \\ 3 \\ 21 \\ +\ 5 \\ \hline \end{array}$

12. $\begin{array}{r} 19 \\ 25 \\ 46 \\ +\ 14 \\ \hline \end{array}$

13. $\begin{array}{r} 62 \\ 70 \\ 2 \\ +\ 54 \\ \hline \end{array}$

14. $\begin{array}{r} 62 \\ 8 \\ 33 \\ +\ 5 \\ \hline \end{array}$

15. $\begin{array}{r} 83 \\ 5 \\ 20 \\ +\ 9 \\ \hline \end{array}$

▶ Find the sum.

16. 39 + 23 + 4 + 33 = ______

17. 16 + 30 + 9 + 21 = ______

Subtract Two-Digit Numbers

Subtract the **ones**.
Regroup as needed.

$$\begin{array}{r} 32 \\ -\ 19 \\ \hline ? \end{array}$$

2 - 9 cannot be done. You must regroup. **3 tens** and **2 ones** is the same as **2 tens** and **12 ones**.

Regroup.
Subtract the **ones**.

$$\begin{array}{r} \scriptsize{2\,12} \\ \not{3}\not{2} \\ -\ 19 \\ \hline 3 \end{array}$$

12 - 9 = **3 ones**

Subtract the **tens**.

$$\begin{array}{r} \scriptsize{2\,12} \\ \not{3}\not{2} \\ -\ 19 \\ \hline 13 \end{array}$$

2 - 1 = **1 ten**
The **difference** is **13**.

Check:

$$\begin{array}{r} \scriptsize{1} \\ 13 \\ +\ 19 \\ \hline 32 \end{array}$$

Add to check your answer.

▶ Find the difference.

1. $\begin{array}{r} 65 \\ -\ 22 \\ \hline \end{array}$
2. $\begin{array}{r} 28 \\ -\ 13 \\ \hline \end{array}$
3. $\begin{array}{r} 63 \\ -\ 24 \\ \hline \end{array}$
4. $\begin{array}{r} 96 \\ -\ 35 \\ \hline \end{array}$
5. $\begin{array}{r} 86 \\ -\ 85 \\ \hline \end{array}$
6. $\begin{array}{r} 78 \\ -\ 33 \\ \hline \end{array}$
7. $\begin{array}{r} 36 \\ -\ 28 \\ \hline \end{array}$
8. $\begin{array}{r} 77 \\ -\ 35 \\ \hline \end{array}$
9. $\begin{array}{r} 80 \\ -\ 31 \\ \hline \end{array}$
10. $\begin{array}{r} 92 \\ -\ 54 \\ \hline \end{array}$
11. $\begin{array}{r} 67 \\ -\ 18 \\ \hline \end{array}$
12. $\begin{array}{r} 36 \\ -\ 27 \\ \hline \end{array}$
13. $\begin{array}{r} 99 \\ -\ 44 \\ \hline \end{array}$
14. $\begin{array}{r} 85 \\ -\ 49 \\ \hline \end{array}$
15. $\begin{array}{r} 82 \\ -\ 55 \\ \hline \end{array}$
16. $\begin{array}{r} 90 \\ -\ 25 \\ \hline \end{array}$

Add and Subtract Two-Digit Numbers

Solve this riddle:
What is the largest land animal?

 Add and subtract to find the answer.

A	B	C	E	F
73 + 17	82 − 17	18 + 33	80 − 34	79 − 19

H	I	L	N	P
70 − 25	88 − 79	14 + 36	91 − 15	93 − 18

R	S	T	U	A
69 + 26	79 + 19	73 − 17	82 + 17	27 18 + 45

E	H	N	A
28 + 18	19 + 26	19 25 + 32	67 + 23

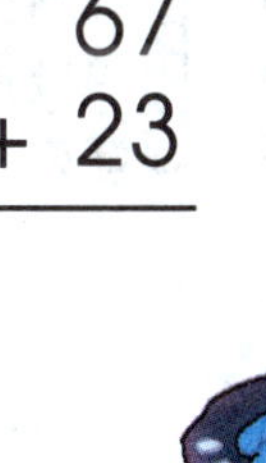

The ___ ___ ___ ___ ___ ___ ___
90 60 95 9 51 90 76

___ ___ ___ ___   ___ ___ ___ ___ ___ ___ ___ ___
65 99 98 45   46 50 46 75 45 90 76 56

Hundreds, Tens, and Ones

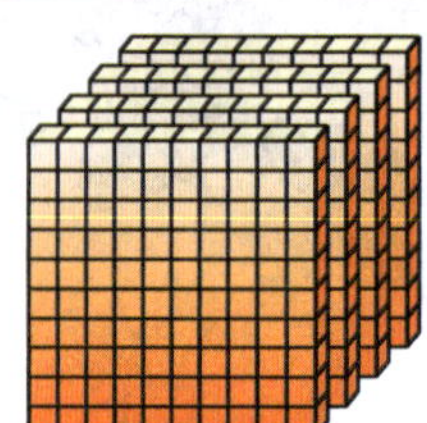
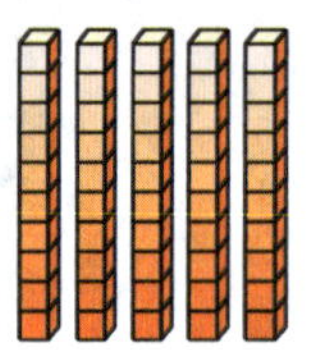

__4__ hundreds __5__ tens __7__ ones

__400__ + __50__ + __7__

__457__

▶ Look at the picture. Count how many hundreds, tens, and ones there are. Then write the number.

1. 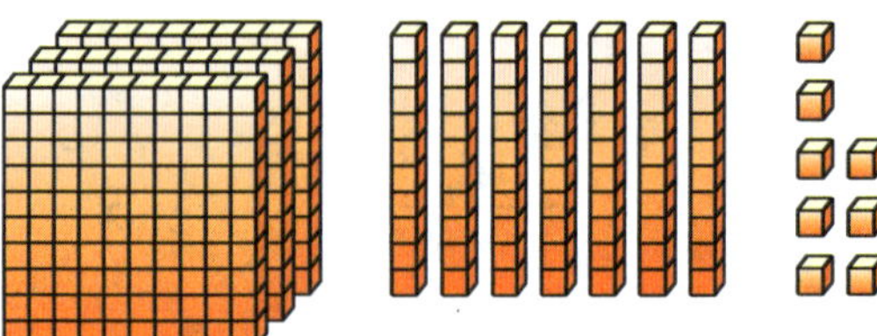

_____ hundreds _____ tens _____ ones

_____ + _____ + _____

____

2. 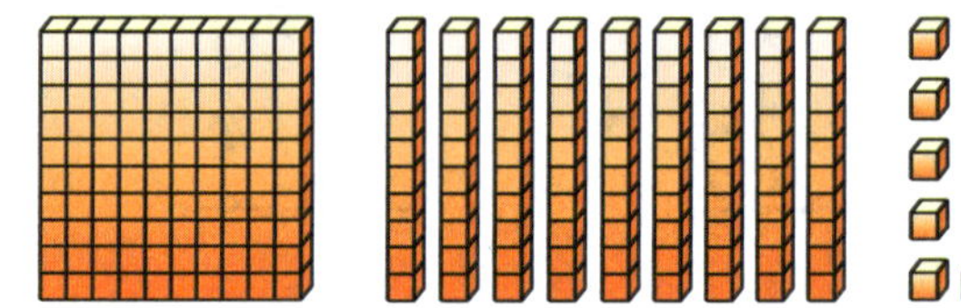

_____ hundred _____ tens _____ ones

_____ + _____ + _____

____

3. 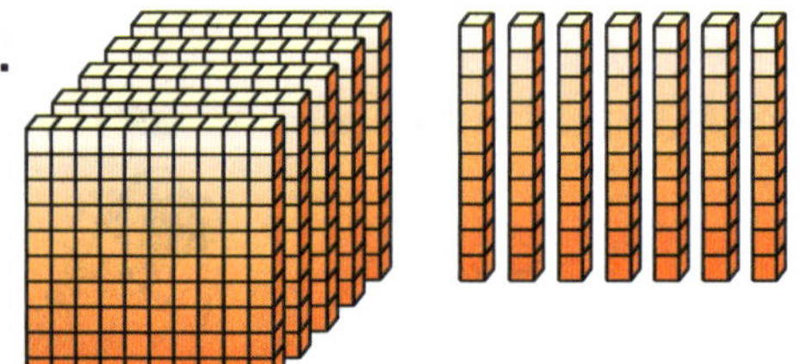

_____ hundreds _____ tens _____ ones

_____ + _____ + _____

____

4. 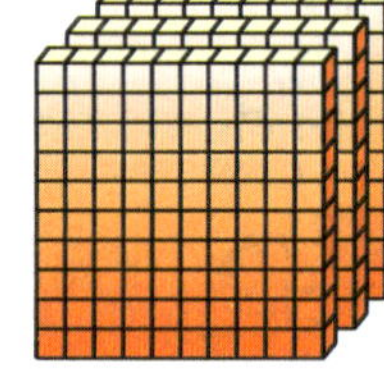

_____ hundreds _____ tens _____ ones

_____ + _____ + _____

____

Expanded Notation

Write the number in **expanded notation** using **words**.

372 = **3** hundreds + **7** tens + **2** ones

Write the number in **expanded notation** using **digits**.

372 = **300** + **70** + **2**

▶ Write the number in expanded notation using words.

1. 749 = ______________ + ______________ + ______________
2. 514 = ______________ + ______________ + ______________
3. 930 = ______________ + ______________ + ______________
4. 398 = ______________ + ______________ + ______________
5. 607 = ______________ + ______________ + ______________

▶ Write the number in expanded notation using digits.

6. 562 = ________ + ________ + ________
7. 953 = ________ + ________ + ________
8. 370 = ________ + ________ + ________
9. 617 = ________ + ________ + ________
10. 109 = ________ + ________ + ________

Greater or Less

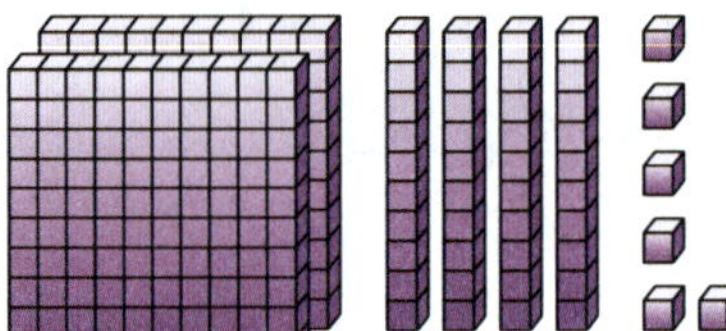
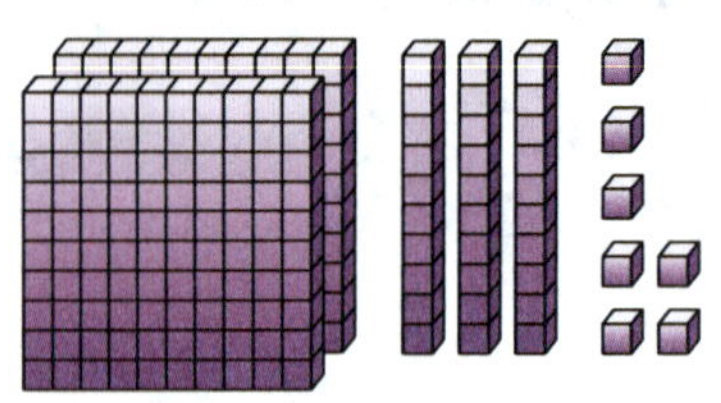

246  237

The symbol points to the number that is less.

246 is **greater** than 237.
246 > 237
or
237 is **less** than 246.
237 < 246

▶ Write the number for each group. Compare the numbers.
Then write < or > in the ☐.

1. 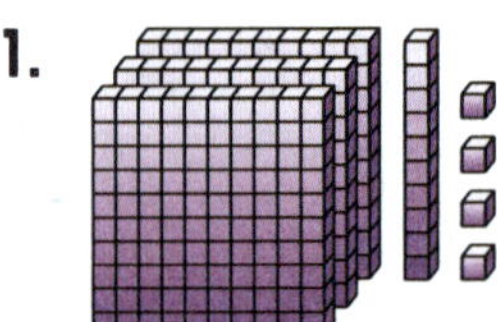 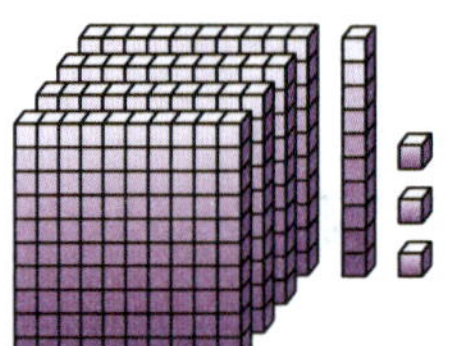

_____ ☐ _____

2. 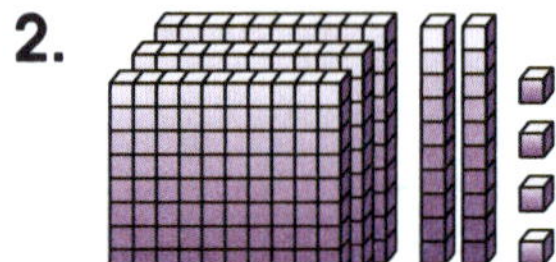 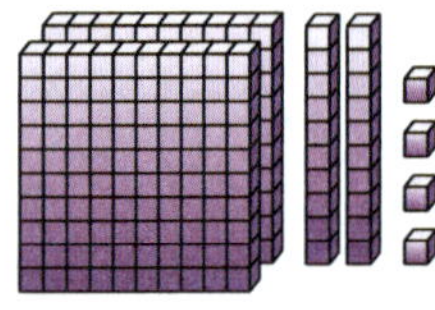

3. 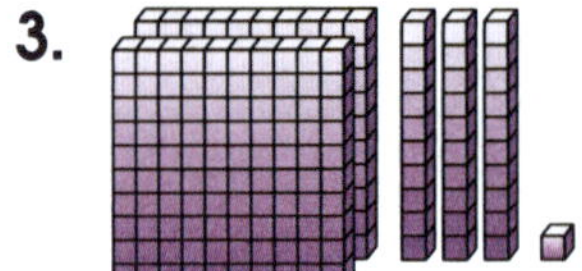 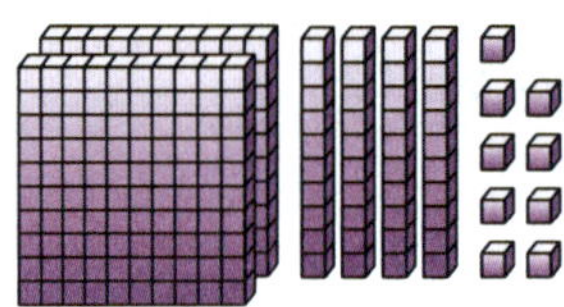

_____ ☐ _____

4. 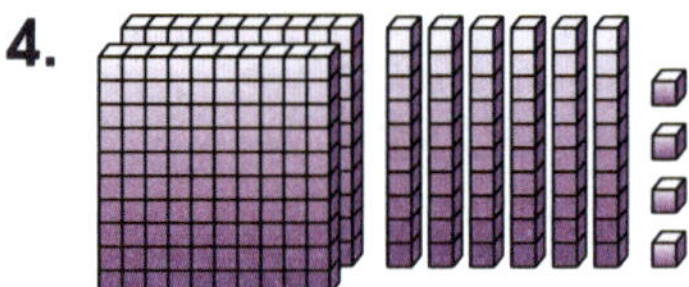 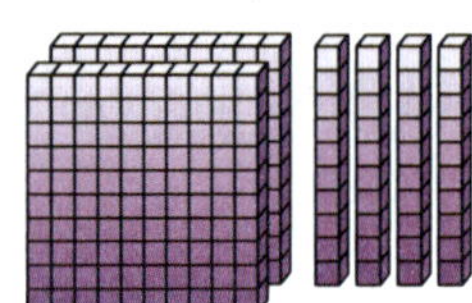

_____ ☐ _____

▶ Compare the numbers. Then write < or > in the ☐.

5. 438  538

6. 572  527

7. 706  670

8. 717  619

9. 390  930

10. 537  573

Numbers in Order

▶ Write the missing numbers.

1. 111, ____, 113, ____, ____, 116, ____, ____, 119, ____
2. 307, ____, 309, ____, 311, ____, ____, 314, ____, 316
3. 555, ____, ____, 558, ____, ____, 561, ____, 563, ____
4. 710, 720, ____, 740, ____, 760, ____, ____, 790, ____
5. 872, 874, ____, 878, ____, 882, ____, ____, 888, ____

▶ Write the numbers in order from least to greatest.

6. 319; 721; 976; 351 ____; ____; ____; ____
7. 572; 897; 711; 999 ____; ____; ____; ____
8. 702; 724; 237; 700 ____; ____; ____; ____
9. 808; 788; 896; 418 ____; ____; ____; ____
10. 987; 813; 381; 789 ____; ____; ____; ____

Round Three-Digit Numbers

To **round** a number to the **nearest hundred**, look at the **tens** place.
If the digit in the tens place is **5 or more**, then **round up**.
If the digit in the tens place is **4 or less**, then **round down**.

Is 235 closer to 200 or 300?

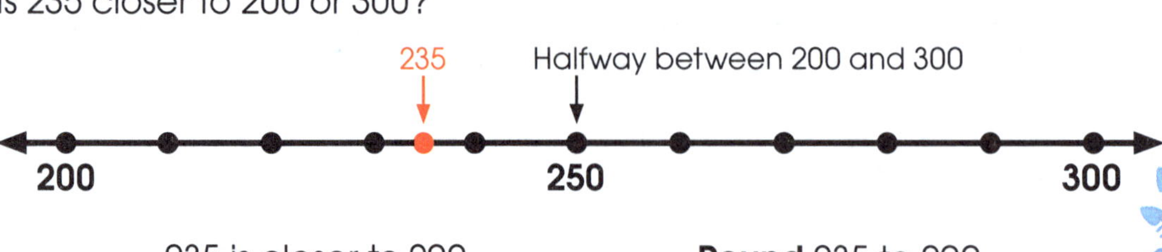

235 is closer to 200. **Round** 235 to 200.

The tens digit is less than 4.

▶ Look at the boldface number. To round, circle the nearest hundred.

1.	**479**	400	500	2.	**716**	700	800	3.	**647**	600	700
4.	**328**	300	400	5.	**761**	700	800	6.	**153**	100	200
7.	**505**	500	600	8.	**350**	300	400	9.	**808**	800	900

▶ Round the number to the nearest hundred.

10. 347 ______ 11. 609 ______ 12. 178 ______

13. 307 ______ 14. 649 ______ 15. 595 ______

16. 370 ______ 17. 469 ______ 18. 350 ______

▶ Round the number to the nearest ten.

19. 138 ______ 20. 246 ______

21. 672 ______ 22. 472 ______

23. 485 ______ 24. 555 ______

Do you remember how to round numbers to the nearest ten? Look at the ones digit.

Estimate Sums and Differences

Estimate the sums and differences by **rounding** to the nearest hundred.

Estimate the sum.

		Estimate:
527	→	500
+ 354	→	+ 400
		900

Estimate the difference.

		Estimate:
718	→	700
− 345	→	− 300
		400

▶ Round the numbers to the nearest hundred.
Write the estimate for the sum or difference.

1.

		Estimate:
671	→	______
+ 238	→	+ ______
		______

2.

		Estimate:
650	→	______
− 109	→	− ______
		______

3.

		Estimate:
475	→	______
− 147	→	− ______
		______

4.

		Estimate:
535	→	______
+ 259	→	+ ______
		______

▶ Estimate the sum or difference.

5. 246 + 381 = ______

6. 815 − 209 = ______

7. 466 − 308 = ______

8. 463 + 295 = ______

9. 809 + 95 = ______

10. 853 − 8 = ______

Add Three-Digit Numbers

Add the **ones**.
Regroup as needed.

$$\begin{array}{r} {}^{1} \\ 346 \\ +\ 286 \\ \hline 2 \end{array}$$

6 + 6 = **12 ones**
12 ones is
1 ten and **2 ones**.

Add the **tens**.
Regroup as needed.

$$\begin{array}{r} {}^{1\,1} \\ 346 \\ +\ 286 \\ \hline 32 \end{array}$$

1 + 4 + 8 = **13 tens**
13 tens is
1 hundred and **3 tens**.

Add the **hundreds**.

$$\begin{array}{r} {}^{1\,1} \\ 346 \\ +\ 286 \\ \hline 632 \end{array}$$

1 + 3 + 2 = **6**
hundreds
The **sum** is **632**.

Estimate:

$$\begin{array}{r} 300 \\ +\ 300 \\ \hline 600 \end{array}$$

▶ Find the sum.

1. 221 + 579	**2.** 398 + 352	**3.** 375 + 246	**4.** 200 + 200
5. 519 + 399	**6.** 600 + 300	**7.** 634 + 200	**8.** 721 + 189
9. 496 + 366	**10.** 100 + 500	**11.** 519 + 181	**12.** 131 + 689
13. 700 + 197	**14.** 400 + 450	**15.** 647 + 188	**16.** 200 + 600

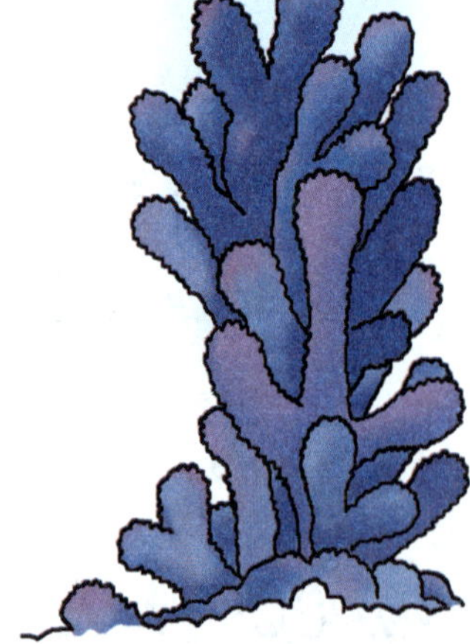

Add Three or More Numbers

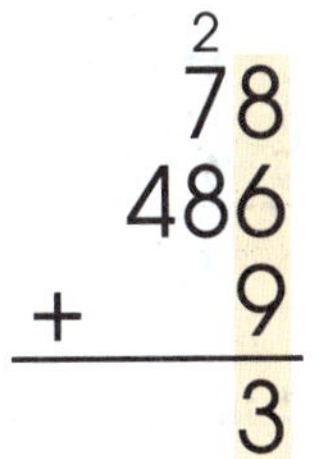
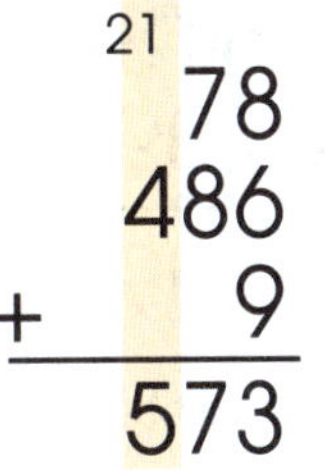

Add: 78 + 486 + 9
Add the **ones**.
Regroup as needed.

$$\begin{array}{r} {}^{2} \\ 78 \\ 486 \\ +\quad 9 \\ \hline 3 \end{array}$$

8 + 6 + 9 = **23 ones**
23 ones is
2 tens and **3 ones**.

Add the **tens**.
Regroup as needed.

$$\begin{array}{r} {}^{1\,2} \\ 78 \\ 486 \\ +\quad 9 \\ \hline 73 \end{array}$$

2 + 7 + 8 = **17 tens**
17 tens is
1 hundred and **7 tens**.

Add the **hundreds**.

$$\begin{array}{r} {}^{21} \\ 78 \\ 486 \\ +\quad 9 \\ \hline 573 \end{array}$$

1 + 4 = **5 hundreds**
The **sum** is **573**.

Estimate:

$$\begin{array}{r} 100 \\ 500 \\ +\quad 0 \\ \hline 600 \end{array}$$

▶ Find the sum.

1. 132 + 206 + 321	**2.** 375 + 132 + 81	**3.** 444 + 44 + 4	**4.** 506 + 56 + 6	**5.** 375 + 86 + 409
6. 514 + 8 + 73	**7.** 193 + 45 + 6	**8.** 765 + 8 + 43	**9.** 140 + 48 + 186	**10.** 349 + 79 + 9
11. 231 + 52 + 5 + 111	**12.** 735 + 8 + 63 + 106	**13.** 321 + 232 + 175 + 109	**14.** 9 + 87 + 654 + 123	**15.** 298 + 197 + 396 + 95

▶ Find the sum.

16. 9 + 65 + 432 = ______

17. 325 + 46 + 9 + 555 = ______

Subtract Three-Digit Numbers

Subtract the **ones**. Regroup as needed.	Subtract the **tens**. Regroup as needed.	Subtract the **hundreds**.	Check:
$\begin{array}{r} {}^{0\,18} \\ 6\not{1}\not{8} \\ -\ 209 \\ \hline 9 \end{array}$	$\begin{array}{r} {}^{0\,18} \\ 6\not{1}\not{8} \\ -\ 209 \\ \hline 09 \end{array}$	$\begin{array}{r} {}^{0\,18} \\ 6\not{1}\not{8} \\ -\ 209 \\ \hline 409 \end{array}$	$\begin{array}{r} {}^{1} \\ 409 \\ +\ 209 \\ \hline 618 \end{array}$
Regroup 1 ten and **8 ones** to **0 tens** and **18 ones**. 18 - 9 = **9 ones**	0 – 0 = **0 tens**	6 – 2 = **4 hundreds** The **difference** is **409**.	Add to check your answer.

▶ Find the difference.

1. $\begin{array}{r} 248 \\ -\ 136 \\ \hline \end{array}$
2. $\begin{array}{r} 274 \\ -\ 143 \\ \hline \end{array}$
3. $\begin{array}{r} 343 \\ -\ 133 \\ \hline \end{array}$
4. $\begin{array}{r} 455 \\ -\ 248 \\ \hline \end{array}$

5. $\begin{array}{r} 353 \\ -\ 205 \\ \hline \end{array}$
6. $\begin{array}{r} 326 \\ -\ 250 \\ \hline \end{array}$
7. $\begin{array}{r} 870 \\ -\ 328 \\ \hline \end{array}$
8. $\begin{array}{r} 258 \\ -\ 196 \\ \hline \end{array}$

9. $\begin{array}{r} 694 \\ -\ 589 \\ \hline \end{array}$
10. $\begin{array}{r} 786 \\ -\ 579 \\ \hline \end{array}$
11. $\begin{array}{r} 971 \\ -\ 226 \\ \hline \end{array}$
12. $\begin{array}{r} 777 \\ -\ 456 \\ \hline \end{array}$

13. $\begin{array}{r} 219 \\ -\ 174 \\ \hline \end{array}$
14. $\begin{array}{r} 493 \\ -\ 188 \\ \hline \end{array}$
15. $\begin{array}{r} 800 \\ -\ 250 \\ \hline \end{array}$
16. $\begin{array}{r} 550 \\ -\ 315 \\ \hline \end{array}$

Add and Subtract Three-Digit Numbers

Solve this riddle:
What is the largest reptile?

▶ Add and subtract to find the answer.

A	C	D	E	I
476 + 309	536 + 164	851 − 333	741 − 423	567 + 321

L	O	R	S	T
820 − 135	626 + 259	987 − 569	858 − 273	409 + 209

W	A	C	E	L
567 + 233	907 − 122	853 − 153	102 106 + 110	246 119 158 + 162

O	R	T
742 + 143	219 + 199	740 − 122

The ___ ___ ___ ___ ___ ___ ___ ___ ___
585 785 685 618 800 785 618 318 418

___ ___ ___ ___ ___ ___ ___ ___ ___
700 418 885 700 885 518 888 685 318

Thousands, Hundreds, Tens, and Ones

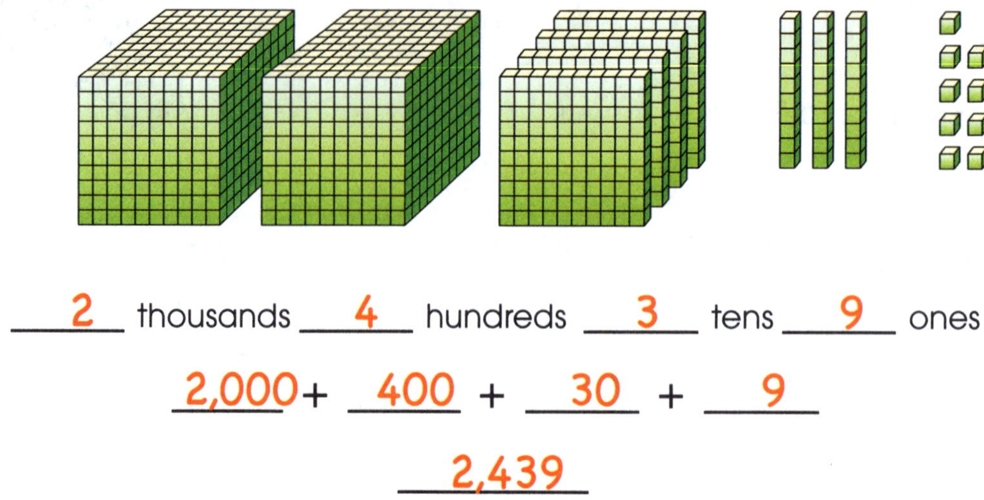

__2__ thousands __4__ hundreds __3__ tens __9__ ones

__2,000__ + __400__ + __30__ + __9__

__2,439__

▶ Look at the picture. Count how many thousands, hundreds, tens, and ones there are. Then write the number.

1.

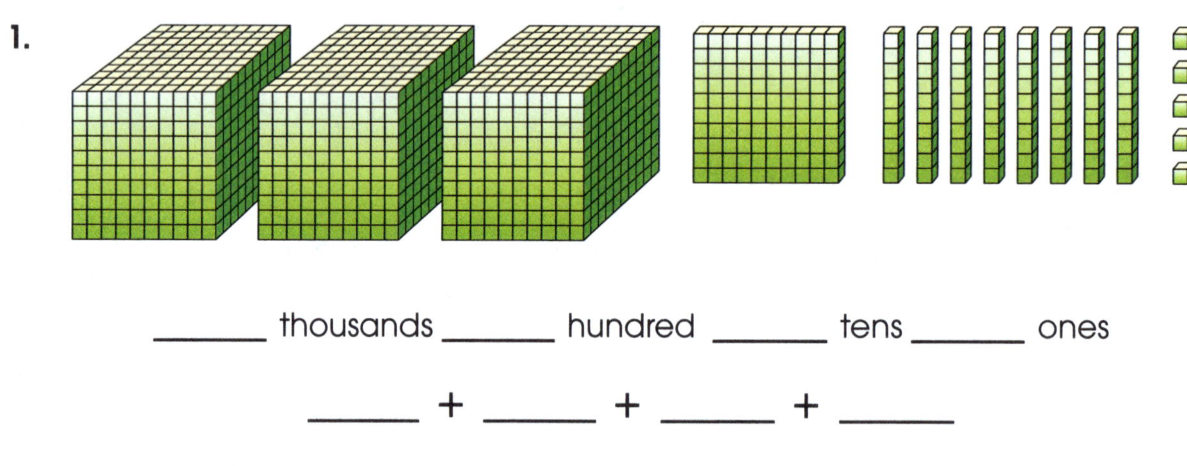

______ thousands ______ hundred ______ tens ______ ones

______ + ______ + ______ + ______

____

2.

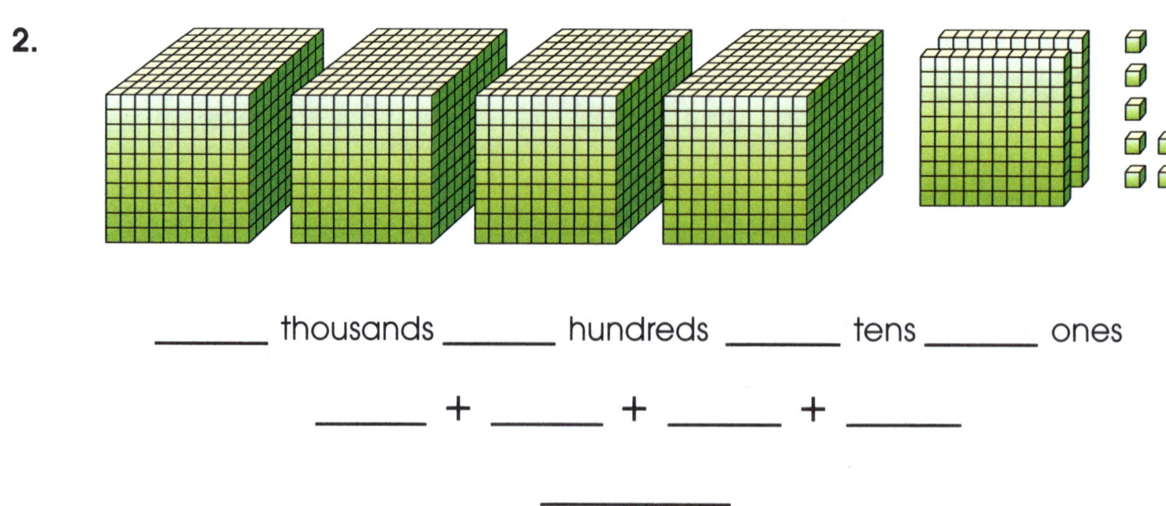

______ thousands ______ hundreds ______ tens ______ ones

______ + ______ + ______ + ______

____

Place Value of Four-Digit Numbers

7,834 = 7 thousands 8 hundreds 3 tens 4 ones

▶ In the number, one digit is in boldface type.
Circle the place value of that digit.

1.	2,43**5**	thousands	hundreds	tens	ones
2.	8,**2**59	thousands	hundreds	tens	ones
3.	**1**,020	thousands	hundreds	tens	ones
4.	**2**,435	thousands	hundreds	tens	ones
5.	9,5**4**1	thousands	hundreds	tens	ones
6.	1,02**0**	thousands	hundreds	tens	ones

▶ Circle the correct digit in the number.

7.	Circle the ones.	8,191
8.	Circle the thousands.	4,275
9.	Circle the hundreds.	1,243
10.	Circle the tens.	9,470
11.	Circle the thousands.	5,437
12.	Circle the hundreds.	9,751

Understand Greater Numbers

Number Words to Know

1	one	10	ten
2	two	20	twenty
3	three	30	thirty
4	four	40	forty
5	five	50	fifty
6	six	60	sixty
7	seven	70	seventy
8	eight	80	eighty
9	nine	90	ninety

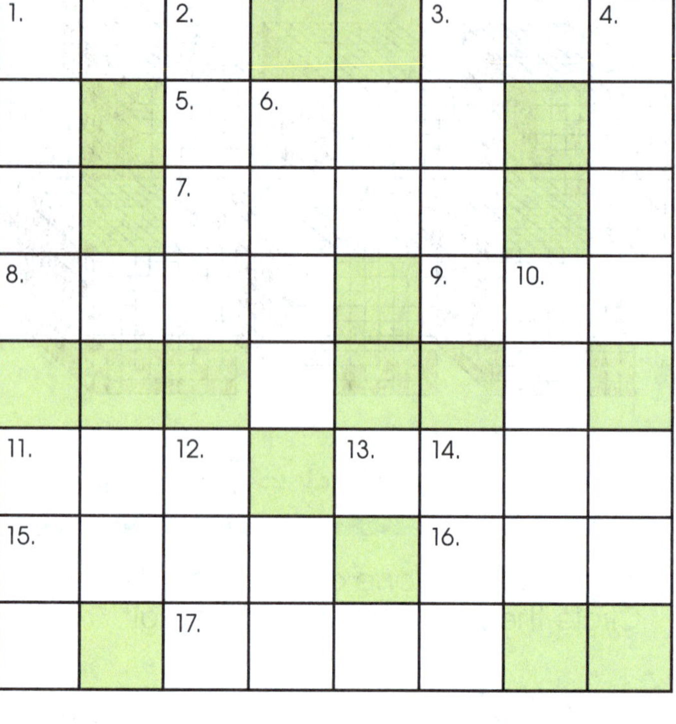

▶ Find the sums and numbers to fill in the puzzle.

Across

1. 2 hundreds + 6 tens + 8 ones
3. 3 hundreds + 9 tens + 7 ones
5. 4 thousands + 7 hundreds + 8 tens + 0 ones
7. three thousand, three hundred thirty-three
8. 9,000 + 30 + 5
9. six hundred twenty-two
11. 6 hundreds + 7 tens + 8 ones
13. 5,000 + 300 + 90
15. 8 thousands + 1 hundred + 2 tens + 6 ones
16. 90 + 100
17. two thousand, five hundred fifty

Down

1. 2 thousands + 9 hundreds + 5 tens + 9 ones
2. eight thousand, four hundred thirty-three
3. 3,000 + 30 + 6
4. 7 thousands + 3 hundreds + 9 tens + 2 ones
6. 4 + 50 + 300 + 7,000
10. two thousand, five hundred ninety-nine
11. 600 + 80 + 5
12. 20 + 2 + 800
14. 3 hundreds + 1 ten

Greater or Less

1,525 is **greater** than 1,520.

1,52<u>5</u> [>] 1,52<u>0</u>   Which digits did you compare? ones

2,650 is **less** than 3,210.

<u>2</u>,650 [<] <u>3</u>,210   Which digits did you compare? thousands

▶ Compare the numbers. Then write < or > in the [ ].

1. 5,148 [ ] 4,185   Which digits did you compare? ________
2. 6,450 [ ] 6,504   Which digits did you compare? ________
3. 5,709 [ ] 5,704   Which digits did you compare? ________
4. 9,205 [ ] 9,250   Which digits did you compare? ________
5. 3,239 [ ] 3,299   Which digits did you compare? ________
6. 4,398 [ ] 2,459   Which digits did you compare? ________
7. 2,879 [ ] 2,814   Which digits did you compare? ________

▶ Write the numbers in order from least to greatest.

8. 6,705; 6,075; 6,507; 675   _____; _____; _____; _____
9. 4,279; 7,942; 987; 4,297   _____; _____; _____; _____
10. 56; 506; 6,052; 6,502   _____; _____; _____; _____

Challenge: Write the greatest four-digit number you can using the digits 3, 9, 1, and 6. ________

Super Challenge: On another sheet of paper, write as many four-digit numbers as you can using the digits 3, 9, 1, and 6. Then put all the numbers in order.

Add Four-Digit Numbers

Add the **ones**. Regroup as needed.	Add the **tens**. Regroup as needed.	Add the **hundreds**. Regroup as needed.	Add the **thousands**.
$\begin{array}{r} ^{1} \\ 7{,}286 \\ +2{,}465 \\ \hline 1 \end{array}$	$\begin{array}{r} ^{1\,1} \\ 7{,}286 \\ +2{,}465 \\ \hline 51 \end{array}$	$\begin{array}{r} ^{1\,1} \\ 7{,}286 \\ +2{,}465 \\ \hline 751 \end{array}$	$\begin{array}{r} ^{1\,1} \\ 7{,}286 \\ +2{,}465 \\ \hline 9{,}751 \end{array}$

▶ Find the sum.

1. $\begin{array}{r} 4{,}840 \\ +1{,}023 \\ \hline \end{array}$

2. $\begin{array}{r} 4{,}462 \\ +1{,}923 \\ \hline \end{array}$

3. $\begin{array}{r} 2{,}640 \\ +3{,}173 \\ \hline \end{array}$

4. $\begin{array}{r} 6{,}540 \\ +2{,}482 \\ \hline \end{array}$

5. $\begin{array}{r} 7{,}731 \\ +1{,}273 \\ \hline \end{array}$

6. $\begin{array}{r} 1{,}847 \\ +6{,}259 \\ \hline \end{array}$

7. $\begin{array}{r} 4{,}787 \\ +1{,}896 \\ \hline \end{array}$

8. $\begin{array}{r} 6{,}354 \\ +2{,}498 \\ \hline \end{array}$

9. $\begin{array}{r} 2{,}743 \\ +5{,}189 \\ \hline \end{array}$

10. $\begin{array}{r} 3{,}086 \\ +5{,}027 \\ \hline \end{array}$

11. $\begin{array}{r} 6{,}259 \\ +1{,}362 \\ \hline \end{array}$

12. $\begin{array}{r} 4{,}274 \\ +3{,}899 \\ \hline \end{array}$

Subtract Four-Digit Numbers

Subtract the **ones**. Regroup as needed.	Subtract the **tens**. Regroup as needed.	Subtract the **hundreds**. Regroup as needed.	Subtract the **thousands**.	Check:
2,637 − 1,715 2	2,637 − 1,715 22	1 16 ~~2~~,~~6~~37 − 1,715 922	1 16 ~~2~~,~~6~~37 − 1,715 922	1 922 + 1,715 2,637
7 − 5 = 2 No regrouping.	3 − 1 = 2 No regrouping.	6 − 7 = ? Regroup.	1 − 1 = 0, but do not write a 0 as the first digit of a number. The **difference** is **922**.	

▶ Find the difference.

1. 4,345 − 3,261

2. 5,916 − 2,842

3. 2,135 − 1,841

4. 8,642 − 7,539

5. 6,757 − 4,902

6. 3,502 − 1,201

7. 8,435 − 5,713

8. 6,149 − 2,076

9. 5,806 − 3,402

10. 4,490 − 1,374

11. 7,261 − 3,521

12. 9,214 − 7,007

Find Sums and Differences

▶ Find the sums and differences to fill in the puzzle.

Across

1. 346 + 62 = ______
3. 873 – 189 = ______
5. 103 – 85 = ______
6. 198 + 6 = ______
7. 435 + 168 + 53 = ______
9. 593 – 199 = ______
11. 66 + 6 = ______
12. 5,540 – 1,234 = ______
13. 99 + 9 + 90 = ______

Down

1. 29 + 291 + 92 = ______
2. 643 + 7,500 = ______
4. 2,053 – 1,168 = ______
7. 4,567 + 1,865 = ______
8. 864 – 258 = ______
10. 732 – 638 = ______
11. 46 + 6 + 19 = ______

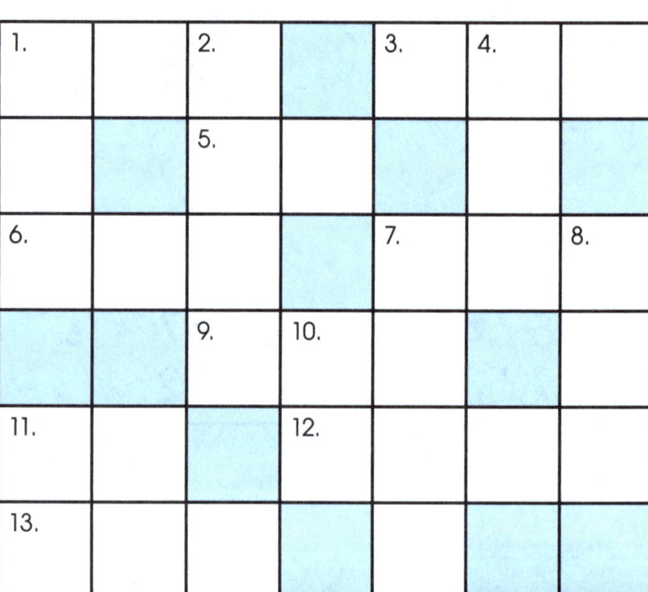

Add or Subtract to Solve Problems

Use these 4 steps to help you solve word problems:

1. **Read** the problem carefully.
2. **Decide** what to do.
3. **Solve** the problem.
4. **Check** to see if the answer makes sense.

Jason found 18 starfish on the beach. Jose found 14 starfish, and Jay found 6 starfish. How many more starfish did Jason find than Jose?

Read: Which boys is the question asking about? Which numbers do you use?

Decide: add or **subtract**

Solve:

$$\begin{array}{r} 18 \\ -\ 14 \\ \hline \end{array}$$

4 starfish

Check: 18 is 4 more than 14.

▶ Read the problem. Circle *add* or *subtract*. Solve the problem. Label your answer.

1. Kayla, Sara, and Maria are at the beach. Kayla found 17 shells, Sara found 46 shells, and Maria found 23 shells. How many shells did they find altogether?

   add or **subtract** ____________

2. Kayla, Sara, and Maria are at the beach. Kayla found 17 shells, Sara found 46 shells, and Maria found 23 shells. Sara sold 28 shells. How many shells does Sara have left?

   add or **subtract** ____________

3. Jason found 18 starfish on the beach. Jose found 14 starfish, and Jay found 46 starfish. How many starfish did Jose and Jay find?

   add or **subtract** ____________

4. Jason found 18 starfish on the beach. Jose found 14 starfish, and Jay found 6 starfish. How many more starfish does Jose have than Jay?

   add or **subtract** ____________

Introduction to Multiplication

There are 3 groups of bats.
There are 2 bats in each group.

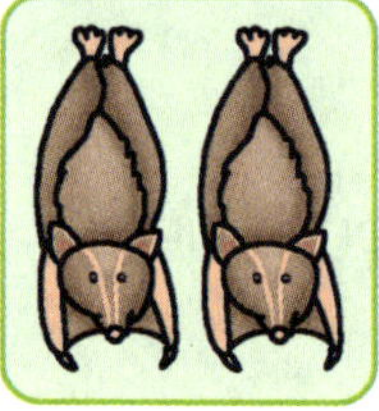
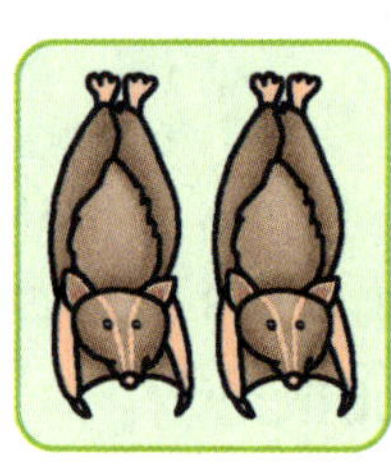
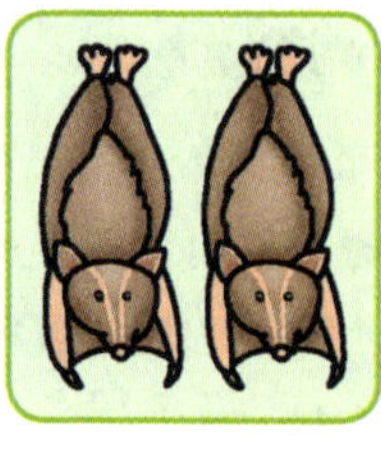

$3 \times 2 = 6$

factors (3, 2) — product (6)

The answer to a multiplication problem is called the **product**.

▶ Look at the picture. Write the missing factor. Then write the product.

1. 2 x ____ = ____

2. 2 x ____ = ____

3. ____ x 6 = ____

4. 3 x ____ = ____

5. 2 x ____ = ____

6. 2 x ____ = ____

Multiply by 0, 1, 2, and 3

You can also think of multiplication as **repeated addition.**

5 + 5 + 5 = 15

3 x 5 = 15

▶ Find the products.

1.

2 x 1 = ____ 2 x 6 = ____
2 x 2 = ____ 2 x 7 = ____
2 x 3 = ____ 2 x 8 = ____
2 x 4 = ____ 2 x 9 = ____
2 x 5 = ____

Count by **2s** to check your answers.

2.

3 x 1 = ____ 3 x 6 = ____
3 x 2 = ____ 3 x 7 = ____
3 x 3 = ____ 3 x 8 = ____
3 x 4 = ____ 3 x 9 = ____
3 x 5 = ____

Count by **3s** to check your answers.

3.

1 x 1 = ____ 1 x 6 = ____
1 x 2 = ____ 1 x 7 = ____
1 x 3 = ____ 1 x 8 = ____
1 x 4 = ____ 1 x 9 = ____
1 x 5 = ____

Hint: Any number times **1** equals that number.

4.

0 x 1 = ____ 0 x 6 = ____
0 x 2 = ____ 0 x 7 = ____
0 x 3 = ____ 0 x 8 = ____
0 x 4 = ____ 0 x 9 = ____
0 x 5 = ____

Hint: Any number times **0** equals **0**.

Multiply by 4 and 5

Changing the order of the factors does not change the product.

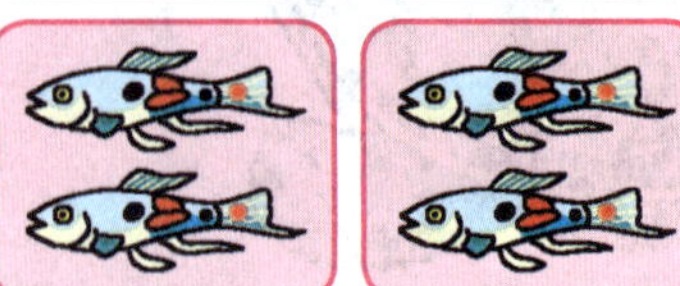

=

4 x 2 = 8 (factors: 4, 2; product: 8)

2 x 4 = 8 (factors: 2, 4; product: 8)

▶ Find the products.

1. 4 x 1 = ____ 4 x 6 = ____
   4 x 2 = ____ 4 x 7 = ____
   4 x 3 = ____ 4 x 8 = ____
   4 x 4 = ____ 4 x 9 = ____
   4 x 5 = ____

   Count by **4s** to check your answers.

2. 5 x 1 = ____ 5 x 6 = ____
   5 x 2 = ____ 5 x 7 = ____
   5 x 3 = ____ 5 x 8 = ____
   5 x 4 = ____ 5 x 9 = ____
   5 x 5 = ____

   Count by **5s** to check your answers.

▶ Practice these facts.

3. 4 x 5 = ____
4. 8 x 0 = ____
5. 3 x 3 = ____
6. 5 x 4 = ____
7. 5 x 7 = ____
8. 3 x 7 = ____
9. 5 x 1 = ____
10. 4 x 8 = ____
11. 3 x 6 = ____
12. 5 x 9 = ____
13. 2 x 7 = ____
14. 2 x 5 = ____
15. 4 x 3 = ____
16. 4 x 4 = ____
17. 2 x 9 = ____
18. 4 x 7 = ____

Multiply by 6 and 7

4 + 4 + 4 + 4 + 4 + 4 + 4 = 28

7 x 4 = 28

▶ Find the products.

1. 6 x 1 = ____ 6 x 6 = ____
   6 x 2 = ____ 6 x 7 = ____
   6 x 3 = ____ 6 x 8 = ____
   6 x 4 = ____ 6 x 9 = ____
   6 x 5 = ____

   Count by **6s** to check your answers.

2. 7 x 1 = ____ 7 x 6 = ____
   7 x 2 = ____ 7 x 7 = ____
   7 x 3 = ____ 7 x 8 = ____
   7 x 4 = ____ 7 x 9 = ____
   7 x 5 = ____

   Count by **7s** to check your answers.

▶ Find the missing factor or product.

3. 5 x ____ = 15
4. 6 x ____ = 0
5. ____ x 7 = 14
6. 4 x 6 = ____
7. 3 x 9 = ____
8. 7 x ____ = 56
9. 2 x ____ = 18
10. ____ x 5 = 35
11. 4 x ____ = 24
12. ____ x 5 = 30
13. 7 x ____ = 7
14. ____ x 9 = 54

Multiply by 8 and 9

Find the products.

1. 8 x 1 = ____
   8 x 2 = ____
   8 x 3 = ____
   8 x 4 = ____
   8 x 5 = ____
   8 x 6 = ____
   8 x 7 = ____
   8 x 8 = ____
   8 x 9 = ____

Count by **8s** to check your answers.

2.

	Find the sum of each product's digits:
9 x 1 = ____	0 + 9 = 9
9 x 2 = ____	1 + 8 = 9
9 x 3 = ____	2 + 7 = ____
9 x 4 = ____	3 + 6 = ____
9 x 5 = ____	4 + ____ = ____
9 x 6 = ____	5 + ____ = ____
9 x 7 = ____	____ + 3 = ____
9 x 8 = ____	____ + 2 = ____
9 x 9 = ____	8 + ____ = ____

When 9 is multiplied by a single digit, the digits of the product always have a sum of 9.

Fill in the multiplication table. Write the products.

x	0	1	2	3	4	5	6	7	8	9
0										
1										
2										
3										
4										
5										
6										
7										
8										
9										

Practice Multiplication Facts

Find the products to fill in the puzzle.

Across

1. 5 x 2
2. 8 x 3
3. 5 x 6
4. 4 x 3
5. 8 x 2
6. 7 x 5
7. 6 x 2
8. 2 x 9
9. 8 x 5
10. 5 x 5
11. 3 x 7
12. 8 x 3

Down

1. 7 x 2
2. 5 x 4
3. 8 x 4
4. 4 x 4
5. 5 x 3
6. 4 x 8
7. 6 x 3
8. 2 x 5
9. 9 x 5
10. 7 x 3
11. 4 x 6
12. 7 x 4

Introduction to Division

You can use division to find the number in each group or the number of groups.

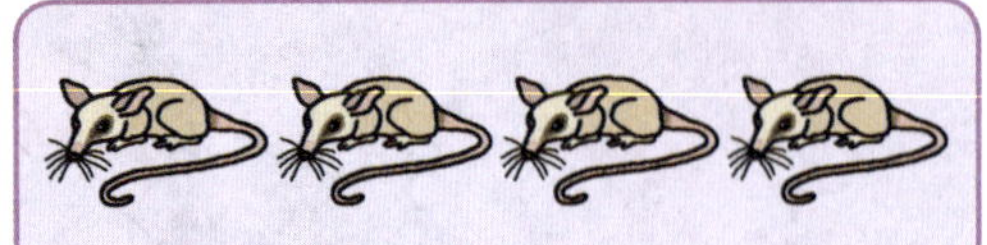

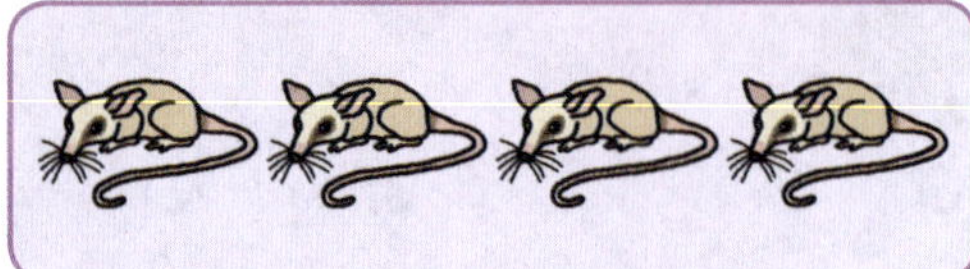

Find the number in each group:

There are 8 in all.
Divide the 8 into 2 groups.
How many are in each group? __4__

$8 \div 2 =$ __4__

Find the number of groups:

There are 8 in all.
There are 4 in each group.
How many groups of 4 are there? __2__

$8 \div 4 =$ __2__

▶ Read the problem. Circle the correct number of groups.
Answer the question and fill in the blank(s).

1. 

There are 12 in all.
There are 4 in each group.
How many groups of 4 are there? _____

$12 \div 4 =$ _____

2. 

There are 15 in all.
Divide the 15 into 3 groups.
How many are in each group? _____

$15 \div 3 =$ _____

3. 

There are _____ in all.
Divide the _____ into 2 groups.
How many are in each group? _____

_____ $\div 2 =$ _____

4. 

There are _____ in all.
Divide the _____ into 4 groups.
How many are in each group? _____

_____ $\div 4 =$ _____

5. 

There are _____ in all.
There are 3 in each group.
How many groups of 3 are there? _____

_____ $\div 3 =$ _____

6. 

There _____ in all.
There are 6 in each group.
How many groups of 6 are there? _____

_____ $\div$ _____ $=$ _____

Divide by 2

How many groups of 2 are in 16? 8

16 ÷ 2 = 8

dividend divisor quotient

▶ Look at the picture. Circle groups of 2. Answer the question. Write the quotient.

1.

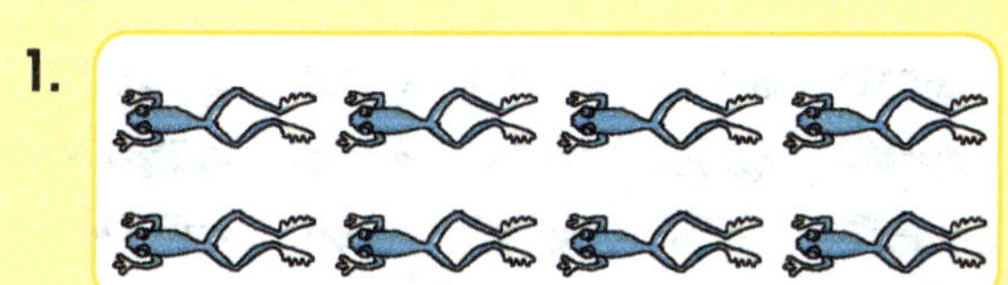

How many groups of 2 are in 8? ____

8 ÷ 2 = ____

2.

How many groups of 2 are in 10? ____

10 ÷ 2 = ____

3.

How many groups of 2 are in 14? ____

14 ÷ 2 = ____

4.

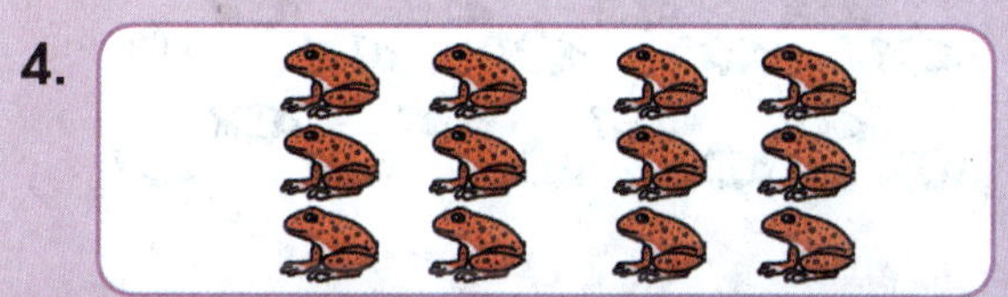

How many groups of 2 are in 12? ____

12 ÷ 2 = ____

▶ Find the quotients.

5. 2 ÷ 2 = ____	8 ÷ 2 = ____	14 ÷ 2 = ____
4 ÷ 2 = ____	10 ÷ 2 = ____	16 ÷ 2 = ____
6 ÷ 2 = ____	12 ÷ 2 = ____	18 ÷ 2 = ____

Divide by 3

How many groups of 3 are in 24? 8

$24 \div 3 =$ 8

▶ Look at the picture. Circle groups of 3. Answer the question. Write the quotient.

1.

How many groups of 3 are in 12? ______

$12 \div 3 =$ ______

2.

How many groups of 3 are in 15? ______

$15 \div 3 =$ ______

3.

How many groups of 3 are in 18? ______

$18 \div 3 =$ ______

4.

How many groups of 3 are in 21? ______

$21 \div 3 =$ ______

▶ Find the quotients.

5. $3 \div 3 =$ ______ $18 \div 3 =$ ______

$6 \div 3 =$ ______ $21 \div 3 =$ ______

$9 \div 3 =$ ______ $24 \div 3 =$ ______

$12 \div 3 =$ ______ $27 \div 3 =$ ______

$15 \div 3 =$ ______

Divide by 4 and 5

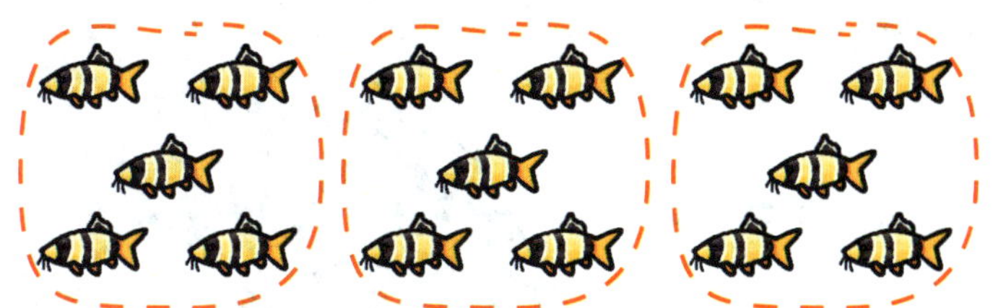

How many groups of 5 are in 15? 3

$15 \div 5 =$ 3

▶ Find the quotients.

1. $4 \div 4 =$ ____
$8 \div 4 =$ ____
$12 \div 4 =$ ____
$16 \div 4 =$ ____
$20 \div 4 =$ ____
$24 \div 4 =$ ____
$28 \div 4 =$ ____
$32 \div 4 =$ ____
$36 \div 4 =$ ____

2. $5 \div 5 =$ ____
$10 \div 5 =$ ____
$15 \div 5 =$ ____
$20 \div 5 =$ ____
$25 \div 5 =$ ____
$30 \div 5 =$ ____
$35 \div 5 =$ ____
$40 \div 5 =$ ____
$45 \div 5 =$ ____

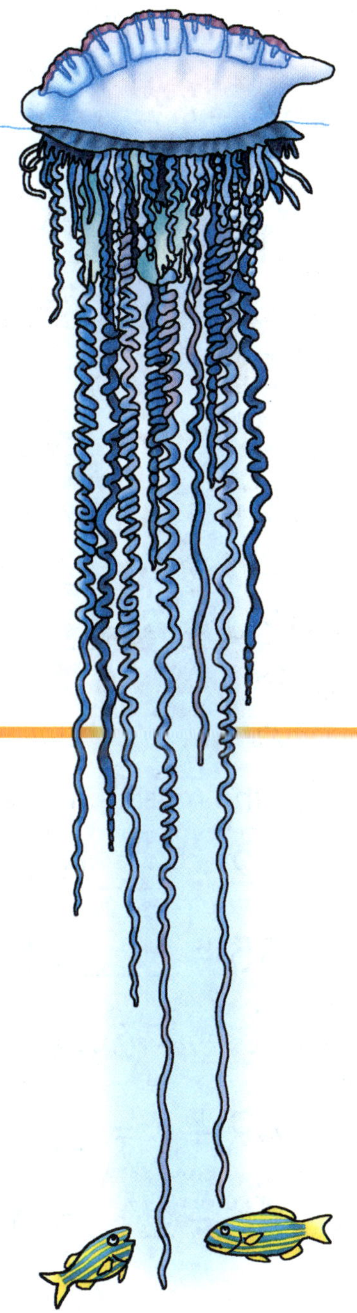

▶ Practice these facts.

3. $6 \div 3 =$ ____
4. $4 \div 2 =$ ____
5. $10 \div 2 =$ ____
6. $15 \div 5 =$ ____
7. $20 \div 4 =$ ____
8. $14 \div 2 =$ ____
9. $20 \div 5 =$ ____
10. $12 \div 3 =$ ____
11. $25 \div 5 =$ ____
12. $18 \div 2 =$ ____
13. $8 \div 4 =$ ____
14. $10 \div 5 =$ ____
15. $16 \div 4 =$ ____
16. $12 \div 2 =$ ____
17. $21 \div 3 =$ ____
18. $28 \div 4 =$ ____

Divide by 6 and 7

Knowing multiplication facts can help you recall division facts.

Here is a multiplication fact: $6 \times 3 = 18$

Here are two related division facts: $18 \div 3 = 6$
$18 \div 6 = 3$

▶ Find the quotients. Recall related multiplication facts if you need help.

1. $6 \div 6 =$ ____
$12 \div 6 =$ ____
$18 \div 6 =$ ____
$24 \div 6 =$ ____
$30 \div 6 =$ ____
$36 \div 6 =$ ____
$42 \div 6 =$ ____
$48 \div 6 =$ ____
$54 \div 6 =$ ____

2. $7 \div 7 =$ ____
$14 \div 7 =$ ____
$21 \div 7 =$ ____
$28 \div 7 =$ ____
$35 \div 7 =$ ____
$42 \div 7 =$ ____
$49 \div 7 =$ ____
$56 \div 7 =$ ____
$63 \div 7 =$ ____

▶ Find the missing dividend, divisor, or quotient.

3. $12 \div$ ____ $= 2$

4. $56 \div$ ____ $= 8$

5. $35 \div$ ____ $= 5$

6. $54 \div 6 =$ ____

7. ____ $\div 6 = 5$

8. ____ $\div 6 = 7$

9. $49 \div 7 =$ ____

10. $7 \div$ ____ $= 1$

11. $48 \div$ ____ $= 8$

12. $36 \div$ ____ $= 6$

Divide by 8 and 9

Think of multiplication facts to find the quotients.

▶ Find the quotients. Recall related multiplication facts if you need help.

1.
8 ÷ 8 = ____
16 ÷ 8 = ____
24 ÷ 8 = ____
32 ÷ 8 = ____
40 ÷ 8 = ____
48 ÷ 8 = ____
56 ÷ 8 = ____
64 ÷ 8 = ____
72 ÷ 8 = ____

2.
9 ÷ 9 = ____
18 ÷ 9 = ____
27 ÷ 9 = ____
36 ÷ 9 = ____
45 ÷ 9 = ____
54 ÷ 9 = ____
63 ÷ 9 = ____
72 ÷ 9 = ____
81 ÷ 9 = ____

Watch the signs!

▶ Find the product or quotient.

3. 5 x 8 = ____
4. 32 ÷ 8 = ____
5. 7 x 9 = ____
6. 21 ÷ 7 = ____
7. 28 ÷ 4 = ____
8. 4 x 7 = ____
9. 7 x 6 = ____
10. 6 x 6 = ____
11. 48 ÷ 6 = ____
12. 30 ÷ 6 = ____
13. 7 x 8 = ____
14. 24 ÷ 3 = ____
15. 7 x 7 = ____
16. 45 ÷ 5 = ____
17. 56 ÷ 7 = ____
18. 4 x 9 = ____
19. 7 ÷ 7 = ____
20. 54 ÷ 9 = ____

Divide with 1 and 0

$4 \div 4 = 1$

4 rabbits divided into 4 groups means that there is 1 rabbit in each group.

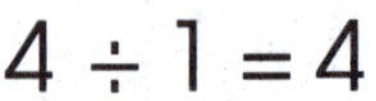

$4 \div 1 = 4$

4 rabbits divided into 1 group means that there are 4 rabbits in that group.

▶ Practice the facts. Match each problem to a division rule.

Here are some division rules:

Any number divided by 1 equals that number.
5 ÷ 1 = 5

Any non-zero number divided by itself equals 1.
5 ÷ 5 = 1

Zero divided by any non-zero number equals 0.
0 ÷ 5 = 0

You cannot divide by zero.
5 ÷ 0/cannot do

1. 3 ÷ 3 = 1
2. 13 ÷ 1 = ____
3. 0 ÷ 6 = ____
4. 10 ÷ 10 = ____
5. 3 ÷ 1 = ____
6. 0 ÷ 15 = ____
7. 8 ÷ 0 = ____
8. 15 ÷ 15 = ____
9. 7 ÷ 7 = ____
10. 12 ÷ 0 = ____
11. 0 ÷ 6 = ____
12. 0 ÷ 17 = ____
13. 9 ÷ 1 = ____
14. 19 ÷ 1 = ____
15. 0 ÷ 0 = ____
16. 20 ÷ 20 = ____

Write Division Facts Two Ways

As you've learned, there are three parts to a division problem. You can write a division problem two ways:

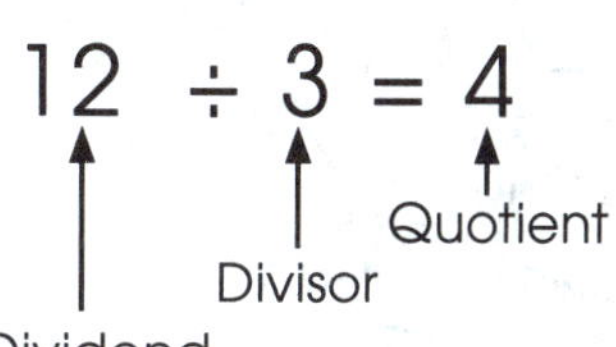

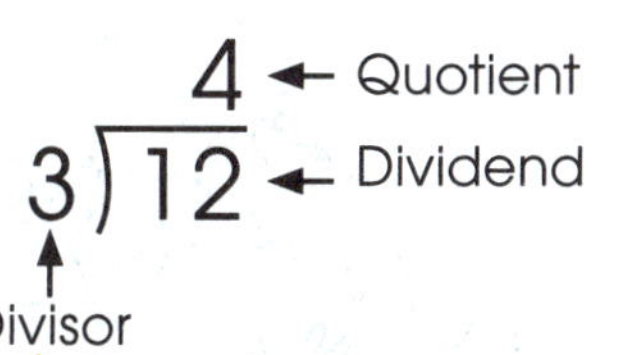

▶ Rewrite the division problem.

1. $32 \div 4 = 8$ $\overline{)\quad}$

2. $18 \div 2 = 9$ $\overline{)\quad}$

3. $28 \div 7 = 4$ $\overline{)\quad}$

4. $48 \div 6 = 8$ 

▶ Complete the problem by finding the divisor or the quotient.

5. $18 \div 3 =$ ____

6. $\_\_\_\_\overset{6}{\overline{)30}}$

7. $\_\_\_\_\overset{5}{\overline{)45}}$

8. $54 \div$ ____ $= 9$

9. $56 \div 7 =$ ____

10. $7\overline{)7}$

▶ Find the quotient.

11. $28 \div 4 =$ ____

12. $6\overline{)48}$

13. $24 \div 3 =$ ____

14. $7\overline{)49}$

15. $56 \div 8 =$ ____

16. $9\overline{)27}$

17. $1\overline{)9}$

18. $35 \div 5 =$ ____

19. $4\overline{)0}$

Fact Families

Remember: All of the problems in a fact family use the same numbers.

If you know your multiplication facts, you can figure out related division facts.

$$\begin{array}{r} 2 \\ \times\ 3 \\ \hline 6 \end{array} \qquad \begin{array}{r} 3 \\ \times\ 2 \\ \hline 6 \end{array} \qquad \begin{array}{l} 6 \div 3 = 2 \\ 6 \div 2 = 3 \end{array}$$

▶ Fill in the missing numbers for the fact family.

1. $\begin{array}{r} 3 \\ \times\ 5 \\ \hline \square \end{array} \quad \begin{array}{r} \square \\ \times\ 3 \\ \hline 15 \end{array}$

$15 \div 5 = \square$

$\square \div 3 = 5$

2. $\begin{array}{r} 2 \\ \times \square \\ \hline 18 \end{array} \quad \begin{array}{r} 9 \\ \times \square \\ \hline 18 \end{array}$

$\square \div 2 = 9$

$18 \div \square = 2$

3. $\begin{array}{r} 6 \\ \times\ 7 \\ \hline \square \end{array} \quad \begin{array}{r} \square \\ \times\ 6 \\ \hline 42 \end{array}$

$42 \div 7 = \square$

$42 \div \square = 7$

4. $\begin{array}{r} \square \\ \times\ 3 \\ \hline 27 \end{array} \quad \begin{array}{r} \square \\ \times\ 9 \\ \hline 27 \end{array}$

$\square \div 3 = 9$

$27 \div \square = 3$

5. $\begin{array}{r} 5 \\ \times \square \\ \hline 30 \end{array} \quad \begin{array}{r} 6 \\ \times\ 5 \\ \hline \square \end{array}$

$30 \div \square = 6$

$30 \div 6 = \square$

6. $\begin{array}{r} 8 \\ \times\ 7 \\ \hline \square \end{array} \quad \begin{array}{r} 7 \\ \times \square \\ \hline 56 \end{array}$

$56 \div \square = 8$

$\square \div 8 = 7$

▶ Find the product. Then write a related division fact or facts.

7. $6 \times 9 =$ _____

_____ ÷ _____ = _____

_____ ÷ _____ = _____

8. $9 \times 8 =$ _____

_____ ÷ _____ = _____

_____ ÷ _____ = _____

9. $8 \times 0 =$ _____

_____ ÷ _____ = _____

Multiplication and Division Facts

▶ Find the product or quotient.

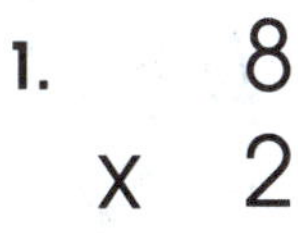

1. 8×2
2. 9×0
3. 5×9
4. 4×8
5. 5×6
6. $2\overline{)14}$
7. $4\overline{)36}$
8. $6\overline{)42}$
9. $3\overline{)27}$
10. $5\overline{)40}$
11. 5×7
12. 7×7
13. 6×9
14. 5×1
15. 7×9
16. $3\overline{)0}$
17. $6\overline{)54}$
18. $8\overline{)48}$
19. $7\overline{)56}$
20. $0\overline{)6}$

▶ Write and solve a number sentence for the problem. Label your answer.

21. Carla wants to buy some animal stickers. She has 28 cents. Each sticker costs 7 cents. How many stickers can she buy?

____

Multiply Two-Digit Numbers

Multiply the **ones**.
Regroup as needed.

```
   3
  18
x  4
----
   2
```

4 x 8 ones = 32 ones
Regroup 32 ones to
3 tens and **2 ones**.

Multiply the **tens**.

4 x 1 ten = 4 tens
4 tens + 3 tens = **7 tens**
The **product** is **72**.

▶ Find the product.

1. 29 x 3	**2.** 12 x 6	**3.** 24 x 8	**4.** 13 x 4
5. 16 x 4	**6.** 33 x 5	**7.** 36 x 3	**8.** 18 x 2
9. 61 x 8	**10.** 52 x 7	**11.** 47 x 3	**12.** 91 x 9
13. 98 x 2	**14.** 34 x 8	**15.** 40 x 6	**16.** 14 x 7

Multiply Three-Digit Numbers

Multiply the **ones**.
Regroup as needed.

```
   3
 128
x  4
----
   2
```

4 x 8 ones = 32 ones
Regroup 32 ones to
3 tens and **2 ones**.

Multiply the **tens**.
Regroup as needed.

```
  1 3
 128
x  4
----
  12
```

4 x 2 tens = 8 tens
8 tens + 3 tens = 11 tens
Regroup 11 tens to
1 hundred and **1 ten**.

Multiply the **hundreds**.

```
 1 3
 128
x  4
----
 512
```

4 x 1 hundred = 4 hundreds
4 hundreds + 1 hundred = **5 hundreds**
The **product** is **512**.

▶ Find each product. Then look for the products in the number search.

1. 318 x 3

2. 164 x 5

3. 408 x 6

4. 237 x 8

5. 128 x 2

6. 333 x 7

7. 350 x 2

8. 508 x 4

9. 143 x 6

8	2	8	5	8	7	9
5	2	7	1	2	1	3
2	1	0	8	8	5	2
0	3	0	2	4	9	5
3	2	4	4	8	5	6
2	2	3	3	1	4	7

Division with Remainders

Count the objects.
Circle groups of 3.

How many objects are there? 16

How many groups of 3 are there? 5

How many are leftover? 1

Follow these steps to divide numbers:
1. **Divide**
2. **Multiply**
3. **Subtract**
4. **Compare**

$$\begin{array}{r} 5\text{R}1 \\ 3\overline{)16} \\ -15 \\ \hline 1 \end{array}$$

1 ← remainder

A remainder is a "leftover."

Divide the dividend by the divisor.

$16 \div 3$

Multiply the divisor by the quotient.

$3 \times 5 = 15$

Subtract $16 - 15 = 1$

Compare the remainder with the divisor. $1 < 3$

If the remainder is greater than the divisor, then the quotient should be greater.

▶ Find the quotient and remainder.

1. $3\overline{)10}$	**2.** $4\overline{)15}$	**3.** $6\overline{)13}$	**4.** $2\overline{)19}$	**5.** $5\overline{)19}$
6. $6\overline{)28}$	**7.** $8\overline{)30}$	**8.** $4\overline{)35}$	**9.** $7\overline{)40}$	**10.** $9\overline{)50}$
11. $8\overline{)35}$	**12.** $5\overline{)33}$	**13.** $6\overline{)50}$	**14.** $4\overline{)30}$	**15.** $7\overline{)60}$
16. $3\overline{)22}$	**17.** $7\overline{)55}$	**18.** $9\overline{)35}$	**19.** $8\overline{)75}$	**20.** $6\overline{)44}$

More Dividing

When you divide with greater numbers, use 5 steps. Think of basic division facts to help you find the quotient.

Follow these steps to divide numbers:

1. Divide
2. Multiply
3. Subtract
4. Compare
5. Bring Down

Divide. Multiply. Subtract. Compare. Bring down.

$$\begin{array}{r} 2 \\ 6\overline{)140} \\ -12\downarrow \\ \hline 20 \end{array}$$

Divide: For 14 ÷ 6, think 12 ÷ 6.

Multiply: 6 x 2 = 12

Subtract: 14 - 12 = 2

Compare: 2 < 6

Bring down the next digit in the dividend.

Divide. Multiply. Subtract. Compare.

$$\begin{array}{r} 23 \text{ R2} \\ 6\overline{)140} \\ -12\downarrow \\ \hline 20 \\ -18 \\ \hline 2 \end{array}$$

Divide: For 20 ÷ 6, think 18 ÷ 6.

Multiply: 6 x 3 = 18

Subtract: 20 - 18 = 2

Compare: 2 < 6

There are no more numbers to bring down, so the dividing is finished.

Multiply and add to check your answer.

$$\begin{array}{rl} \overset{1}{2}3 & \leftarrow \text{quotient} \\ \times \quad 6 & \leftarrow \text{divisor} \\ \hline 138 & \\ + \quad 2 & \leftarrow \text{remainder} \\ \hline 140 & \leftarrow \text{dividend} \end{array}$$

▶ Find the quotient. The quotient may have a remainder.

1. $3\overline{)44}$ 2. $2\overline{)72}$ 3. $4\overline{)45}$ 4. $6\overline{)90}$ 5. $5\overline{)62}$

6. $4\overline{)94}$ 7. $3\overline{)95}$ 8. $2\overline{)86}$ 9. $5\overline{)76}$ 10. $7\overline{)80}$

11. $2\overline{)125}$ 12. $3\overline{)205}$ 13. $4\overline{)156}$ 14. $5\overline{)222}$ 15. $9\overline{)234}$

Multiply to Solve Problems

To solve multiplication word problems, look for clue words like **how many** and **how much**. Multiplication clue words are similar to addition clue words.

Remember the 4 problem-solving steps:

1. **Read** the problem carefully.
2. **Decide** what to do.
3. **Solve** the problem.
4. **Check** to see if the answer makes sense.

A cheetah can cover as many as **20** feet in one stride when moving at top speed. How many feet could it cover in **6** strides?

$$\begin{array}{r} 20 \\ \times \quad 6 \\ \hline 120 \text{ feet} \end{array}$$

A cheetah can cover **120 feet** in **6** strides.

▶ Read and solve the problem. Label your answer.

1. If a gibbon can cover 12 feet in a single swing through the rainforest, how many feet can it cover in 9 swings? ________________

2. An elephant in the wild needs about 400 pounds of food a day. How many pounds of food would it need in 7 days? ________________

3. A grizzly bear may eat 85 pounds of fish, grasses, and leaves a day during the summer and fall months. How many pounds of food would it eat in 8 days? ________________

Divide to Solve Problems

To solve division word problems, look for clue words like **share, how many groups**, or **how many in each group**.

Remember the 4 problem-solving steps:

1. **Read** the problem carefully.
2. **Decide** what to do.
3. **Solve** the problem.
4. **Check** to see if the answer makes sense.

Eric has **60** fish and **4** fish bowls. How many fish are in each bowl if each bowl holds the same number of fish?

$$\begin{array}{r} 15 \text{ fish} \\ 4\overline{)60} \\ -4 \\ \hline 20 \\ -20 \\ \hline 0 \end{array}$$

There are **15** fish in each fish bowl.

▶ Read and solve the problem. Label your answer.

1. Emily has 21 birds in 7 cages. She has the same number of birds in each cage. How many birds are in each cage?

   ____

2. There are 9 elephants at the zoo. The zookeeper has 45 loaves of bread. The zookeeper will give the same number of loaves to each elephant. How many loaves will each elephant get?

   ____

3. Six monkeys are going to share 30 bananas. How many bananas will each monkey eat?

   ____

4. There are 63 lions at the park. The lions are separated into 9 groups. How many lions are in each group?

   ____

Multiply or Divide to Solve Problems

Mrs. Smith is going on a field trip to the zoo next Tuesday at 2 o'clock. There are **20** students in the class. Each school van can carry **5** students. How many vans are needed?

Remember:

1. **Read**
2. **Decide**
3. **Solve**
4. **Check**

Read: What do you know? Which numbers do you use?

Decide: multiply or **divide**

Solve: 20 ÷ 5 = 4 vans

Check: 5 students in each of **4** vans is equal to **20** students.

▶ Read the problem. Circle *multiply* or *divide*. Solve the problem. Label your answer.

1. There are 24 pounds of fish to feed 8 seals. If each seal gets an equal amount of fish, how many pounds of fish do you give each seal?

   multiply or **divide** ______________

2. Latisha has 15 animal cards. Ryan has 9 animal cards. Nicole has 3 times as many cards as Ryan. How many cards does Nicole have?

   multiply or **divide** ______________

3. There are 7 chimpanzees at the zoo. A mother chimpanzee usually has a baby every 4 years. How many babies could she have in 28 years?

   multiply or **divide** ______________

4. Shana has 48 flowers. She wants to give the same number of flowers to each of her 3 friends. How many flowers will each friend get?

   multiply or **divide** ______________

Add, Subtract, Multiply, or Divide to Solve Problems

▶ Read the problem carefully. Add, subtract, multiply, or divide to solve the problem. Label your answer.

Remember:

1. **Read**
2. **Decide**
3. **Solve**
4. **Check**

1. The school library has 42 books about animals. Six students are sharing the books for a project. How many books will each student have to read?

____

2. Ken read 8 books about tigers. Laura read 9 books about lions. Kevin read 10 books about house cats. How many books did Ken and Kevin read?

____

3. Eric has 27 animal stickers. Juan has 45 animal stickers. Jesse has 19 animal stickers. How many more animal stickers does Juan have than Jesse?

____

4. Emma has 14 stuffed animals. Josh has 8 stuffed animals. Hannah has 2 times as many stuffed animals as Josh. How many stuffed animals does Hannah have?

____

What I Learned about Numbers

▶ Write the missing numbers.

1. 276; 277; ____; 279; ____; ____; 282; ____

2. 3,425; ____; 3,427; ____; 3,429; ____; ____; 3,432

▶ Compare the numbers. Then write < or > in the ☐.

3. 78 ☐ 87   4. 463 ☐ 476   5. 581 ☐ 518

6. 607 ☐ 670   7. 5,326 ☐ 5,236   8. 9,803 ☐ 9,830

▶ Write the numbers in order from least to greatest.

9. 67; 76; 70; 66   ____; ____; ____; ____

10. 579; 597; 759; 575   ____; ____; ____; ____

11. 3,283; 3,481; 3,318; 3,287   ____; ____; ____; ____

▶ Round the number to the nearest ten.

12. 79 ____   13. 65 ____   14. 346 ____

▶ Round the number to the nearest hundred.

15. 509 ____   16. 828 ____   17. 450 ____

▶ Write the number in standard form.

18. 8 hundreds + 4 tens + 3 ones   ____

19. 2 thousands + 5 hundreds + 8 ones   ____

What I Learned about Numbers

▶ Circle the correct letter for each problem.

1. Which statement is not true?

   A. 67 < 70 B. 427 > 419

   C. 480 > 804 D. 4,720 > 4,719

2. Which number makes _____ > 3,467 true?

   A. 3,465 B. 3,461

   C. 3,476 D. 3,408

3. Which number shows 65 rounded to the nearest ten?

   A. 50 B. 60 C. 70 D. 100

4. Which number shows 478 rounded to the nearest hundred?

   A. 400 B. 470 C. 480 D. 500

5. Which numbers come next?
   566, 567, 568, _____, _____, _____

   A. 570, 572, 574

   B. 568, 569, 570

   C. 569, 570, 571

   D. 578, 588, 598

6. Which statement shows 609 in expanded notation?

   A. 6 hundreds + 9 ones

   B. 6 hundreds + 10 tens + 9 ones

   C. 6 hundreds + 9 tens

   D. 9 hundreds + 6 ones

7. Which numbers are in order from least to greatest?

   A. 868; 876; 880; 808

   B. 880; 876; 868; 808

   C. 808; 880; 876; 868

   D. 808; 868; 876; 880

8. Which number matches this statement: 6,000 + 500 + 9?

   A. 659

   B. 6,509

   C. 6,059

   D. 6,000,509

What I Learned about Addition and Subtraction

▶ Estimate the sum or difference by rounding the numbers to the nearest ten.

1. 37 + 52 = _____

2. 89 – 55 = _____

▶ Estimate the sum or difference by rounding the numbers to the nearest hundred.

3. 725 – 390 = _____

4. 235 + 350 = _____

▶ Find the sum or difference.

5. $\begin{array}{r} 78 \\ +\ 43 \\ \hline \end{array}$

6. $\begin{array}{r} 85 \\ -\ 49 \\ \hline \end{array}$

7. $\begin{array}{r} 483 \\ +\ 265 \\ \hline \end{array}$

8. $\begin{array}{r} 853 \\ -\ 527 \\ \hline \end{array}$

9. $\begin{array}{r} 78 \\ 63 \\ +\ 9 \\ \hline \end{array}$

10. $\begin{array}{r} 358 \\ +\ 163 \\ \hline \end{array}$

11. $\begin{array}{r} 733 \\ -\ 163 \\ \hline \end{array}$

12. $\begin{array}{r} 619 \\ 65 \\ +\ 7 \\ \hline \end{array}$

13. $\begin{array}{r} 4{,}375 \\ -\ 2{,}632 \\ \hline \end{array}$

14. $\begin{array}{r} 2{,}468 \\ +\ 1{,}357 \\ \hline \end{array}$

15. 186 + 40 + 75 = _____

16. 8 + 48 + 487 = _____

▶ Solve the problem. Be sure to label your answer.

17. Maria collects stamps. She has 37 stamps from Mexico, 45 stamps from Canada, and 124 stamps from the United States. How many more stamps does she have from the United States than from Mexico?

____

18. Maria has 37 stamps from Mexico. Jason has 46 stamps from Mexico. Eric has 28 stamps from Mexico. How many stamps do Jason and Maria have from Mexico?

____

What I Learned about Addition and Subtraction

▶ Circle the correct letter for each problem.

1. Estimate: $46 + 35$

A. 60 B. 70
C. 80 D. 90

2. Estimate: $835 - 250$

A. 300 B. 400
C. 500 D. 600

3. $\begin{array}{r} 90 \\ -\ 36 \\ \hline \end{array}$

A. 54
B. 64
C. 66
D. 126

4. $\begin{array}{r} 705 \\ -\ 378 \\ \hline \end{array}$

A. 327
B. 473
C. 1,073
D. 1,083

5. $58 + 508 + 8$

A. 566
B. 574
C. 1,888
D. 6,564

6. $573 + 296$

A. 277
B. 323
C. 869
D. 879

7. $\begin{array}{r} 5{,}733 \\ +\ 1{,}908 \\ \hline \end{array}$

A. 3,825
B. 4,235
C. 7,631
D. 7,641

8. $\begin{array}{r} 4{,}760 \\ -\ 439 \\ \hline \end{array}$

A. 370
B. 3,700
C. 4,321
D. 4,439

What I Learned about Multiplication and Division

▶ Find the product.

1. $\begin{array}{r} 6 \\ \times\ 7 \\ \hline \end{array}$

2. $\begin{array}{r} 0 \\ \times\ 9 \\ \hline \end{array}$

3. $\begin{array}{r} 8 \\ \times\ 7 \\ \hline \end{array}$

4. $\begin{array}{r} 7 \\ \times\ 1 \\ \hline \end{array}$

5. $\begin{array}{r} 9 \\ \times\ 6 \\ \hline \end{array}$

6. $\begin{array}{r} 7 \\ \times\ 5 \\ \hline \end{array}$

7. $\begin{array}{r} 18 \\ \times\ 3 \\ \hline \end{array}$

8. $\begin{array}{r} 26 \\ \times\ 4 \\ \hline \end{array}$

9. $\begin{array}{r} 45 \\ \times\ 2 \\ \hline \end{array}$

▶ Find the quotient.

10. $8\overline{)40}$

11. $7\overline{)49}$

12. $9\overline{)72}$

13. $7\overline{)63}$

14. $6\overline{)0}$

15. $0\overline{)5}$

16. $5\overline{)46}$

17. $6\overline{)62}$

18. $7\overline{)94}$

▶ Solve the problem. Be sure to label your answer.

19. Pete has 44 baseball cards. Nate has 2 times as many baseball cards as Pete. How many baseball cards does Nate have?

____

20. Jenna has 36 stickers. She wants to give the same number of stickers to 4 of her friends. How many stickers will each friend get?

____

What I Learned about Multiplication and Division

▶ Circle the correct letter for each problem.

1. $8 \times 3 =$ ____

   A. 11 B. 18

   C. 24 D. 32

2. $9 \times 0 =$ ____

   A. 0 B. 1

   C. 9 D. 81

3. Which number makes $8 \times$ ____ $= 48$ true?

   A. 5 B. 6

   C. 7 D. 8

4. Which number makes $7 \div$ ____ $= 7$ true?

   A. 49 B. 7

   C. 1 D. 0

5. $\begin{array}{r} 36 \\ \times \quad 3 \\ \hline \end{array}$

   A. 12
   B. 33
   C. 39
   D. 108

6. $\begin{array}{r} 216 \\ \times \quad 4 \\ \hline \end{array}$

   A. 54
   B. 212
   C. 220
   D. 864

7. $6\overline{)50}$

   A. 8
   B. R1
   C. 8 R2
   D. 9

8. $3\overline{)72}$

   A. 24
   B. 2 R2
   C. 20 R4
   D. 216

Play Ball!

Remember, **multiplication** is a short way to add equal groups.

How many groups? __3__

How many in each group? __2__

How many in all? __6__

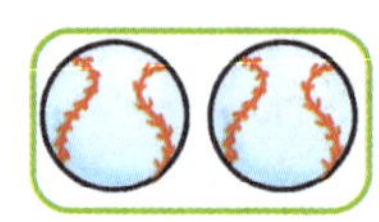 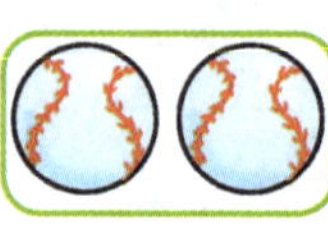 

__2__ + __2__ + __2__ = __6__

__3__ groups of __2__ = __6__

__3__ X __2__ = __6__

▶ How many are there? Fill in the blanks.

1.

__5__ + ______ = ______

__2__ groups of __5__ = ______

______ X __5__ = ______

2.

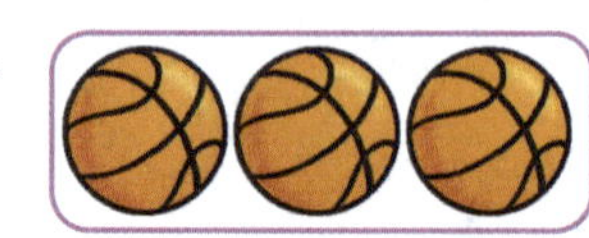 

__3__ + __3__ + ______ + ______ = ______

__4__ groups of ______ = ______

__4__ X ______ = ______

3.

______ + ______ + ______ = ______

______ groups of ______ = ______

______ X ______ = ______

4.

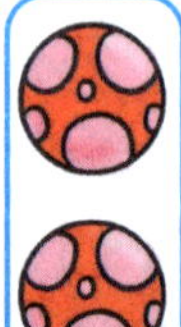        

______ + ______ + ______ + ______ = ______

______ groups of ______ = ______

______ X ______ = ______

Animal Roundup

Use multiplication to show equal groups.

How many groups? __2__

How many in each group? __3__

How many in all? __6__

__2__ X __3__ = __6__

▶ Write a multiplication sentence to find how many.

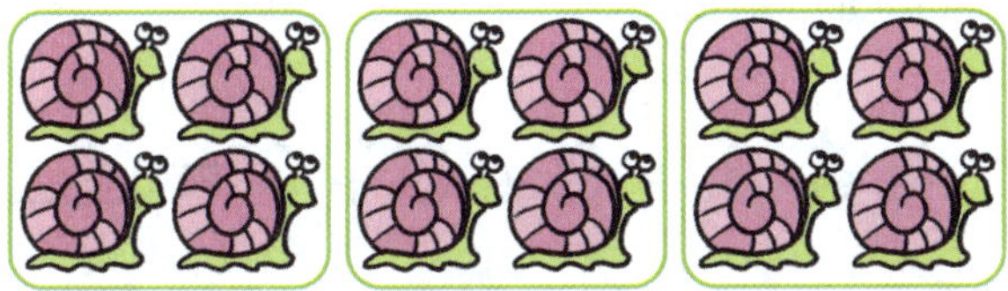

1. ______ X ______ = ______

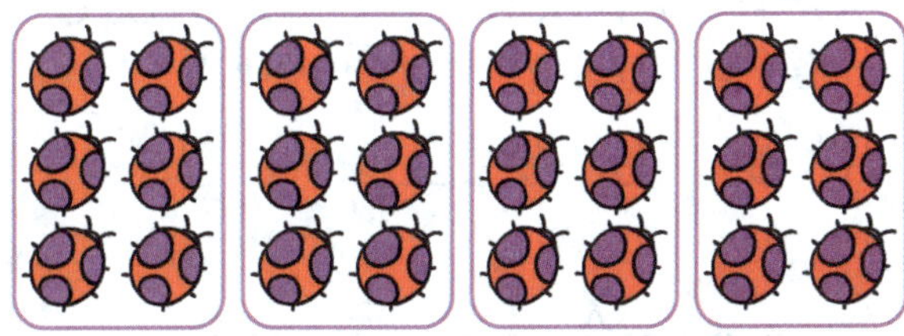

2. ______ X ______ = ______

3. ______ X ______ = ______

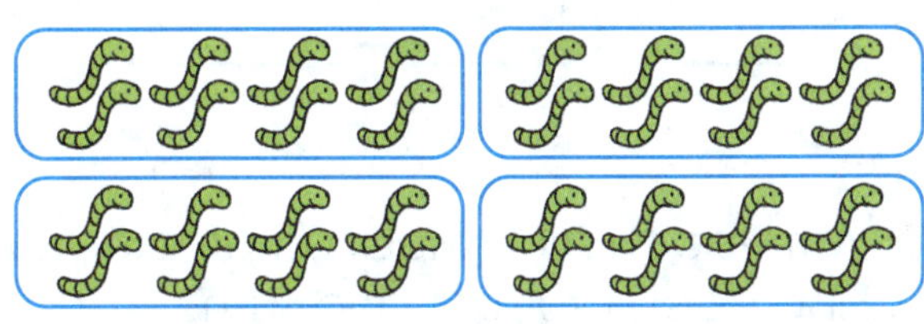

4. ______ X ______ = ______

5. ______ X ______ = ______

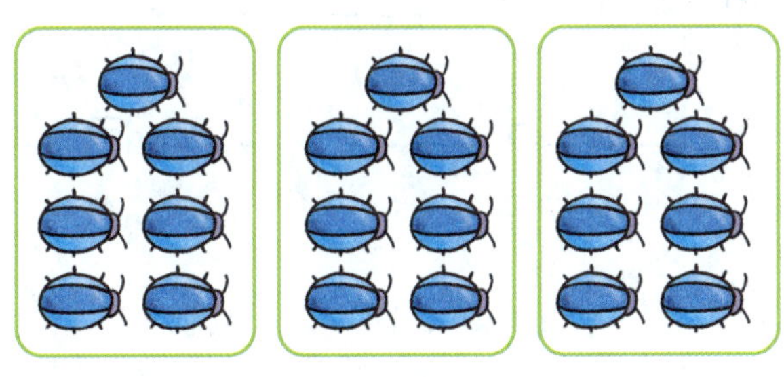

6. ______ X ______ = ______

Addition, Addition

Multiplication is a different form of addition.

In addition, the answer is called the **sum**. The numbers that are added are called **addends**.

In multiplication, the answer is called the **product**. The numbers that are multiplied are called **factors**.

addends → 5 + 5 + 5 + 5 = 20 ← sum

4 x 5 = 20

factors   product

▶ Write each addition problem as a multiplication problem. Find each sum and product.

1. 8 + 8 = ____

   2 x ____ = ____

2. 3 + 3 + 3 + 3 + 3 = ____

   ____ x ____ = ____

3. 7 + 7 + 7 + 7 = ____

   ____ x ____ = ____

4. 6 + 6 + 6 = ____

   ____ x ____ = ____

▶ Write each multiplication problem as an addition problem. Find each product and sum.

5. 5 x 4 = ____

   ____ + ____ + ____ + ____ + ____ = ____

6. 3 x 7 = ____

   ____ + ____ + ____ = ____

7. The sum and the product are the same in each problem.

   Multiplying is a different way of ______________.

Draw a Winner

When two numbers are multiplied, they can be in **any order**. The products are the same.

3 groups of 2

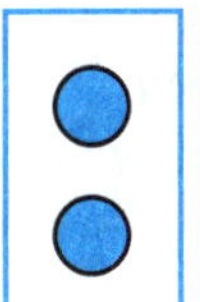
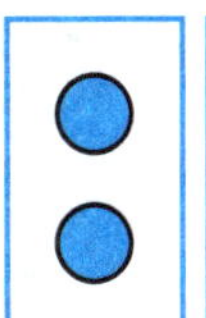

3 x 2 = 6

2 groups of 3

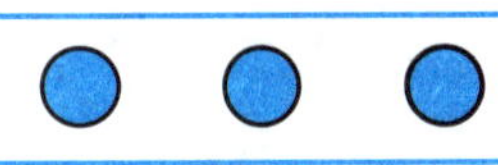

2 x 3 = 6

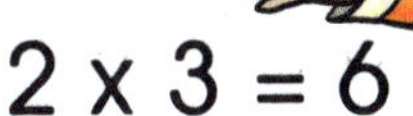

▶ Draw groups of ◯ to show each problem. Then **write the product.**

1. 4 x 2 = ____

2 x 4 = ____

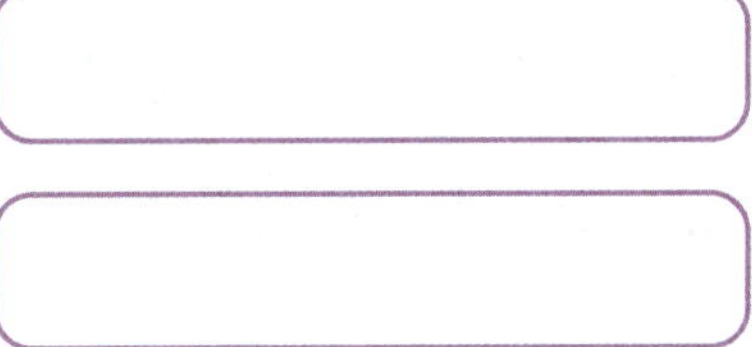

2. 5 x 3 = ____

3 x 5 = ____

3. 3 x 4 = ____

4 x 3 = ____

You're a Problem Solver!

A book of stamps has 2 rows with 4 stamps in each row.
How many stamps are there?

4 + 4 = 8

2 x 4 = 8

▶ Solve each problem using repeated addition and multiplication.

1. Ed reads 2 books a week. How many books will he read in 6 weeks?

_____ + _____ + _____ + _____ + _____ + _____ = _____

_____ X _____ = _____

2. Maria babysits for 4 different families. If each family has 3 children, how many children does she babysit?

_____ + _____ + _____ + _____ = _____

_____ X _____ = _____

3. Kai's dog eats 2 times a day. How many times does the dog eat in 5 days?

_____ + _____ + _____ + _____ + _____ = _____

_____ X _____ = _____

4. Four golfers each have 9 golf balls. How many golf balls are there in all?

_____ + _____ + _____ + _____ = _____

_____ X _____ = _____

Multiply by 1 and 0

Any number times 1 equals that number. Any number times 0 equals 0.

1 group of 3 = 3
1 x 3 = 3

3 groups of 1 = 3
3 x 1 = 3

3 groups of 0 = 0
3 x 0 = 0

0 groups of 3 = 0
0 x 3 = 0

▶ Fill in the blanks.

1.

How many groups? ______

How many in each group? ______

______ x ______ = ______

2.

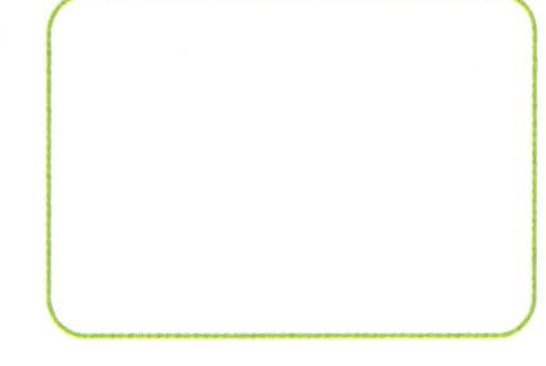

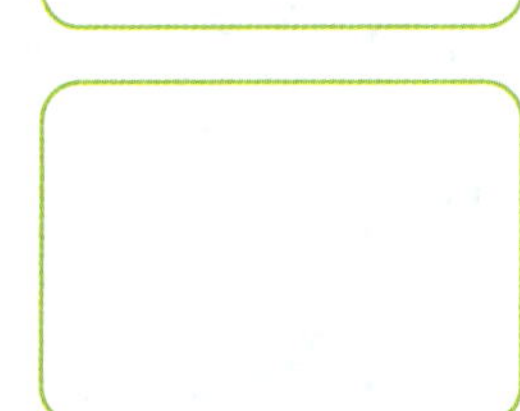

How many groups? ______

How many in each group? ______

______ x ______ = ______

▶ Find the product.

3. 1 x 8 = ______ **4.** 4 x 1 = ______ **5.** 0 x 5 = ______

6. 8 x 0 = ______ **7.** 1 x 7 = ______ **8.** 0 x 4 = ______

9. 6 x 1 = ______ **10.** 0 x 7 = ______ **11.** 3 x 0 = ______

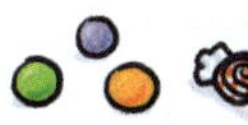

Easy Ones!

▶ Complete the table.

x	0	1	2	3	4	5	6	7	8	9
0										
1										

1. Any number times 0 equals ______.

2. Any number times 1 equals ________________________.

▶ Find the product.

3. 1 x 3 = ______

4. 0 x 3 = ______

5. 5 x 1 = ______

6. 4 x 0 = ______

7. 1 x 8 = ______

8. 0 x 8 = ______

9. 6 x 1 = ______

10. 7 x 0 = ______

11. 1 x 4 = ______

12. 0 x 9 = ______

13. 9 x 1 = ______

14. 0 x 0 = ______

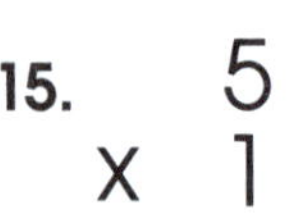

15. 5 x 1

16. 3 x 0

17. 1 x 4

18. 0 x 4

19. 6 x 0

20. 9 x 1

21. 4 x 0

22. 8 x 1

23. 25 x 0

24. 37 x 1

25. 43 x 1

26. 97 x 0

27. 60 x 1

28. 99 x 0

Skip on the Line

Learning to skip count will help you count things faster.
Use a number line to help you skip count.

▶ Use the number line to finish each row.

1. Skip count by twos.

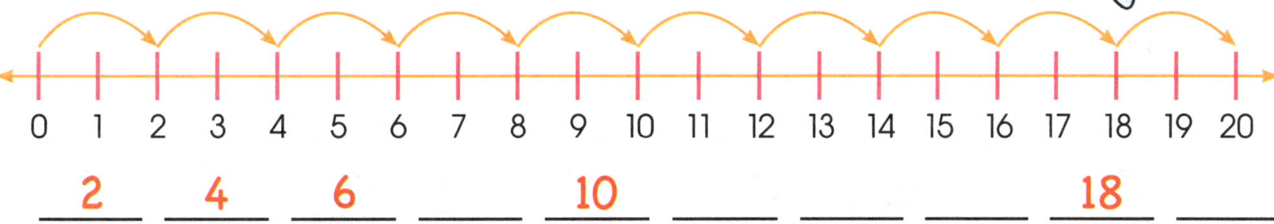

2 4 6 ____ 10 ____ ____ ____ 18 ____

2. Skip count by threes.

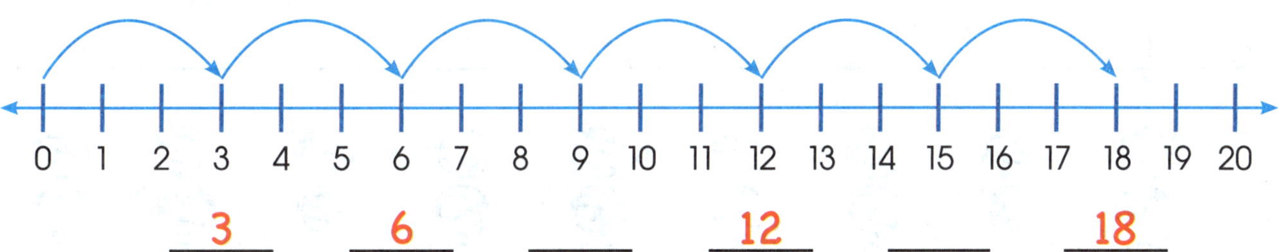

3 6 ____ 12 ____ 18

3. Skip count by fours.

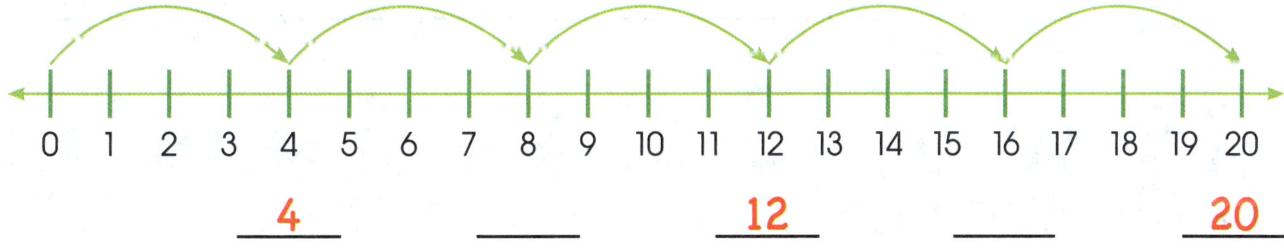

4 ____ 12 ____ 20

4. Skip count by fives.

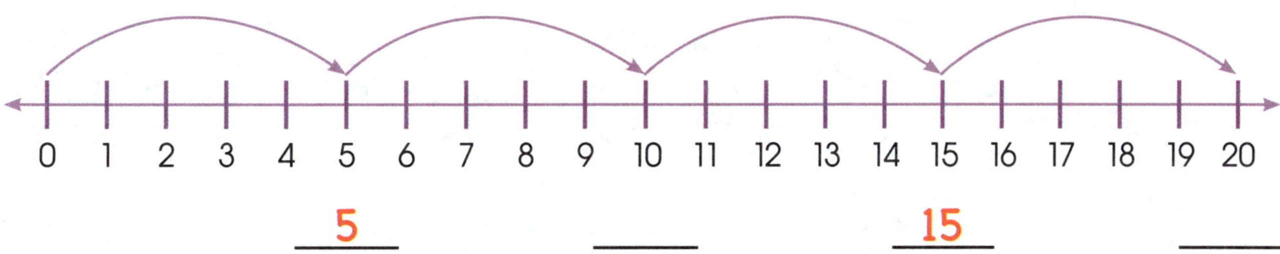

5 ____ 15 ____

Skip Ahead

When objects are in equal groups, skip count to find how many there are in all.

▶ Skip count to finish each row.

1. 2, ____, 6, ____, ____, ____, 14, ____, ____

2. 3, 6, ____, ____, 15, ____, ____, ____, ____

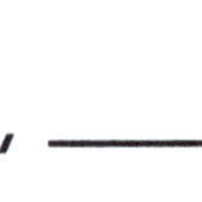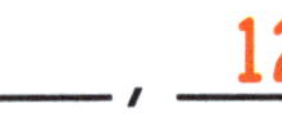

3. 4, ____, 12, ____, ____, ____, ____, ____, ____

4. 5, ____, ____, 20, ____, ____, ____, ____, ____

5. 10, ____, 30, ____, ____, ____, ____, ____, ____

Twice the Fun!

To multiply by 2, skip count by twos to find the product.

▶ Find the product.

1. 2 x 2 = _____
2. 2 x 8 = _____
3. 2 x 5 = _____
4. 2 x 7 = _____
5. 2 x 1 = _____
6. 2 x 6 = _____
7. 2 x 9 = _____
8. 2 x 3 = _____
9. 2 x 4 = _____

▶ Start at the arrow to find the cake.
Follow the path in the same order as your answers above.

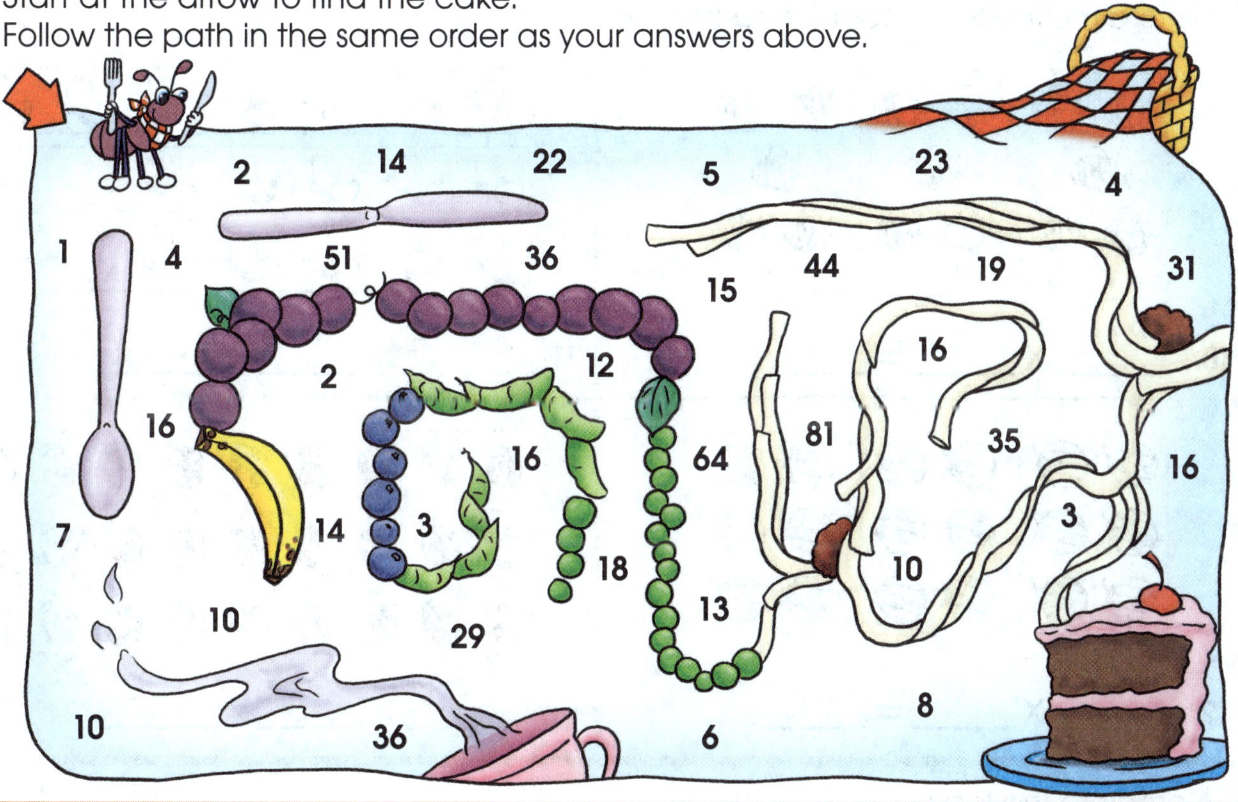

2 14 22 5 23 4
1 4 51 36 15 44 19 31
2 12 16
16 16 64 81 35 16
7 14 3 3
18 10
10 13 29
8
10 36 6

▶ Complete the table.

x	0	1	2	3	4	5	6	7	8	9
2										

Three's a Breeze!

3 x 1	3 x 2	3 x 3	3 x 4	3 x 5	3 x 6	3 x 7	3 x 8	3 x 9
3	6	9	12	15	18	21	24	27

▶ Find the product.

1. 3 x 4 = _____
2. 3 x 1 = _____
3. 3 x 5 = _____
4. 3 x 6 = _____
5. 3 x 8 = _____
6. 3 x 2 = _____
7. 3 x 7 = _____
8. 3 x 9 = _____
9. 3 x 3 = _____

▶ Write a multiplication fact for each problem.

10. _____ X _____ = _____

11. _____ X _____ = _____

12. _____ X _____ = _____

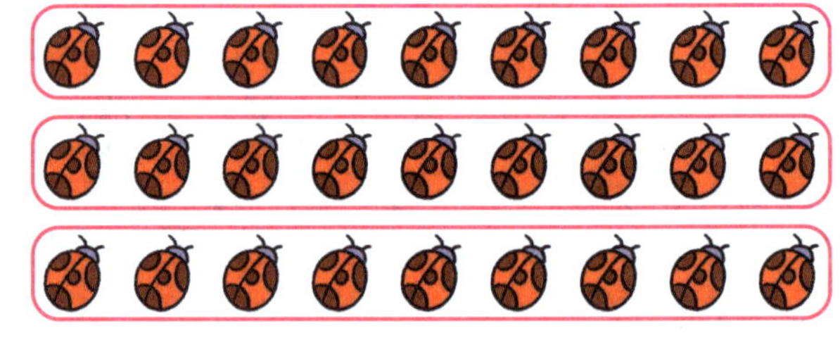

13. _____ X _____ = _____

▶ Complete the table.

x	0	1	2	3	4	5	6	7	8	9
3										

What's an Array?

An **array** shows objects in rows and columns. You can use an array to multiply. One factor is the number of rows. The other factor is the number of columns.

▶ Write a multiplication sentence to describe each array.

1. 

_____ X _____ = _____
rows columns

2. 

_____ X _____ = _____

3.  

_____ X _____ = _____

4. 

_____ X _____ = _____

5.  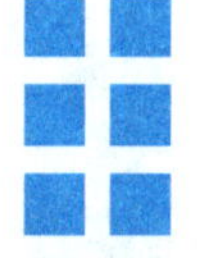

_____ X _____ = _____

6.  

_____ X _____ = _____

▶ Circle the pictures that show arrays.
Write a multiplication sentence for each array.

7. 

____

8. 

____

9. 

____

Explore the Fours!

4 x 1	4 x 2	4 x 3	4 x 4	4 x 5	4 x 6	4 x 7	4 x 8	4 x 9
4	8	12	16	20	24	28	32	36

▶ Find the product.

I

1. $\begin{array}{r} 1 \\ \times\ 4 \\ \hline \end{array}$

N

2. $\begin{array}{r} 3 \\ \times\ 4 \\ \hline \end{array}$

L

3. $\begin{array}{r} 7 \\ \times\ 4 \\ \hline \end{array}$

A

4. $\begin{array}{r} 5 \\ \times\ 4 \\ \hline \end{array}$

E

5. $\begin{array}{r} 9 \\ \times\ 4 \\ \hline \end{array}$

B

6. $\begin{array}{r} 4 \\ \times\ 4 \\ \hline \end{array}$

T

7. $\begin{array}{r} 6 \\ \times\ 4 \\ \hline \end{array}$

S

8. $\begin{array}{r} 2 \\ \times\ 4 \\ \hline \end{array}$

▶ Use your answers to decode the riddle.
Write the letter for each answer on the correct blank.

What can you serve but never eat?

___ 20 ___ 24 ___ 36 ___ 12 ___ 12 ___ 4 ___ 8   ___ 16 ___ 20 ___ 28 ___ 28

▶ Complete the table.

x	0	1	2	3	4	5	6	7	8	9
4										

Five Alive!

5 x 1	5 x 2	5 x 3	5 x 4	5 x 5	5 x 6	5 x 7	5 x 8	5 x 9
5	10	15	20	25	30	35	40	45

▶ Find the product.

1. 3×5
2. 1×5
3. 5×5
4. 8×5
5. 6×5
6. 2×5
7. 7×5
8. 6×5
9. 4×5
10. 9×5
11. 5×4
12. 5×7

13. When you multiply by 5, the product ends with a ______ or a ______.

▶ Complete the table.

x	0	1	2	3	4	5	6	7	8	9
5										

Try a Table

You can use a multiplication table to learn new facts and to find products.

In 4 x 2 = _____ , the factors are 4 and 2.

The factors are shown in the top row and in the first column.

Step 1: Find the 4 row.

Step 2: Find the 2 column.

Step 3: Find where the 4 row and the 2 column meet. That is the product of 4 x 2.

4 x 2 = 8

x	0	1	2	3	4	5
0	0	0	0	0	0	0
1	0	1	2	3	4	5
2	0	2	4	6	8	10
3	0	3	6	9	12	15
4	0	4	8	12	16	20
5	0	5	10	15	20	25

▶ Name the factors. Then use the multiplication table to find the product.

	Factors		Product
1. 3 x 2 =	_____	_____	_____
2. 5 x 5 =	_____	_____	_____
3. 0 x 1 =	_____	_____	_____
4. 2 x 4 =	_____	_____	_____
5. 5 x 0 =	_____	_____	_____
6. 4 x 3 =	_____	_____	_____
7. 3 x 3 =	_____	_____	_____
8. 1 x 5 =	_____	_____	_____

Gopher It, Six!

6 x 1	6 x 2	6 x 3	6 x 4	6 x 5	6 x 6	6 x 7	6 x 8	6 x 9
6	12	18	24	30	36	42	48	54

▶ Help the gopher find his way home. Multiply and then color the even number products. (Even numbers end in 2, 4, 6, 8, or 0.)

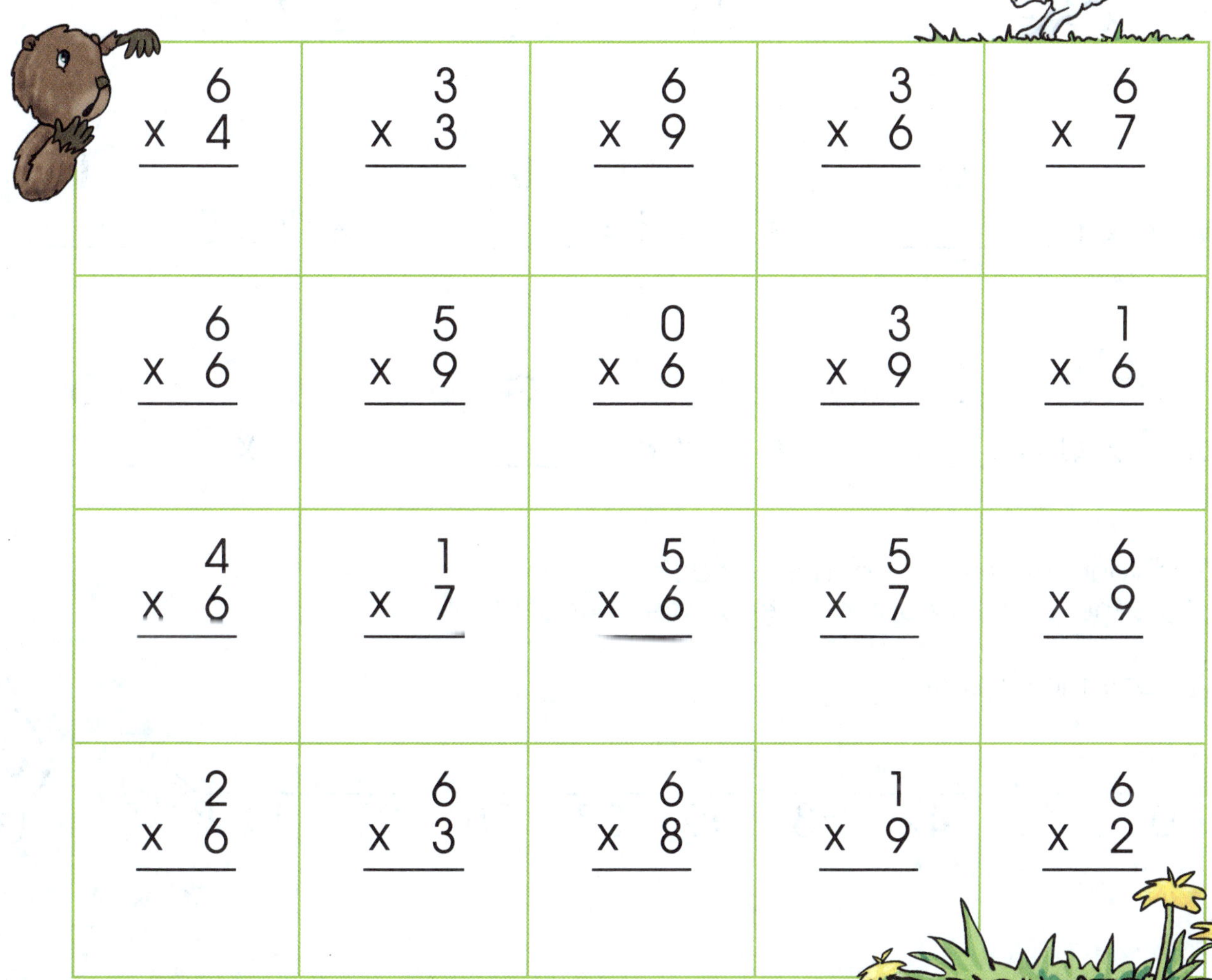

6 x 4	3 x 3	6 x 9	3 x 6	6 x 7
6 x 6	5 x 9	0 x 6	3 x 9	1 x 6
4 x 6	1 x 7	5 x 6	5 x 7	6 x 9
2 x 6	6 x 3	6 x 8	1 x 9	6 x 2

▶ Complete the table.

x	0	1	2	3	4	5	6	7	8	9
6										

Lucky Seven!

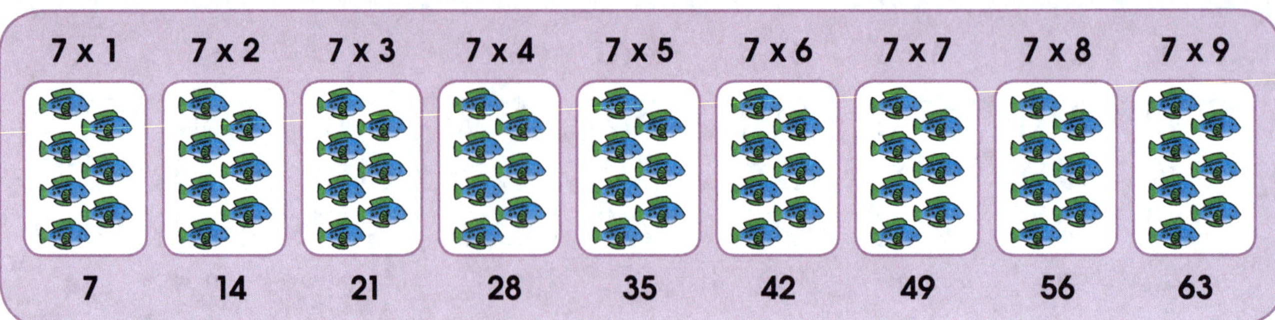

▶ Find the product.

F 1. 7 x 4 = ____	L 2. 7 x 9 = ____	H 3. 7 x 2 = ____
O 4. 7 x 6 = ____	S 5. 7 x 3 = ____	I 6. 7 x 5 = ____
A 7. 7 x 0 = ____	G 8. 7 x 8 = ____	D 9. 7 x 7 = ____

▶ Use your answers to decode the riddle.
Write the letter for each answer on the correct blank.

What is the richest fish?

____ ____ ____ ____ ____ ____ ____ ____ ____
0 56 42 63 49 28 35 21 14

▶ Complete the table.

x	0	1	2	3	4	5	6	7	8	9
7										

Products in a Pyramid

▶ Multiply. Write the products in the puzzle.

Across

1. 7 x 5 = 35
2. 4 x 4 = ____
3. 7 x 8 = ____
5. 3 x 8 = ____
6. 4 x 8 = ____
8. 6 x 8 = ____
9. 2 x 7 = ____
11. 8 x 4 = ____
12. 7 x 0 = ____

Down

1. 4 x 9 = ____
2. 2 x 7 = ____
4. 7 x 9 = ____
5. 4 x 7 = ____
7. 3 x 7 = ____
8. 7 x 6 = ____
10. 5 x 8 = ____

Eight Is Great!

If you know your 4s facts, you can double them to know the 8s facts.

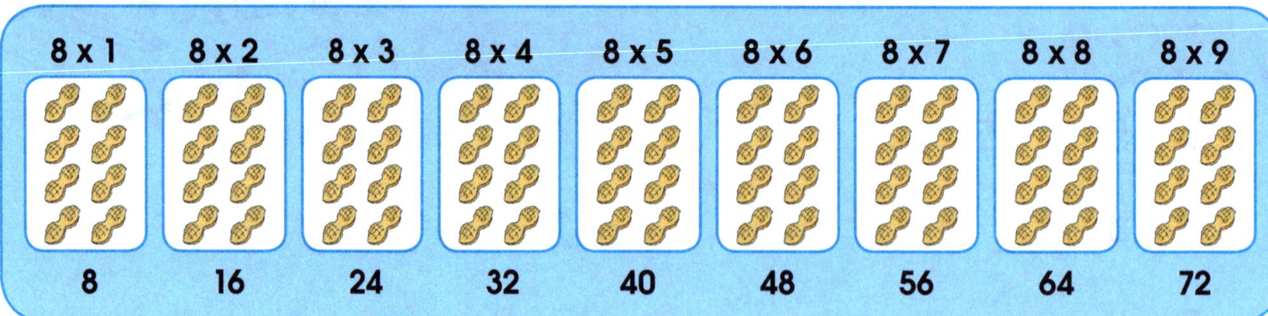

▶ Find the product.

1. 8 x 3 = ____ E
2. 8 x 6 = ____ L
3. 8 x 4 = ____ P
4. 8 x 8 = ____ B
5. 8 x 1 = ____ A
6. 8 x 9 = ____ Y
7. 8 x 5 = ____ H
8. 8 x 7 = ____ N
9. 8 x 2 = ____ T

▶ Use your answers to decode the riddle.
Write the letter for each answer on the correct blank.

What does an elephant have that no other animals have?

A ____ ____ ____ ____
64 8 64 72

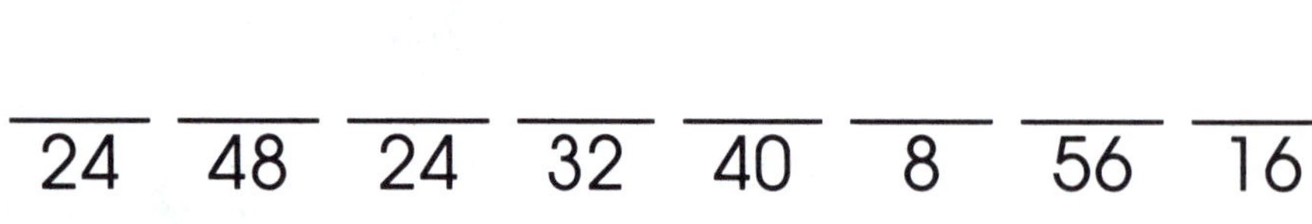

▶ Complete the table.

x	0	1	2	3	4	5	6	7	8	9
8										

Nine is Fine!

9 x 1	9 x 2	9 x 3	9 x 4	9 x 5	9 x 6	9 x 7	9 x 8	9 x 9
9	18	27	36	45	54	63	72	81

▶ Find the product.

1.	3 x 9	5 x 9	7 x 9	1 x 9	8 x 9	0 x 9	6 x 9	2 x 9
2.	4 x 9	9 x 6	9 x 3	9 x 0	9 x 5	9 x 7	9 x 9	9 x 8

▶ Start at the arrow to find the carrot.
Follow the path in the same order as your answers above.

▶ Complete the table.

x	0	1	2	3	4	5	6	7	8	9
6										

Any Order

As you've learned, you can multiply factors in any order and get the same product.

4 x 3 = 12 3 x 4 = 12

▶ Multiply. Draw lines that connect the matching problems.

7 x 9 = _____ •	W R	•0 x 8 = _____
6 x 8 = _____ •	T I	•9 x 7 = _____
8 x 7 = _____ •	N	•6 x 9 = _____
8 x 0 = _____ •	S D E	•7 x 5 = _____
5 x 7 = _____ •	A	•8 x 6 = _____
9 x 6 = _____ •	O	•9 x 8 = _____
7 x 6 = _____ •	W P C M	•6 x 7 = _____
8 x 9 = _____ •	S	•7 x 8 = _____

▶ To answer the riddle, write the letters from top to bottom that aren't crossed out.

What invention allows you to see through walls?

_____ _____ _____ _____ _____ _____ _____

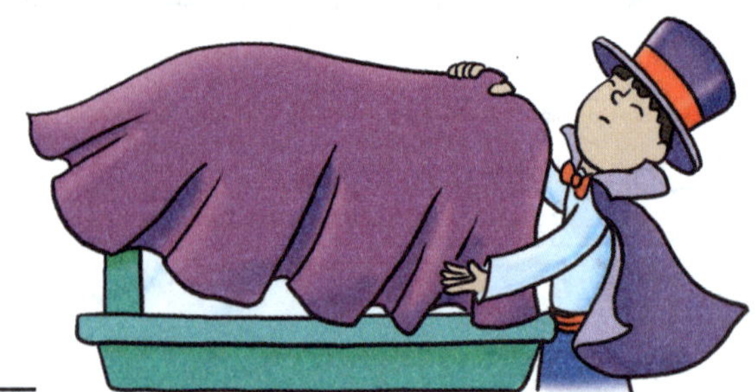

Home Run Riddle

▶ Complete the multiplication table.

The first factor is the row, and the second factor is the column.

x	0	1	2	3	4	5	6	7	8	9
0		0						0		
1				3						
2	0							14		
3										27
4		4								
5						25				
6	0									
7					28					63
8										
9							54			

▶ Solve the problems.

7 x 4 = 28　　3 x 6 = ____　　4 x 3 = ____　　5 x 8 = ____

2 x 5 = ____　　6 x 3 = ____　　8 x 5 = ____　　4 x 7 = ____

3 x 4 = ____　　7 x 6 = ____　　5 x 2 = ____　　6 x 7 = ____

▶ Color the squares with the answers to the problems in the table to solve the riddle. Which gem has something in common with baseball?

____

Out of This World

▶ Multiply. Use your answers to color the picture.

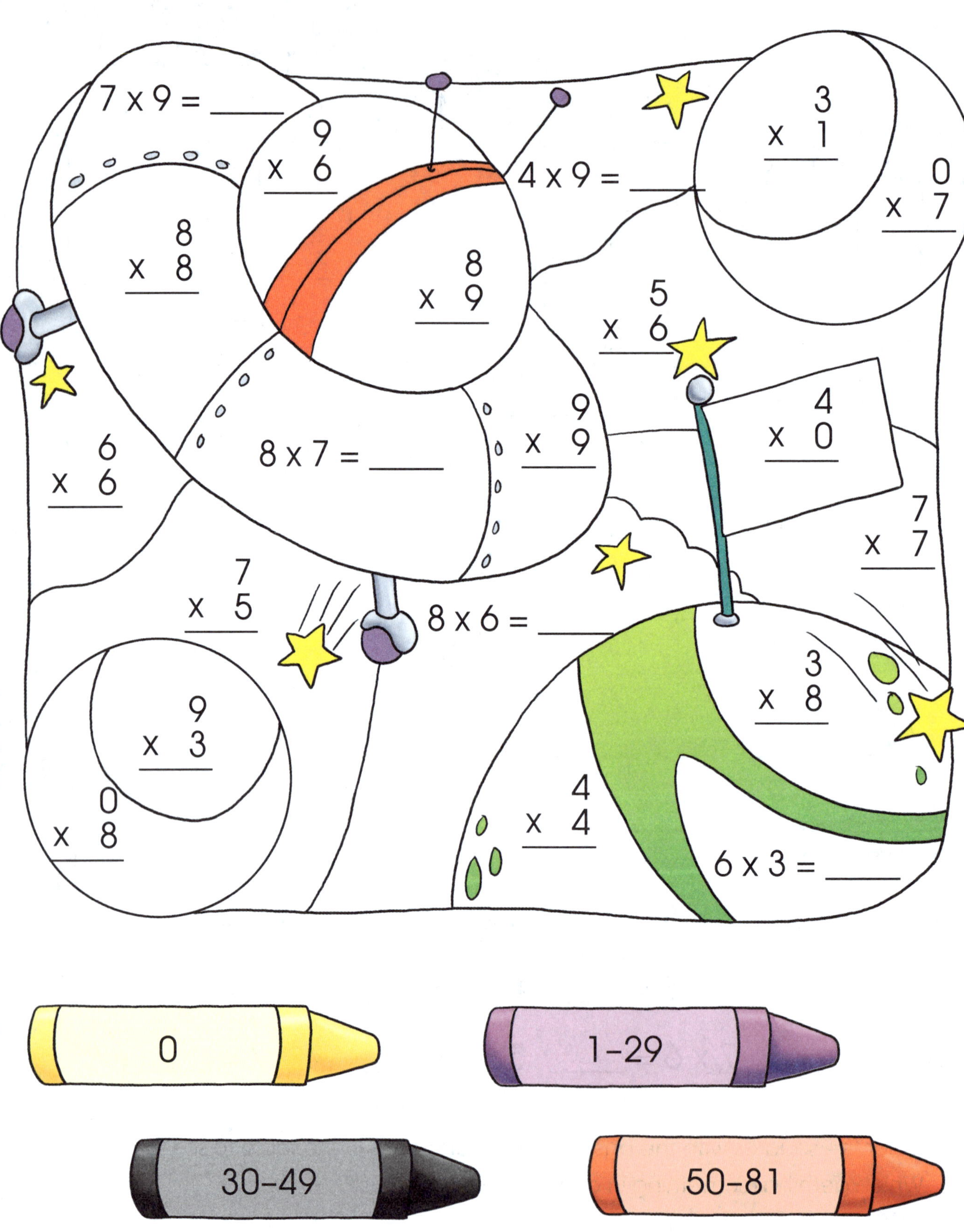

Triangle Times

▶ Multiply. Use the numbers in the triangle as factors. Write a product in each circle.

Fast Facts!

▶ Practice the facts. Time yourself.
Can you solve all of these problems in less than 10 minutes?

1. 2 x 8 = ____ 4 x 5 = ____ 6 x 4 = ____ 3 x 7 = ____
2. 5 x 3 = ____ 3 x 8 = ____ 5 x 5 = ____ 4 x 8 = ____
3. 7 x 4 = ____ 4 x 9 = ____ 7 x 3 = ____ 8 x 6 = ____
4. 5 x 9 = ____ 6 x 1 = ____ 2 x 9 = ____ 6 x 6 = ____
5. 8 x 3 = ____ 7 x 2 = ____ 5 x 8 = ____ 8 x 7 = ____
6. 7 x 9 = ____ 8 x 8 = ____ 3 x 6 = ____ 0 x 9 = ____
7. 4 x 7 = ____ 9 x 6 = ____ 6 x 8 = ____ 9 x 7 = ____
8. 9 x 9 = ____ 3 x 0 = ____ 8 x 4 = ____ 6 x 9 = ____
9. 5 x 8 = ____ 7 x 7 = ____ 4 x 6 = ____ 7 x 8 = ____
10. 9 x 5 = ____ 5 x 7 = ____ 8 x 0 = ____ 9 x 8 = ____
11. 4 x 4 = ____ 7 x 6 = ____ 5 x 9 = ____ 7 x 4 = ____
12. 9 x 3 = ____ 0 x 7 = ____ 8 x 9 = ____ 0 x 0 = ____

What's Missing?

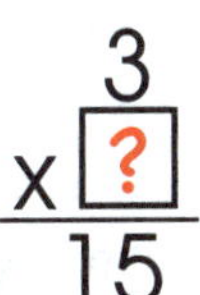

3 times what number equals 15?

The **missing factor** is 5 because 3 x 5 = 15.

▶ Write the missing factor for each number sentence.

Y	A	I	A
1. 4 x ☐ = 20	2. ☐ x 8 = 48	3. 5 x ☐ = 45	4. ☐ x 7 = 42

N	L	F	G
5. 8 x ☐ = 16	6. ☐ x 8 = 24	7. 9 x ☐ = 63	8. 3 x ☐ = 12

Z	I	P	Z
9. 5 x ☐ = 40	10. ☐ x 4 = 36	11. 4 x ☐ = 4	12. ☐ x 7 = 56

▶ Use the numbers you wrote to decode the riddle.
Write the letter for each number on the correct blank.

What is a pie in the sky?

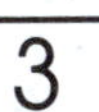
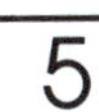

___ ___ ___ ___ ___ ___ ___
6 7 3 5 9 2 4

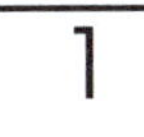

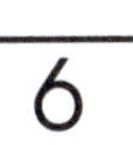

___ ___ ___ ___ ___
1 9 8 8 6

Ten Again

Look at each product. When you multiply a number by 10, it's like writing the number and zero.

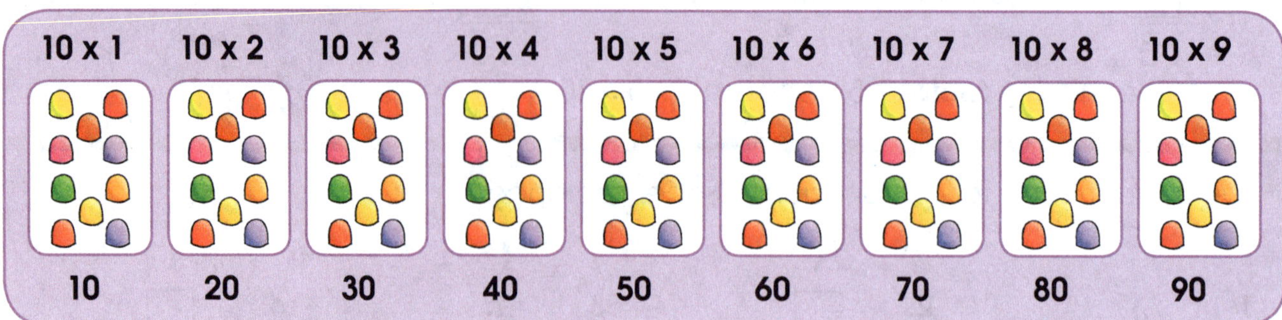

▶ Find the product.

1. 10 x 6 = _____
2. 10 x 4 = _____
3. 1 x 10 = _____
4. 10 x 3 = _____
5. 5 x 10 = _____
6. 10 x 8 = _____
7. 7 x 10 = _____
8. 10 x 0 = _____
9. 2 x 10 = _____
10. 9 x 10 = _____
11. When you multiply a number times 10, the product ends with a ______.

▶ Complete the table.

x	0	1	2	3	4	5	6	7	8	9
10										

Double-Digit Time

To multiply 11 by a number from 1 through 9, remember this clue:
The product is a two-digit number that repeats the factor.

▶ Find the product. Then look across and down to find the problems and products in the number search.

1. 11 x 3 = 33

2. 11 x 7 = ____

3. 11 x 9 = ____

4. 11 x 4 = ____

5. 11 x 2 = ____

6. 11 x 8 = ____

7. 11 x 5 = ____

8. 11 x 1 = ____

9. 11 x 0 = ____

10. 11 x 6 = ____

11	17	1	28	11	7	77
5	11	4	44	16	48	11
55	32	63	11	0	0	3
0	11	8	88	11	38	33
24	9	56	71	1	15	41
65	99	36	23	11	2	22
18	11	6	66	43	0	17

▶ Complete the table.

x	0	1	2	3	4	5	6	7	8	9
11										

Delve into Twelves

Interesting Facts: 12 objects = 1 dozen and 12 inches = 1 foot

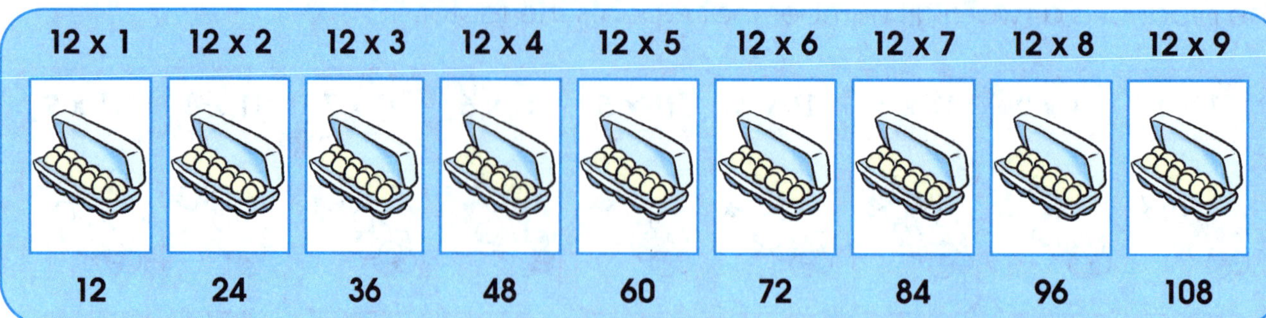

▶ Find the product.

1. 12 x 2 = ____ **N**
2. 12 x 5 = ____ **O**
3. 12 x 4 = ____ **A**
4. 12 x 8 = ____ **I**
5. 12 x 1 = ____ **C**
6. 12 x 7 = ____ **E**
7. 12 x 6 = ____ **U**
8. 12 x 9 = ____ **R**
9. 12 x 3 = ____ **P**

▶ Use your answers to decode the riddle.
Write the letter for each answer on the correct blank.

What pine has the sharpest needles?

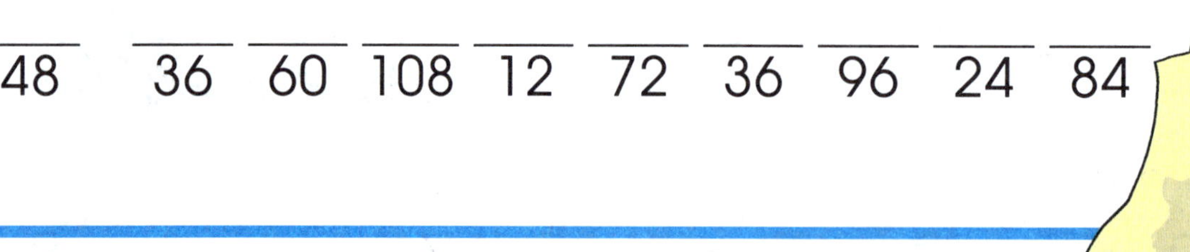

▶ Complete the table.

x	0	1	2	3	4	5	6	7	8	9
12										

Multiplication Table

▶ Complete the table.

x	0	1	2	3	4	5	6	7	8	9	10	11	12
0													
1													
2													
3													
4													
5													
6													
7													
8													
9													
10													
11													
12													

Addition Clue Words

Some clue words tell you to **add**. These clue words are: **in all**, **altogether**, **sum**, and **total**. Remember the 4 steps to follow when solving all problems.

1. **Read** the problem carefully.
2. **Decide** what to do.
3. **Solve** the problem.
4. **Check** to see if the answer makes sense.

Sara saw **23** butterflies when she was walking in the field. When she stopped to rest, she saw **10** grasshoppers. How many insects did she see **altogether**?

Solve:

$$\begin{array}{r} 23 \\ +\ 10 \\ \hline 33 \end{array}$$

The answer:

Sara saw **33** insects altogether.

▶ Underline the word or words that give you the clue to add. Then solve the problem. Write your answer in a complete sentence.

1. While hiking in the woods, Calvin picked up 34 rocks. He then spotted 12 new rocks and picked them up also. What is the total number of rocks that Calvin found?

____

____

2. Yesterday Jamie saw 14 birds in her yard. Today she saw 39 birds in her yard. How many birds did she see in all?

____

____

Addition Word Problems

▶ Underline the word or words that give you the clue to add. Solve the problem. Write your answer in a complete sentence.

1. Stephanie had 25 dolls in her collection. She received 11 more for her birthday. What is the total number of dolls Stephanie has in her collection?

____

2. Dalton had 31 baseball cards. His dad gave him 22 more. How many baseball cards does he have in all?

____

3. Andy counted 64 dandelions. Beth counted 26 violets. What is the sum of the flowers they counted?

____

4. Adam found 91 small twigs and 29 larger twigs for the campfire. How many twigs did he find altogether?

____

5. In her week of camping, Krista saw 15 chipmunks run for the safety of their homes. She also saw 15 squirrels climb into the trees. How many animals did Krista see in all?

____

6. Alesha caught 52 fish. Yumiko caught 39 fish. What is the total number of fish they caught?

____

Subtraction Clue Words

Some clue words tell you to **subtract**. These clue words are: **how many more, how many are left,** and **difference.** The same 4 steps you used for addition can also be used for subtraction problems.

1. **Read** the problem carefully.
2. **Decide** what to do.
3. **Solve** the problem.
4. **Check** to see if the answer makes sense.

Steve played **12** games with his baseball team. His team will be playing **57** games this season. How many more games will Steve need to play to complete the season?

Solve:

$$\begin{array}{r} 57 \\ -\ 12 \\ \hline 45 \end{array}$$

The answer:

Steve needs to play **45** more games to complete the season.

▶ Underline the word or words that give you the clue to subtract. Then solve the problem. Write your answer in a complete sentence.

1. Chelsea threw the ball 29 feet. Meagan threw the ball 27 feet. What was the difference between their throws in feet?

   ____

2. Yesterday John kicked the soccer ball 68 times during the game. Today he kicked the ball 49 times. How many more times did he kick the ball yesterday?

   ____

Subtraction Word Problems

▶ Underline the word or words that give you the clue to subtract. Then solve the problem. Write your answer in a complete sentence.

1. Sue delivered 46 newspapers. Tom delivered 35 newspapers. How many more newspapers did Sue deliver?

___

2. Jennifer sold 72 candy bars. Patti sold 56 candy bars. How many more candy bars did Jennifer sell?

___

3. Kim wants to do 75 cartwheels. She has already done 16 cartwheels. How many cartwheels are left for Kim to do?

___

4. Eric ran the race in 43 seconds. Scott ran the race in 46 seconds. What was the difference between their times in seconds?

___

5. Elliot wants to hit the tennis ball against the wall 100 times. He has hit the ball against the wall 66 times. How many hits are left for him to do?

___

Add or Subtract

On this page you will need to decide whether to **add** or **subtract**. Remember the 4 steps.

1. **Read** the problem carefully.
2. **Decide** what to do.
3. **Solve** the problem.
4. **Check** to see if the answer makes sense.

Decide:

There are **178** sixth grade students and **106** fifth grade students. How many more sixth grade students are there?

add or **subtract**

The answer:

There are **72** more sixth grade students.

Read the problem. Circle *add* or *subtract*. Then solve the problem. Write your answer in a complete sentence.

1. In our school there are 328 girls and 297 boys. How many children are there in our school altogether? **add** or **subtract**

   ____

2. The class painted 10 pictures on Monday and 13 pictures on Tuesday. How many more pictures did they paint on Tuesday? **add** or **subtract**

   ____

3. Jessica brought 45 pennies to school and Sam brought 25 pennies to school. How many pennies did they bring in all? **add** or **subtract**

   ____

4. Miss Bracken had 160 pieces of chalk. She broke 73 of them. How many pieces were left unbroken? **add** or **subtract**

   ____

Addition & Subtraction Problems

▶ Write the number sentence. Solve the problem. Label your answer.

1. There were 16 spotted butterflies in the field. They were joined by 18 plain butterflies. What is the sum of the butterflies in the field?

____

2. There are 15 spiders on the porch. If 10 of those spiders leave the porch, how many spiders will be left?

____

3. There are 98 grasshoppers in the grass. There are also 65 beetles in the grass. How many more grasshoppers are there?

____

4. There were 120 brown ants and 92 black ants marching down the ant hill. How many more brown ants were there?

____

5. There are 127 big flies buzzing around the pond. Also buzzing are 112 little flies. How many flies are there altogether?

____

6. There are 25 bees and 13 hornets flying near the bush. How many insects are there in all?

____

Addition & Subtraction Problems

When adding money, keep the decimal point in line.

Jacob bought a pencil for **$0.92** He also bought an eraser for **$0.37**. How much money did he spend altogether?

Solve:

	$0.92
+	**$0.37**
	$1.29

The answer:

He spent **$1.29** altogether.

▶ Solve the problem. Show your work.

1. Molly bought a box of cat food for $1.64. She then went to the candy store and bought some gum for $0.35. How much money did she spend in all?

   ____

2. Mandi bought a book that cost $5.00. Her friend Justin bought a used book that cost $0.25. How much more did Mandi spend?

   ____

3. Jaric saw a bottle of shampoo that cost $1.72. He also saw conditioner that cost $1.18. If he purchased both items, what would the sum be?

   ____

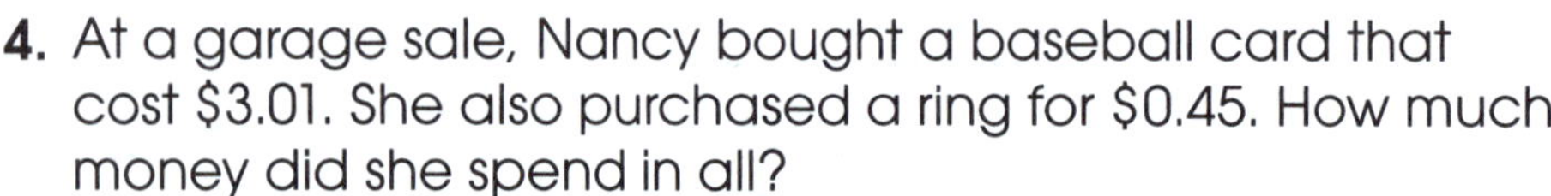

4. At a garage sale, Nancy bought a baseball card that cost $3.01. She also purchased a ring for $0.45. How much money did she spend in all?

   ____

5. Lauren bought some beads for $2.60. She later bought some string for $0.55. How much more money did she spend on the beads?

   ____

Addition & Subtraction Problems

▶ Solve the problem. Label your answer.

1. The band marched 65 minutes in the morning and 45 minutes in the afternoon. How many minutes did the band march altogether?

____

2. The band has 25 tubas and 19 trombones. How many more tubas does the band have?

____

3. The band went on a field trip. It traveled 275 miles going and 280 miles returning. How many miles did the band travel in all?

____

4. There are 29 flutes in the band and 20 drums. What is the difference in number between these instruments?

____

5. There are 125 people in the band. There are only 65 uniforms. How many more uniforms are needed?

____

6. Jill knows how to play 26 marching songs. Jack knows how to play 32. What is the total number of songs they know?

____

Drawing Multiplication Word Problems

It is sometimes helpful to draw a picture of the information given to you in word problems. Using a graph will help you to organize and keep your information accurate. Here is an example:

Miss Halt stopped **5** rows of cars.

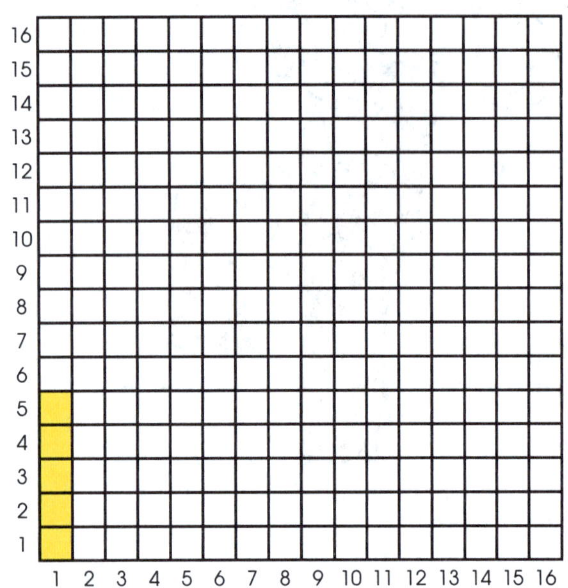

There were **9** cars in each row.

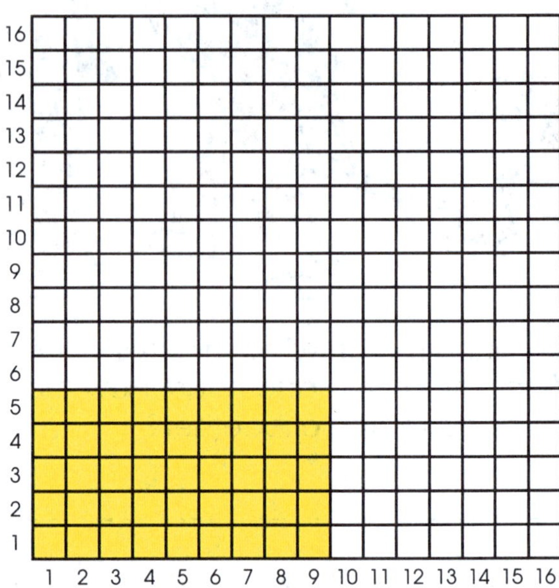

How many cars did Miss Halt stop?
Count all of the colored boxes in the final drawing. The answer is **45**.

▶ Read and solve each problem using the drawing method shown above.

1. Miss Halt helps about 15 people across the street each week.

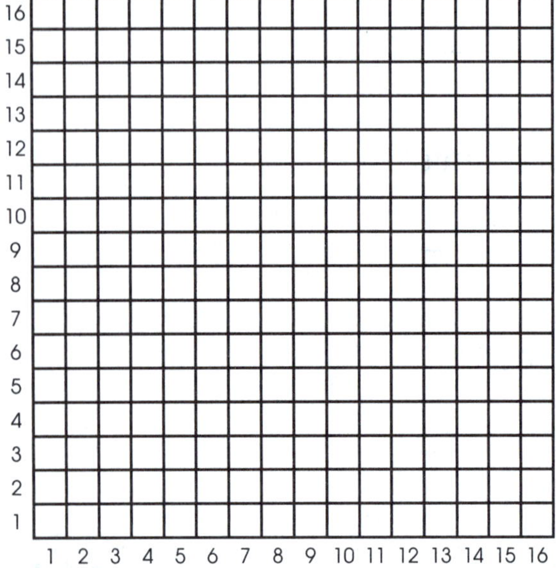

How many people does she help in 4 weeks? ________

2. Suppose Miss Halt gave 12 tickets in a day.

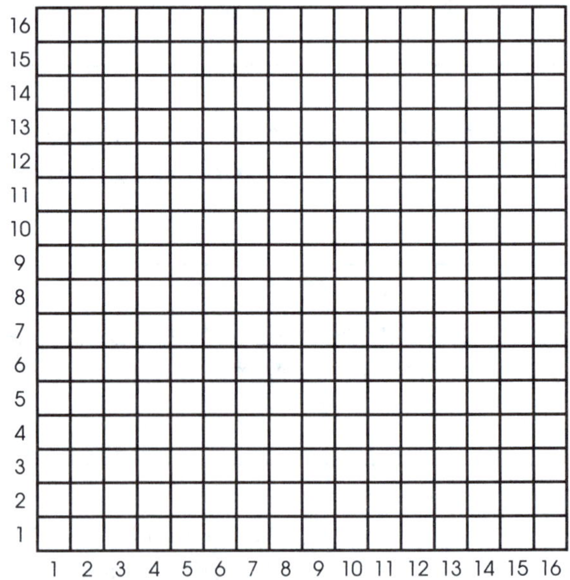

If she did this for 6 days, how many tickets would she give? ________

Drawing Multiplication Word Problems

▶ Read and solve each problem using the drawing method shown on page 280.

1. Miss Halt practiced directing traffic. She practiced for 7 hours a day. She practiced for 11 days.

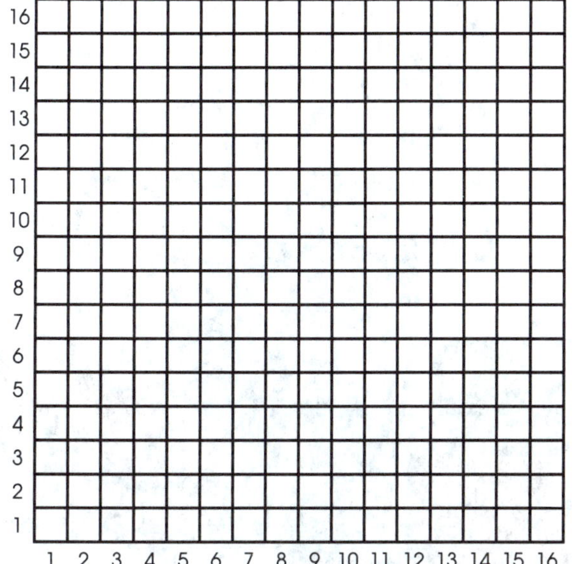

How many hours did she practice? ___________

2. Miss Halt has 10 boxes. In each box she has 10 whistles.

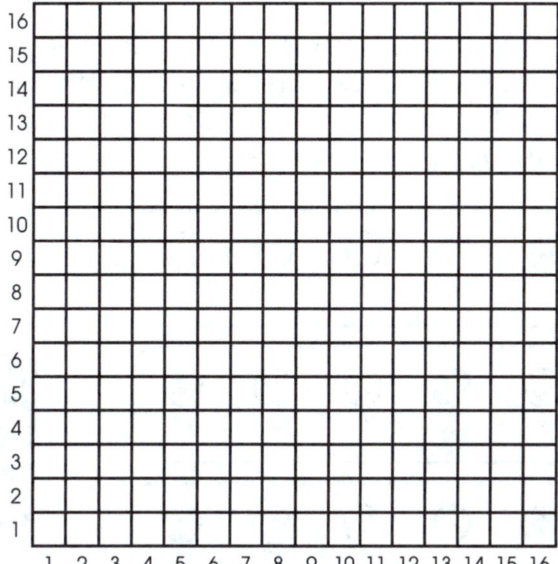

How many whistles does she have? ___________

3. Miss Halt blew her whistle 12 times in one day. Let's say she blew it that many times for 3 days.

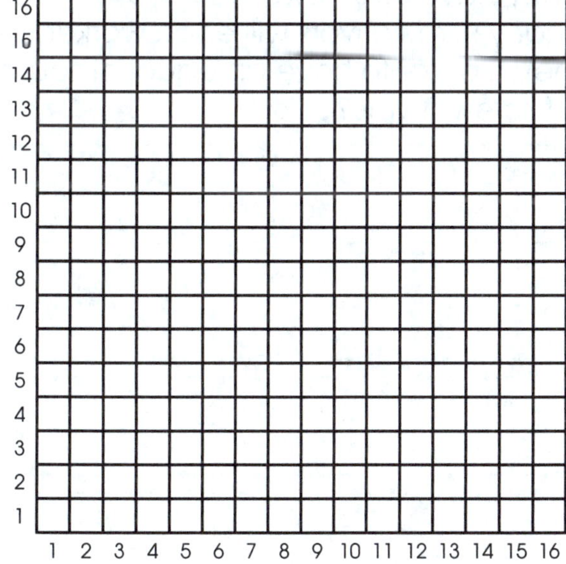

How many times would she blow her whistle? ___________

4. Miss Halt gave directions to 14 people. Each person asked 5 questions.

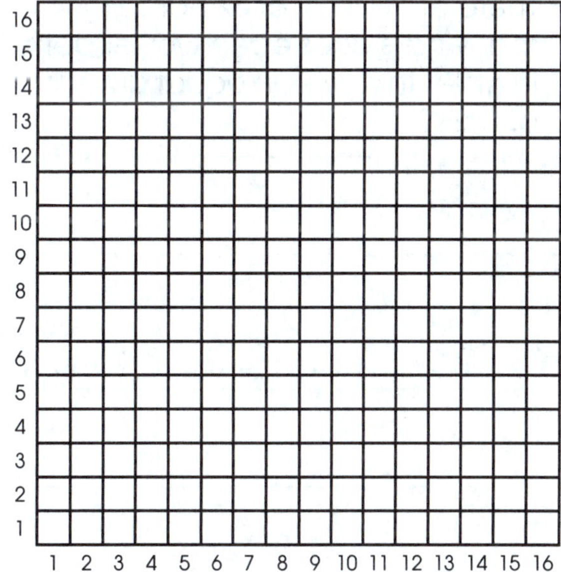

How many questions were asked? ___________

Drawing Division Word Problems

It is sometimes helpful to draw a picture of the information given to you in word problems. Here is another example:

Carl has **3** toolboxes. He needs to divide **15** hammers equally into all his toolboxes.

First draw **3** toolboxes. Then, beginning with the first box, draw one dot in each box. Each dot will represent one hammer. Repeat until all **15** hammers are drawn.

1	4	7	10	13
2	5	8	11	14
3	6	9	12	15

How many hammers will he place in each box?
Count the number of dots that were drawn in one box. The answer is **5**.

▶ Read and solve each problem using the drawing method shown above.

1. There are 4 construction workers. There are a total of 32 nails. How many nails does each worker get in order to have an equal amount of nails?

2. There are 8 construction workers. They have 56 screwdrivers. How many screwdrivers will each worker get in order to have an equal amount of screwdrivers?

Drawing Division Word Problems

▶ Read and solve each problem using the drawing method shown on page 282.

1. There are 4 trucks. There are 32 pieces of wood. How many pieces of wood would be placed into each truck so that each truck has an equal amount of wood?

2. There are 7 toolboxes. There are 49 saws. How many saws will be in each box in order to have an equal amount in each box?

3. There were 8 people with drills. There were 48 holes drilled into the wall. Each person drilled an equal number of holes. How many holes did each person drill?

4. There were 6 toolboxes. There were 42 wrenches. Each toolbox contained an equal number of wrenches. How many wrenches were in each box?

Multiplication Clue Words

Some clue words tell you to **multiply**. These clue words are: **how many** and **how much**. Remember that multiplying is a quicker form of addition. Use the 4 steps to help you solve the story problems.

There were **15** people ready to begin the race. Each person had **2** water bottles at the finish line. **<u>How many</u>** water bottles were there at the finish line?

Solve:

$$\begin{array}{r} 15 \\ \times\ \ 2 \\ \hline 30 \end{array}$$

The answer:

There were **30** water bottles at the finish line.

▶ Underline the clue words that tell you to multiply.
Then solve the word problem. Write your answer in a complete sentence.

1. There are 7 swimmers waiting for their finishing ribbons. Each swimmer will receive 3 ribbons. How many finishing ribbons are there altogether?

____

____

2. Amy trained for 5 hours every day to get ready for her big game. She trained for 30 days. How much time, in hours, did she spend training?

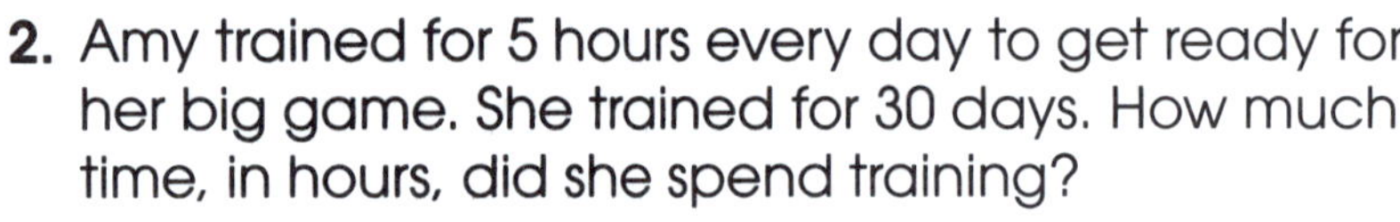

____

____

3. There were 72 bikers at the start of the race. Each biker had 1 helmet. How many helmets were there?

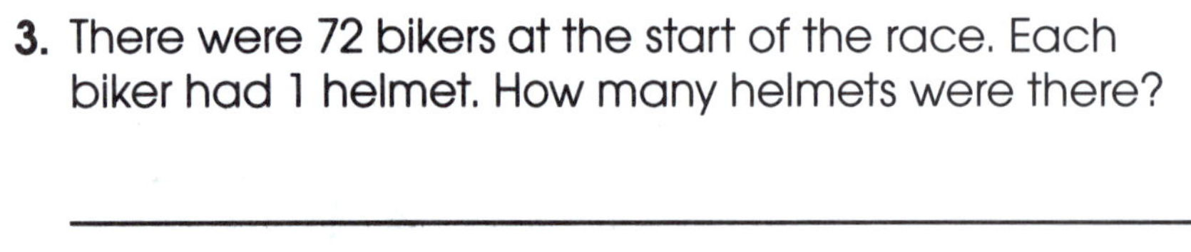

____

____

Multiplication Word Problems

Underline the clue words that tell you to multiply. Then solve the problem. Label your answer.

1. There were 16 golfers from each school at the tournament. 5 schools participated. How many golfers were there altogether?

____

2. Dana drove his snowmobile 37 miles a day for 8 days. How many miles did he drive in all?

____

3. Curtis trained for 39 days to get ready for the race. He drank 8 glasses of water every day that he trained. How much water did Curtis drink throughout his training?

____

4. There were 8 rows of bikers. There were 6 bikers in each row. How many bikers were there altogether?

____

5. There were 96 swimmers waiting to race. Each swimmer brought 4 friends to watch the race. How many friends were there at the race?

____

More Multiplication Word Problems

Solve the problem. Show your work.

1. There were 57 skaters at the start of the race. Each skater had 2 knee pads. How many knee pads were there?

____

2. Keli practiced for 19 days to prepare for her dance recital. Every day she practiced for 3 hours. How many hours did she practice in all?

____

3. Daniel has 3 cases to hold his toy planes. Each case holds 18 planes. How many planes can Daniel store in his cases?

____

4. Nadia's classroom has 12 rows of chairs. Each row has 5 chairs. How many chairs are in Nadia's classroom?

____

Division Clue Words

Some clue words mean to **divide**. These clue words are: **how many** and **each**. Use the 4 steps to solve division word problems.

Kim planted **32** flowers. In **each** row there were **4** flowers. **How many** rows of flowers were there?

Solve: $\begin{array}{r} 8 \\ 4\overline{)32} \end{array}$

The answer:

There were **8** rows of flowers.

Underline the clue words that tell you to divide. Then solve the problem. Write your answer in a complete sentence.

1. Alesha planted 7 rows of carrots in her garden. Later, she pulled up the same number of carrots from each row. She counted 56 carrots. How many carrots did she pull from each row?

____

2. Scott and Brad had 48 flowers. They put 6 flowers in each vase. How many vases did they have?

____

3. Amy and John planted 30 rose bushes in 10 rows. Each row had the same number of bushes. How many rose bushes were in each row?

____

Division Word Problems

▶ Underline the word or words that give you the clue to divide. Then solve the problem. Write your answer in a complete sentence.

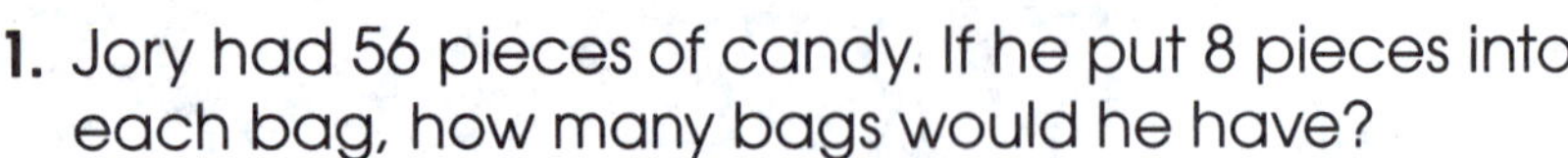

1. Jory had 56 pieces of candy. If he put 8 pieces into each bag, how many bags would he have?

   ____

2. Jamal planted 20 rows of onions in his garden. He pulled the same number of onions from each row. He counted 100 onions. How many onions did he pull from each row?

   ____

3. James was planting pine trees for his parents' tree farm. He planted 81 trees. There were 9 trees in each row. How many rows were there?

   ____

4. Margie has 45 plants in the tray she bought. The tray is divided into 9 rows. How many plants are in each row?

   ____

5. George picked 63 apples from 7 trees. He picked the same number of apples from each tree. How many apples did he pick from each tree?

   ____

More Division Word Problems

▶ Solve the problem. Show your work.

1. Katlin had 30 dolls. She divided them equally between herself and four friends while playing. How many dolls did each of the 5 girls have?

____

2. Jason swam 81 laps over a 9-day period. If he swam the same distance every day, how many laps did he swim each day?

____

3. Dorry likes to send postcards to her friends. She mailed 24 postcards to 12 of her friends. Each friend received the same number of cards. How many postcards did each friend receive?

____

4. If a stamp costs $0.29, how many stamps could you buy with $14.50?

____

Multiplication & Division Word Problems

▶ Solve the problem. Show your work.

1. Jamie bought 17 stamps. Andrew bought 3 times as many stamps. How many stamps did Andrew buy?

____

2. There are 40 letters in the mail bag. They are for 5 people. If each person gets the same number of letters, how many letters will each person get?

____

3. Miss James delivered 48 packets of letters. Each packet had 9 letters in it. How many letters did Miss James deliver?

____

4. Donna has pen pals in 15 countries. Suppose she has 3 pen pals in each country. How many pen pals would she have?

____

5. Mr. Koontz had 72 postcards. He put them in 9 equal piles. How many postcards were in each pile?

____

6. Miss James delivered 63 packages. She took 9 packages to each house. How many houses had packages delivered to them by Miss James?

____

Multiplication & Division Word Problems

▶ Solve the problem. Show your work.

1. The Smiths drove 55 miles an hour for 5 hours. How many miles did they drive?

____

2. Tina Smith collects postcards. She has 81 postcards. She keeps equal amounts of them in 9 envelopes. How many postcards are in each envelope?

____

3. Mrs. Smith took pictures of the trip. If she took 125 pictures a day for 7 days, how many pictures would she take?

____

4. Ann Smith saw bears on 9 mountains. Suppose each mountain had 32 bears on it. How many bears would there be?

____

5. Mr. Smith packed 12 shirts. He packed them into 4 suitcases. If there were an equal number of shirts in each suitcase, how many shirts would be in each?

____

6. The Smiths rode on a cable car. There were 25 people waiting in line. Each cable car holds 5 people. How many cable cars were needed?

____

Fractions

A **fraction** is a number that names part of a whole.

$\frac{2}{3}$ — **numerator** / — **denominator**

$\frac{2}{3}$ = **2** pieces out of **3** equal parts.

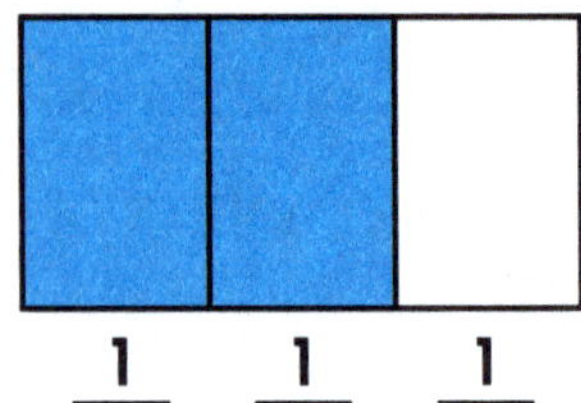

$\frac{1}{3}$ $\frac{1}{3}$ $\frac{1}{3}$

$\frac{2}{3}$ pieces colored / pieces in all

$\frac{2}{3}$ pieces are triangles / pieces in all

▶ Write each fraction using the method shown above.

1.

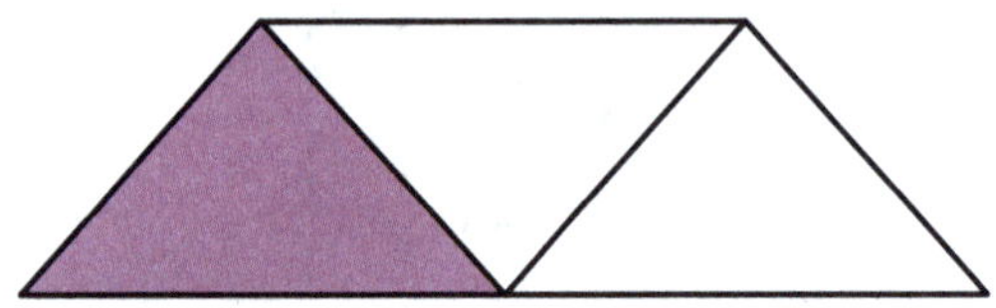

How many pieces are colored?

______

How many pieces are in the whole?

2.

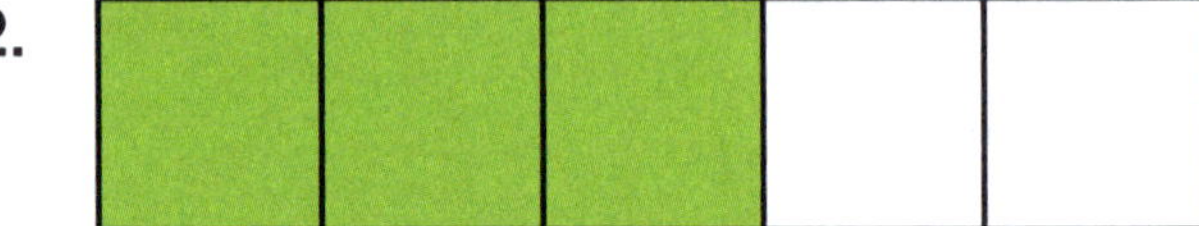

How many pieces are colored?

______

How many pieces are in the whole?

3.

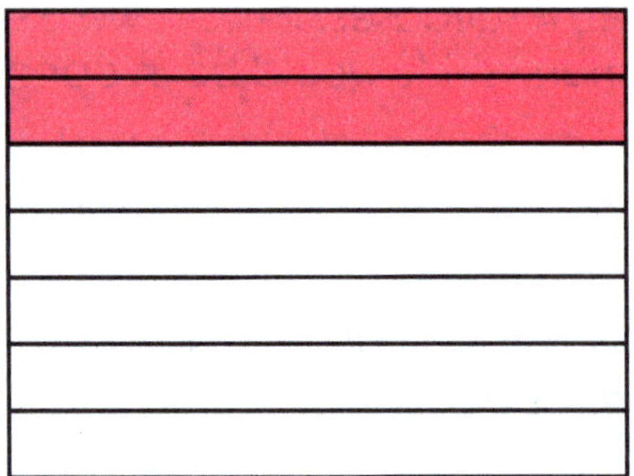

How many pieces are colored?

______

How many pieces are in the whole?

4.

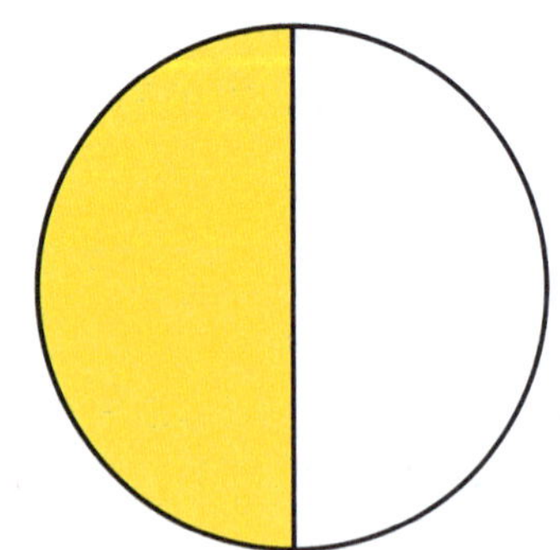

How many pieces are colored?

______

How many pieces are in the whole?

Adding & Subtracting Fractions

When you add or subtract fractions, you use only the top numbers (numerators). Below is an example:

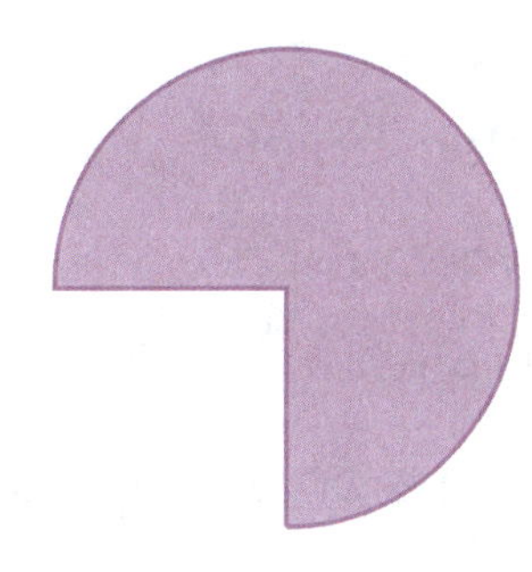

$\frac{1}{4}$ + $\frac{2}{4}$ = $\frac{3}{4}$

▶ Write a fraction for each colored part. Solve the problem.

1.

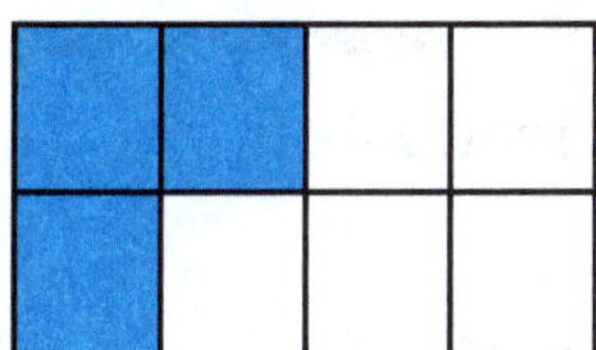
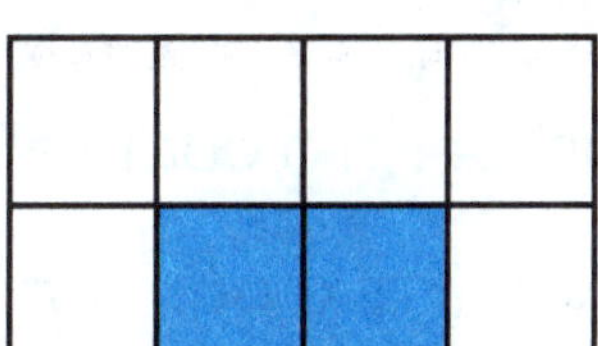

______ + ______ = ______

2.

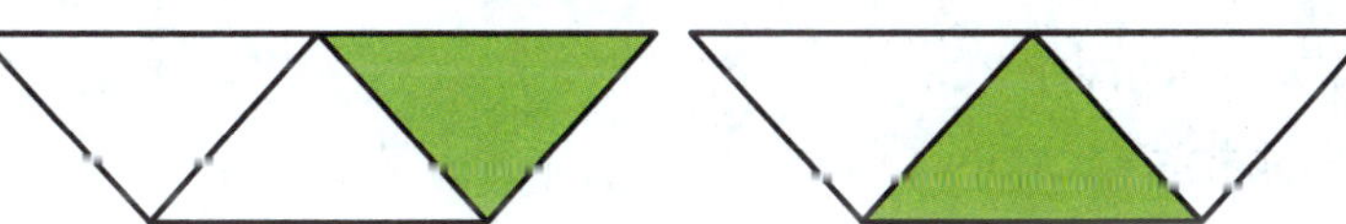

______ – ______ = ______

3.

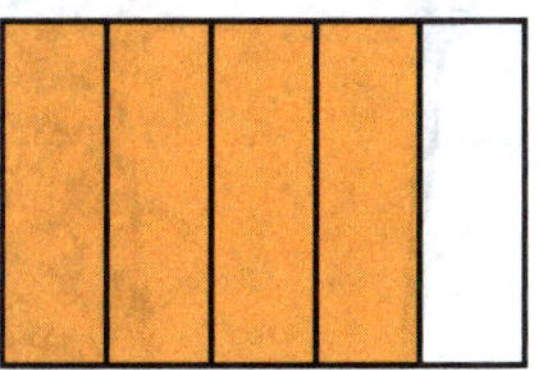
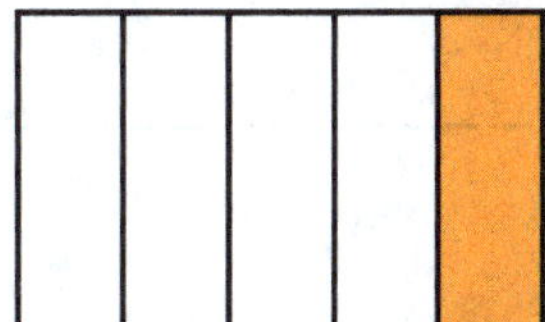

______ – ______ = ______

Fractions in Word Problems

Sometimes you have fractions in word problems. Look for the clue words that tell you to add or subtract. Remember to add or subtract only the top number (numerator) of the fractions.

1. **Read** the problem carefully.
2. **Decide** what you must do.
3. **Solve** the problem.
4. **Check** to see if the answer makes sense.

Mary planted $\frac{2}{7}$ of the garden with corn and $\frac{3}{7}$ with beans. How much of the garden did she use?

Solve: $\frac{2}{7} + \frac{3}{7} = \frac{5}{7}$

The answer:

Mary used $\frac{5}{7}$ of the garden.

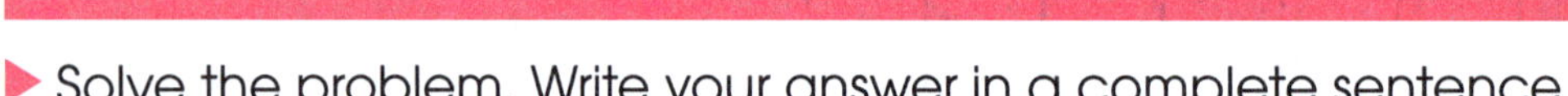

▶ Solve the problem. Write your answer in a complete sentence.

1. Wanda picked corn. She picked $\frac{8}{9}$ of a bushel on Wednesday. She picked $\frac{5}{9}$ of a bushel on Thursday. How much more did she pick on Wednesday than Thursday?

   ____

2. Kim dug $\frac{2}{4}$ of the garden in the morning and $\frac{1}{4}$ in the evening. How much of the garden did she dig altogether?

   ____

3. Suzanne must plant $\frac{8}{16}$ of the garden. She has planted $\frac{2}{16}$ so far. How much more must she plant?

   ____

More Fractions in Word Problems

Solve the problem. Write your answer in a complete sentence.

1. Todd bought $\frac{3}{8}$ of a yard of red fabric and $\frac{2}{8}$ of a yard of purple fabric. How much fabric did Todd buy?

   ____

2. Mom has only $\frac{9}{12}$ of an hour to paint. She painted for $\frac{3}{12}$ of an hour. How much more time does Mom have to paint?

   ____

3. Karen bought $\frac{5}{7}$ of a roll of flowered wallpaper. She used $\frac{3}{7}$. How much wallpaper does she have left?

   ____

4. Lucky used $\frac{2}{3}$ of a can of paint to paint a chair. He used $\frac{1}{3}$ of a can to paint a stool. How much more paint did it take for the chair?

   ____

5. Luis used $\frac{1}{4}$ cup of paste in one tray and $\frac{2}{4}$ cup in the other How much paste did he use altogether?

   ____

6. Margie has one piece of wallpaper that is $\frac{12}{18}$ of a yard long. She has another that is $\frac{6}{18}$ of a yard long. What is the difference?

   ____

Logic Puzzles

Word problems give you information that helps you solve a problem. These puzzles below give you a limited amount of information, but enough to solve the puzzle if you take some time to think. All of these puzzles will have a chart provided for you to record important information.

There are three children named Patti, Mary, and Paul. Each has a different favorite food of chicken, pizza, or spaghetti. You need to decide what food is the favorite for each child using the information below.

Patti does not like chicken.

	Patti	Mary	Paul
Pizza			
Spaghetti			
Chicken	no		

Mary will not eat foods that have tomatoes in them. (*Hint: If Mary does not like foods with tomato, then she must like chicken.*)

	Patti	Mary	Paul
Pizza		no	
Spaghetti		no	
Chicken	no	yes	

Paul likes a food that starts with the same letter as his name. (*Hint: If Paul likes pizza, then spaghetti or chicken must not be his favorite.*)

	Patti	Mary	Paul
Pizza		no	yes
Spaghetti		no	no
Chicken	no	yes	no

1. What is each child's favorite food according to the information given?

Patti ______________________

Mary ______________________

Paul ______________________

Logic Puzzles

▶ Here are a few logic puzzles for you to try. The charts are provided for you to record important information. Have fun!

1. Rachel's height is in between Nick's and Sam's.
Nick is taller than Sam.
What is the height of each child?

	Rachel	Nick	Sam
4′2″			
4′5″			
4′7″			

Rachel ______________________

Nick ______________________

Sam ______________________

2. Maggie is 9 years old. Susan is older than Maggie. James is younger than Susan. Joe is the oldest. Can you discover the ages of Maggie, Susan, Joe, and James?

	Maggie	Susan	Joe	James
8 years				
9 years				
10 years				
11 years				

Maggie is ______________________

Susan is ______________________

Joe is ______________________

James is ______________________

Two-Step Problems

Sometimes you must use two steps to solve a problem. These problems are called two-step word problems.

There are **9** girls on the basketball team. Each girl needs a shirt and shorts for the games. A shirt costs **$3.50**. A pair of shorts cost **$5.00**. What is the total cost of all the outfits?

Step 1: Add to get the cost of one outfit.
Step 2: Multiply to get the cost of all the outfits.

Step 1:

	$5.00	for a pair of shorts
+	**$3.50**	for a shirt
	$8.50	total per outfit

Step 2:

	$8.50	per outfit
x	**9**	number of girls
	$76.50	for 9 outfits

The answer:

The total cost of all the outfits is **$76.50**.

▶ Write the two equations needed to solve the problem. Label your answer.

1. Angie has gym class 40 minutes a day. She has it 3 times a week. Nancy has gym class 90 minutes a week. How much longer does Angie have gym class compared to Nancy?

____

____

2. Craig put 208 tennis balls into 4 wire baskets. He put the same number of balls in each basket. Then he took 3 baskets of balls outdoors. How many tennis balls did Craig take outdoors?

____

____

3. P.J. sold 4 rabbits for $3.75 each and 1 rabbit for $4.50. How much money did he get altogether?

____

____

4. Tim bought 6 tickets to the County Fair. Each ticket cost $1.50. How much change did he get from $10.00?

____

____

Venn Diagrams

A Venn diagram uses circles to represent sets and their relationships.

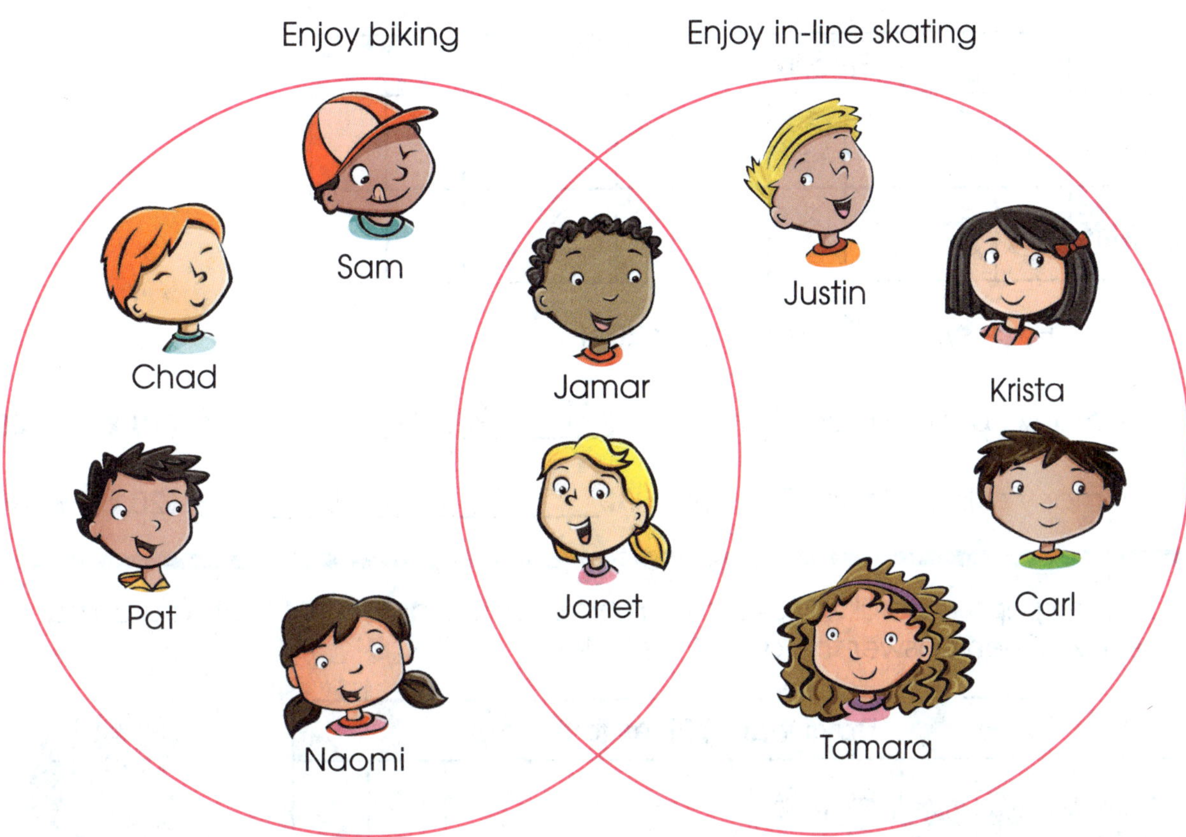

▶ Ten children were surveyed to discover whether they enjoyed bicycling, in-line skating, or both. The Venn diagram above gives you all the information you need to answer the following questions. Hint: Where the Venn diagram intersects, the children are in both circles.

1. Which activity does Tamara enjoy? ______________________

2. Naomi and Sam enjoy the same activity. Which one is it? ______________

3. How many children enjoy biking? ______________________

4. How many children enjoy in-line skating? ______________________

5. Who enjoys both biking and in-line skating? ______________________

6. How many children enjoy both biking and in-line skating? ______________

Picture Graphs

A picture graph gives you information. Read it carefully. Make certain you understand what facts are being presented.

Each symbol stands for **20** students.

1. How many boys are in Joy School? 120 boys **(20 x 6 = 120)**

2. How many girls are in Joy School? 140 girls **(20 x 7 = 140)**

▶ Read the graph carefully. Make certain you understand what facts are being presented. Then answer the questions below.

	Days Riding Bikes to School
Nancy	
Kim	
Luis	
Ramona	
Fred	

Each bike stands for **3** days.

1. Who rode to school the most days? ____________________

2. How many days did he or she ride to school? ____________________

3. How many days did Luis ride to school? ____________________

4. Nancy rode to school more days than Kim.
   How many more days did Nancy ride to school? ____________________

Bar Graphs

A bar graph gives you information. Read it carefully. Make sure you understand what facts are being presented.

	Attendance at the School Play														
	50	100	150	200	250	300	350	400	450	500	550	600	650	700	750
WED.															
THURS.															
FRIDAY															

1. On what day did the most people attend the play? Thursday
2. How many people came that day? 650
3. How many people came altogether? 1,800

▶ Study the graph. Then answer the questions below.

	Tickets sold to the School Play				
	10	20	30	40	50
Albert					
Jennifer					
Lucy					
Todd					
Shirley					

1. Who sold the most tickets? ____________
2. How many did Albert and Jennifer sell altogether? ____________
3. How many did Lucy and Todd sell in total? ____________
4. Todd sold more tickets than Shirley.
   How many more tickets did Todd sell? ____________
5. Shirley sold more tickets than Albert.
   How many more tickets did Shirley sell? ____________

Answer Key

Page 1
1. bridge
2. glass
3. stems
4. wheels
5. A's
6. trapeze ropes

Page 2
1. My Bones Are Missing!
2. think
3. Dog used them.
4. not think about what you do
5. bone picture

Page 3
1st mouse played a drum
2nd mouse hummed along
3rd mouse danced around
4th mouse clapped his hands
5th mouse sang a song

Page 4
1. picture 2
2. picture 2
3. picture 2
4. picture 1

Page 5

Across
1. shaker
3. shovel
5. path
6. hose
7. ear

Down
2. rake
3. shoe
4. vase

Page 6
1. No T
2. No H
3. Yes E
4. Yes R
5. Yes A
6. Yes I
7. No N
8. THE RAIN

Page 7
1. a cat who uses a computer
2. yes
3. no
4. yes
5. picture of cat at computer

Page 8
1. Henry's Dream
2. a lion chasing him
3. in the jungle
4. a bad dream
5. was red.
   were always white.
   woke up.

Page 9
1. a note
2. next week
3. maple, oak, and elm
4. keep it green
5. picture of people planting trees

Page 10
two zebras
one elephant
ten snakes
one giraffe
four monkeys

Pictures will vary.

Page 11

Across
3. horse
4. bear
7. elephant
8. panda
9. snake

Down
1. monkey
2. zebra
5. anteater
6. seal

Page 12
1. a note
2. Kris
3. Jackie's friend
4. shoot
5. Tuesdays
6. very good

Page 13
1. white
2. running
3. snow
4. spring
5. round
6. showers
7. day

Page 14
1. a milk bottle
   some markers
   some tape
   a grown-up
2. 6 1
   5 2
   3 4

Page 15
1. yes
2. no
3. yes
4. yes
5. no
6. no
7. yes
8. no
9. no
10. yes

Page 16
1. Mr. Ramirez s
2. The band s
3. Cory and Rosa c
4. Jeannette s
5. Leroy and his brother c
6. The bus s
7. Our driver s
8. Mia and I c
9. Parents and students c
10. They s

Page 17
1. crawled out of the ocean s
2. dug in the sand and laid her eggs c
3. covered the eggs with sand s
4. shone on the sand and warmed the eggs c
5. dug up an egg and ate it c
6. took some eggs for soup s
7. finally hatched s
8. climbed out of the sand s
9. ran down the sand and swam into the sea c
10. will come back and lay eggs c

Page 18
1. I like pizza, but I hate mushrooms on it.
2. Greg dislikes pizza, and he doesn't like hot dogs either.
3. not a compound sentence
4. Dee makes her own pizza sauce, but she buys crust.
5. Pizza has a lot of fat calories, but it sure is good.
6. My mom doesn't eat pizza, and neither does my dad.
7. not a compound sentence

Page 19
1. .
2. .
3. .
4. ?
5. ?
6. ?
7. .
8. .
9. .
10. ?

Answer Key

Page 20
1. Don't give away the ending to the movie.
2. Yikes, it's an alien!
3. Wow, I was really scared!
4. Tell your friend what time the movie starts.
5. Pay for the popcorn at the food stand.
6. Oh, gross, there's gum on my shoe!
7. Cover your eyes at the scary parts.

Page 22
1. a pig and a spider
2. The second paragraph should be circled.
3. The book report writer likes the characters and the information about animals.

Page 21
1. star patterns
   Constellations are patterns of stars.
2. just after sunset
   Dusk is the time of day just after the sun sets.
3. shooting his bow and arrow
   An archer is a person who shoots a bow and arrow.
4. brighter and dimmer
   To shimmer is to get brighter and dimmer.
5. unbelievable
   Incredible means unbelievable.
6. Earth, eight other planets, and the Sun.
   A solar system is a group of planets and a star.

Page 23
Responses will vary.

Page 24
Responses will vary.

Page 25
James and the Giant Peach
Roald Dahl
Delete sentence 4 and the last sentence.
Other responses will vary.

Page 26
Responses will vary.

Page 27
1. west
2. arm
3. brother, hospital
4. hospital, doctor, cast
5. home
6. dog
7. uncle, skis
8. bike

Person	Place	Animal	Thing
brother	west	dog	arm
doctor	home		cast
uncle	hospital		skis
			bike

Page 28
1. trucks
2. guys, crates
3. bananas
4. clerks, customers
5. apples, oranges
6. lemons
7. pies, cakes
8. grapes
9. dollars
10. pears

Page 29
1. buses, classes
2. boxes, lunches
3. dishes, glasses
4. stories
5. butterflies, branches, bunnies

Page 30
1. Miss Sampson asked about our summer vacations.
2. Teddy and Barb showed pictures of the Everglades.
3. The Tafts liked Florida better than Texas.
4. Leroy saw wolves at Yellowstone Park.
5. Eli and the Cohens went canoeing in Michigan.
6. Roger's dad, Doctor Madison, helped a sick camper.
7. Randy and Maria loved the Grand Canyon.
8. The Gurwitzes just escaped Hurricane George.

Page 31
1. Thursday
2. Halloween
3. summer
4. Monday
5. New Year's Day
6. birthday
7. weekend
8. Fourth of July
9. April
10. Thanksgiving

Page 32
1. Dr., St.
2. Jr., T.L.
3. Mr., Ms., Ave.
4. G.P., Blvd.
5. Gen., Mrs.
6. Mr., Mrs., St., Ct.

Page 33
1. mother's
2. mammals'
3. rabbit's
4. Kangaroos'
5. marsupials'
6. kangaroos'
7. baby's
8. Australia's

Page 34
1. b
2. a
3. b
4. a

Exact wording of answers will vary.

5. kind of toy, highest
6. want, lengthy or not short
7. puts or drops, things that grow on trees
8. look out for, timepiece worn on wrist

Page 35
1. C 2. B
3. A 4. B
5. C 6. A
7. B 8. A
9. B 10. C

Answer Key

Page 36
1. has
2. had
3. has
4. has
5. has
6. have
7. have
8. have

Page 37
1. present
2. present
3. present
4. past
5. past
6. present
7. past
8. past

Page 38
1. present
2. past
3. past
4. past
5. present
6. present
7. present
8. present
9. present
10. present, present

Page 39
1. Our class will start a school garden.
2. We will spend time in our garden each week.
3. We think the flowers will make the schoolyard pretty.
4. We also will grow vegetables in the garden.
5. We will give some vegetables to feed hungry people.
6. Suni will plant beans.
7. I will pick peas, and Grant will dig carrots.
8. We all will weed the garden regularly.

Page 40
1. went
2. come
3. see, do
4. ran
5. ate, came
6. go
7. came
8. ate, did
9. eat
10. came

Page 41
1. The writer does not want an office building built in the park.
2. ruin the park
3. The park is a place for animals to live. It is a place for people to do many things.
4. come to the City Council meeting, and try to save the park

Page 42
Responses will vary.

Page 43
Responses will vary.

Page 44
I believe Jan Parker should be elected student council president. She listens to everybody and has good leadership qualities. Who could do a better job?

Delete sentences 4 and 8. Other responses will vary.

Page 45
Responses will vary.

Page 46
The class is studying animals. We saw a movie about snakes today. I don't know why people are frightened of snakes. They are fascinating animals. You could not race the fastest snakes and win, since they can move up to twelve miles per hour. We saw a big python in the movie that was as big around as a person's leg. Tania said it was really gross. But then we saw a close-up of the snake's scales. Tania said the colors and patterns were pretty. Now she thinks snakes are neat. It seems to me that snakes probably think we are the scary ones.

Sentences will vary but should include pronouns.

Page 47
1. he
2. it
3. they
4. She
5. it
6. they
7. she
8. he
9. They

Page 48
1. them
2. it
3. him
4. me
5. you
6. her
7. it

Page 49
1. I
2. me
3. me
4. I
5. me
6. me
7. I
8. I
9. me
10. I

Page 50
1. my
2. his
3. their
4. theirs
5. my, her
6. our
7. ours
8. his
9. mine
10. hers

Page 51
1. "Go to warp speed!" shouted the captain.
2. "I can't," answered the first officer. "Our warp engines are down."
3. "Does anybody have any ideas?" asked the captain.
4. The engineer replied, "We could reverse the engines to push the ship backward."
5. "Try it!" ordered the captain. "We have to try everything!"
6. "It's working!" yelled the first officer.
7. "We're going backward, but the asteroid is still too close," she added.
8. Suddenly the engineer cried, "The warp engines are back up. Let's get out of here!"
9. "Please steer clear of asteroids for a while," sighed the captain. "That's an order!"
10. "Is anybody hungry?" asked the cook. "It's time for lunch."

Page 52

1. Did you read the editorial "Why Vote?" in today's paper?
2. Yes, and I liked the letter to the editor entitled "The Responsibilities of a Citizen."
3. I think "Candle in the Wind" is a very sad song.
4. But the article "The Death of a Princess" was much sadder.
5. I've always loved "Rocky Mountain High" by John Denver.
6. I prefer "Take Me Home, Country Roads" myself.
7. The poem "Steam Shovel" compares the machine to a dinosaur.
8. Yes, and the poem "Garden Hose" compares the hose to a snake.
9. There's a piece in the paper today called "Save the Park."
10. That's because last week someone wrote "Build the Mall."
11. Is "The Telltale Heart" one of Edgar Allen Poe's short stories?
12. Yes, but Jack London wrote "To Build a Fire."

Notes will vary but should use quotation marks for song and story titles.

Page 53

1. terrible
2. biggest
3. huge, excellent
4. thundering, large
5. smaller
6. adult
7. Young, muddy
8. sharp, keen
9. huge, leafy
10. meat, plant, warmer
11. gray, green
12. cooler
13. plunging
14. Some, yesterday's, today's
15. New, amazing

Sentence will vary but should include an adjective.

Page 54

1. tall, white
2. long, black
3. several, red
4. few, magic
5. famous, two, locked
6. many, heavy
7. two, huge, water
8. one
9. grand

Adjectives will vary but should describe how many and what kind.

Page 55

1. a
2. an, the
3. the, a
4. an
5. a, an
6. a
7. the
8. an, the

Page 56

1. most
2. oldest
3. highest
4. tallest, higher
5. better
6. largest
7. rare, rarer
8. strangest

Page 57

1. Jerry, Ashley, Andy
2. a mountainside in a snowstorm
3. The characters have been hiking and suddenly a storm has come up. They cannot see where they are going, and they don't know where a safe place is.

Page 58

Responses will vary.

Page 59

Responses will vary.

Page 60

"Throw it over here!" yelled Marcia.

"No, throw it here!" shouted tony. the two children

were playing football with their father. Suddenly

mr. Vento tripped and fell. "Ouch," he hollered. "I

think I broke my leg!"

Other responses will vary.

Page 61

Responses will vary.

Answer Key

Page 62

1. noisily (how)
2. cautiously (how)
3. sometimes (when)
4. over (where)
5. suddenly (how or when)
6. close (where)
7. playfully (how)
8. near (where)
9. loudly (how)
10. madly (how)

Sentences will vary but should include adverbs that tell how, when, and where.

Page 63

1. immediately
2. quickly
3. completely
4. promptly
5. quietly
6. extremely
7. easily
8. painfully
9. icily
10. coolly
11. impatiently
12. slowly
13. unhappily
14. safely

Page 64

1. adjective
2. adverb
3. adjective
4. adjective
5. adverb
6. adjective
7. adjective
8. adjective
9. adverb
10. adverb
11. adjective
12. adjective

Page 65

1. inside
2. down
3. everywhere
4. behind
5. ahead
6. away
7. outside
8. close
9. there, up
10. inside

Sentences will vary but should include adverbs.

Page 66

1. soon
2. later
3. now
4. yesterday
5. already
6. before

Page 67

1. high, higher, highest
2. faster, fast, fastest
3. harder, hardest, hard
4. tall, taller, tallest
5. soon, soonest, sooner

Page 68

1. Nothing
2. not
3. none
4. nobody
5. No one
6. never
7. nowhere
8. None
9. no
10. not

Page 69

1. The ideas for (many common) inventions may have come from animals.
2. The turtle has (solid, armor) plates for protection. Humans use tanks that move slowly and carry soldiers safely.
3. The rattlesnake shakes its (loud) rattle if an enemy walks nearby. People can protect their homes with (noisy) alarms to warn of burglars.
4. Birds carefully avoid the (bright red) ladybug, which contains poison. (Red) signals warn traffic to stop regularly.
5. Insects and birds fly easily by rapidly beating their wings. Air moves over a wing on an airplane and causes the wing to move upward.
6. Beavers have (large, sharp) teeth for cutting down trees. People use chisels to shape wood carefully.
7. Bats make (high) sounds that bounce against (small) insects. These echoes help bats locate food instantly. People use sonar, a (sound) system for locating objects underwater.
8. Ducks have (soft, downy) feathers which trap layers of (warm) air. Their young can sleep comfortably. People make (special) material in the same way for campers to wear outside.

Answer Key

Page 70
1. Doesn't
2. don't
3. shouldn't
4. isn't
5. can't
6. couldn't
7. won't
8. Don't
9. Aren't
10. couldn't
11. doesn't
12. haven't

Page 71
1. Should we go skating, or should we play catch?
2. Ben is going to the gym, and I want to go with him.
3. We could use the treadmill, or we could use the weights.
4. I could be as strong as Ben, but I don't work out regularly.
5. Tammi likes to play hockey best, but sometimes she plays soccer.
6. Tammi likes to play goalie, and Andy likes to be a forward.
7. Let's go outside and practice, or we could watch sports on TV.
8. I love to play sports, and I like to watch them, too.

Page 72
1. noun and verb
2. one
3. beam
4. Sentences will vary but should include scheme used as a verb.

Page 73
1. snake
2. snapshot
3. snarl
4. sneak
5. sneeze
6. sniff
7. snore
8. snorkel

Page 74
1. alligator
2. asteroid
3. blizzard
4. guitar
5. magnet
6. propeller
7. Saturn
8. snake

Page 75

Across
2. stray
5. mistake
6. decay
7. plain
8. trail
10. whale

Down
1. snake
2. spray
3. brain
4. locate
7. place
9. paint

Page 76
1. money
2. female
3. east
4. speed
5. Neon
6. valley
7. agree
8. grease
9. Turkey
10. freeze
11. degree
12. season

```
G M O N E Y V F Q C
W G G F R E E Z E V
D E G R E E H E A A
A S P E E D L A B L
G R H I A A L R N L
R V O E M S S J E E
E N G E L S T E O Y
E W F S E A S O N E
T U R K E Y E S K M
```

Page 77

Across
2. lilac
4. silent
5. Divide
8. shy
9. invite
12. icy
13. child

Down
1. pilot
3. kindly
6. deny
7. beside
8. sign
10. rhyme
11. mild

Answer Key

Page 78
Across
1. goal
2. ocean
6. slope
7. tomato
10. robot
11. obey

Down
1. globe
3. ago
4. coast
5. lonely
8. vote
9. float

Page 79
1. pupil
2. value
3. perfume
4. amuse
5. useful
6. fuel
7. future
8. human
9. usual
10. regular
11. refuse
12. units

```
V R P U P I L R S
A U E P U N I T S
L S R E G U L A R
U E F U E L H M E
E F U S U A L U F
H U M A N C B S U
D L E Y S M N E S
R S C F U T U R E
```

Page 80
1. ounces
2. scissors
3. dance
4. center
5. lesson
6. scene
7. scent
8. pencil
9. address
10. press

```
K R C E N T E R S
T P A P R E S S O
F E R D A N C E U
Z N L P D B L V N
S C E N T R R M C
G I R M S C E N E
D L E S S O N S S
R S C I S S O R S
```

Page 81
Across
3. subject
5. germs
6. budge
7. gentle
8. jelly
9. giant

Down
1. ledge
2. fudge
4. engine
8. jest

Page 82
Across
1. Foxes
3. friends
5. hunches
7. wishes
8. taxes
9. dishes

Down
1. flashes
2. passes
4. nickels
6. matches

Page 83
1. forest
2. laugh
3. trophy
4. finger
5. alphabet
6. enough
7. coffee
8. telephone
9. office
10. rough

Page 84
Across
2. chest
4. choose
5. author
7. wheat
8. thick

Down
1. leash
3. share
4. cloth
6. both
7. whim

Page 85
1. verb
2. curve
3. dirty
4. surprise
5. burned
6. further
7. thirsty
8. every
9. serve
10. shirt

```
K R B U R N E D S
T F V E R B E B U
H C U R V E V C R
I S E R V E E O P
R D I R T Y R M R
S T R L T H Y B I
T R O T E W E C S
Y R S H I R T R E
```

Page 86
1. sport
2. start
3. garden
4. orange
5. labor
6. smart
7. apart
8. morning
9. market
10. thorns

Page 87
1. fault
2. thaw
3. crawl
4. autumn
5. pause
6. gauze
7. lawn
8. awful
9. taught
10. dawn

Page 88
Across
1. loyal
3. enjoy
4. point
5. voyage
7. choice
8. oyster

Down
2. annoy
3. employ
5. voice
6. noise

Page 89
1. about
2. crowd
3. flowers
4. shout
5. cloud
6. fowl
7. proud
8. power
9. aloud
10. frown

Page 90
1. wrote
2. Knock
3. gnaw
4. comb
5. knife
6. knot
7. gnat
8. wreck
9. kneel
10. tomb

```
K R W R E C K R
K N O C K H P B
G K I G N A T C
N N J F Q L S O
A O K N E E L M
W T R L T O M B
W R O T E W F C
```

Page 91
Across
2. relief
4. niece
7. weigh
9. deceive
10. believe

Down
1. sleigh
3. receive
5. eight
6. field
8. ceiling

Page 92
1. carried
2. tried
3. denied
4. married
5. buried
6. copied
7. driving
8. rising
9. exciting
10. writing
11. voting
12. smiling

Page 93
Across
1. broke
2. roast
3. growth
5. pillow
6. cocoa
7. most

Down
1. borrow
3. global
4. hollow
5. protect

Page 94
1. happiest
2. softer
3. prettiest
4. shorter
5. busiest
6. sweetest
7. fastest
8. cleaner
9. noisier
10. rougher

Answer Key

Page 95
Across
3. renew
4. incorrect
6. untied
8. disagree

Down
1. indirect
2. unjust
3. rewrite
5. rebuild
6. unhappy
7. dislike

Page 96
1. softly
2. homeless
3. beautiful
4. loudly
5. neatly
6. endless
7. priceless
8. safely
9. thankful
10. helpful

B A P R I C E L E S S L W
Y E S R N J H L G F E O H
T S A R E G L C N V N U O
X O F U A V R W R F D D M
C F E Z T W G X B D L L E
S T L C L I H R T S E Y L
D L Y T Y Y F K Q Y S Q E
C Y P J K M G U K C S X S
S T H E L P F U L F H R S
D C T H A N K F U L T K T

Page 97
1. short
2. lose
3. start
4. sour
5. laugh
6. easy
7. slow
8. dirty
9. light
10. big

L A U G H P Q S
O L B I G Y H L
S O U R N O L O
E H N C R E I W
C T P T K A G X
S T A R T S H R
D I R T Y Y T K

Page 98
Across
4. noisy
5. roast
7. select
8. welcome
9. weak

Down
1. jolly
2. quiet
3. harm
6. solid
7. speak

Page 99
1. peace
2. piece
3. their
4. there
5. Write
6. right
7. week
8. weak
9. hear
10. here

S R G F H E A R H
P I T T W H T B W
E G T H E H R Q R
A H N C E L S P I
C T P I K R X M T
E H R K J H E R E
P I E C E W E A K

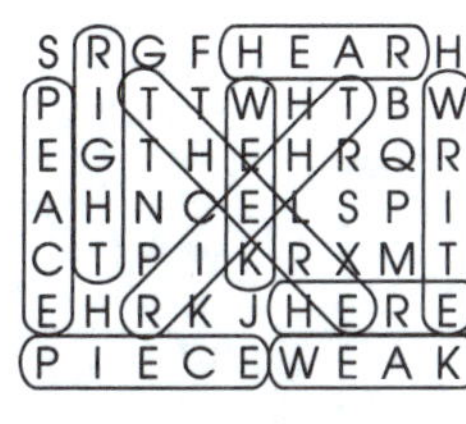

Page 100
Across
1. lives
3. Calves
4. elves
5. shelves
7. knives

Down
1. Leaves
2. wives
6. halves

Page 101
1. slamming
2. trotted
3. slipped
4. melted
5. carrying
6. walked
7. pointed
8. reaching
9. dripping
10. stepped

S A M E L T E D C H B
C R S T E P P E D D G
R E L L H W C Q E R P
W A I C A O R T F I O
A C P L K M T M H P I
L H P K J O M L R P N
K I E N R C T I C I T
E N D T V R G K N N E
D G C A R R Y I N G D

Page 102
Across
1. swung
3. froze
4. wrote
6. left
8. tore

Down
2. grew
3. fought
5. drove
7. felt

Page 103
1. busy
2. flatter
3. easy
4. happy
5. make every effort
6. be quiet
7. lead person
8. get angry
9. tell a secret
10. asleep

Page 104
Fairy Tales
Jack and the Beanstalk
Cinderella

Biographies
The Truth About John Henry
Martin Luther King, Jr.

Mysteries
The Mona Lisa Is Missing!
Death at the Opera

Poetry
Mother Goose Rhymes
Verses for Spring

Science Fiction
Trouble on Planet Zot
The Monster from Space

Nonfiction
Discoveries About Dinosaurs
Grow Your Own Salad

Page 105
Nouns
mother
barn
poodle

Adjectives
red
exciting
fluffy
huge

Adverbs
quickly
silently

Prepositions
under
into

Verbs
think
make

Pronouns
she
they

Page 106
1. b a t c h
2. h a b i t
3. s c h o o l

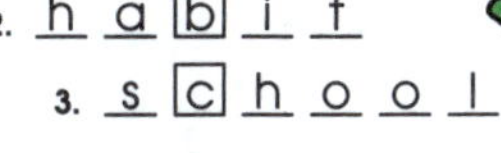

4. c a b i n
5. t o o t h
6. b a s e b a l l
7. d r u m
8. s p r i n g
9. c r i b
10. d o o r b e l l
11. a n o t h e r

Page 107
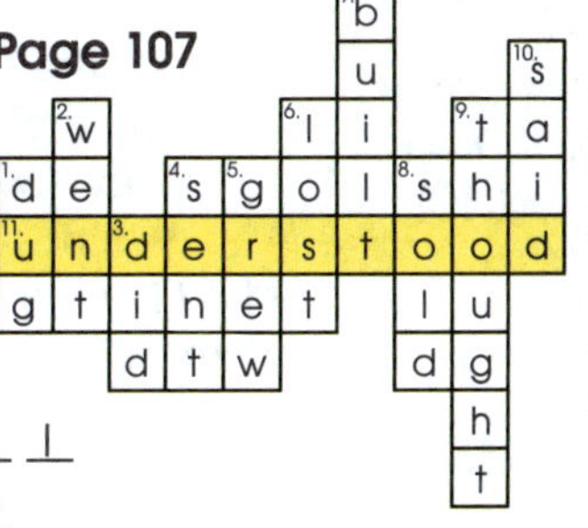

Page 108
The most common words include the following:

motherless; motherly
dishonest; honestly
fearless; fearful
disquiet; quietness; quietly
beautifully
slowness; slowly
disable; unable
repaint
uncomfortable; comfortableness
rethought; thoughtless; thoughtful
yearly
goodness
careless; careful
unkind; kindness; kindly
joyless; joyful
quickly
disagree
rewrite
discontinue
unhappy

Answer Key

Page 109

Page 110

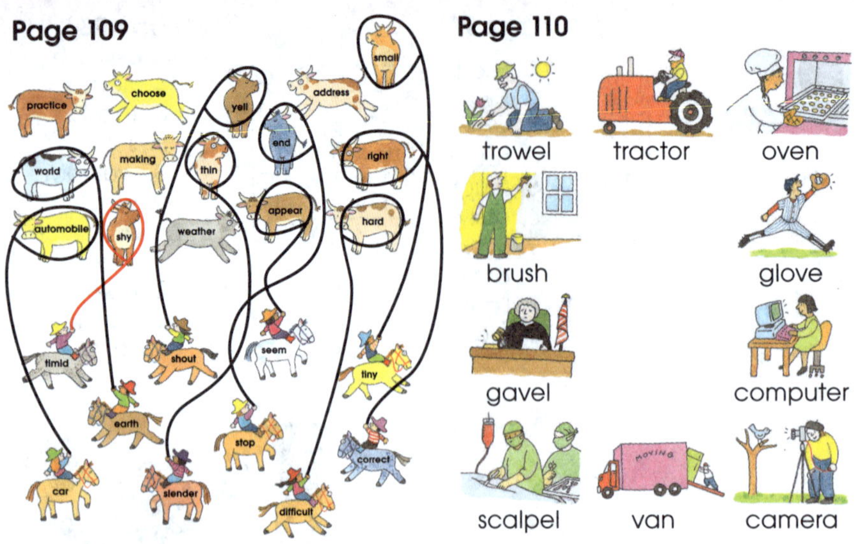

Page 111

skateboard
sandbox
popcorn
sunglasses
playground
baseball

Page 113

1. beet
2. pale
3. chilly
4. hoarse
5. cellar
6. pale pail
7. beat beet
8. chilly chili
9. hoarse horse
10. cellar seller

Page 112

Person	Place	Thing
scientist	laboratory	monster
brother	closet	discovery
	museum	newspaper
		photograph

Page 114–115

Check paragraph. Fashion firsts should be circled, and dates underlined.

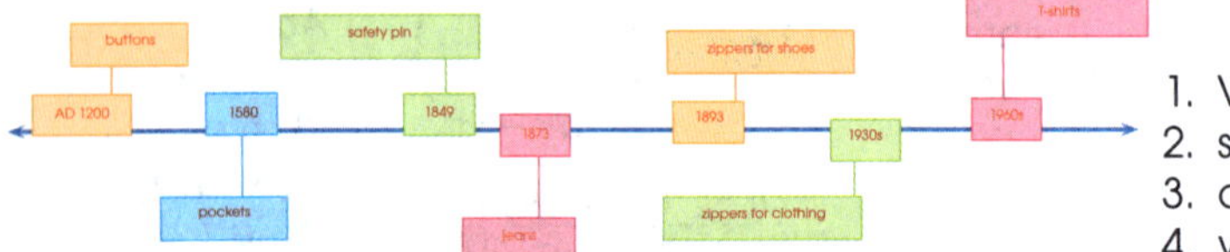

1. Velcro
2. spinning wheel
3. crayon
4. wool

Page 116

1. Theodore Roosevelt was President from 1901 to 1909, and ~~President Roosevelt~~ he lived at 1600 Pennsylvania Avenue.
2. When President Roosevelt lived in the White House, ~~the White House~~ it was home for six fun-loving children.
3. The children had lots of room to play, and ~~the children~~ they thought of new things to do each day.
4. Visitors knew about the mischief in the White House, and ~~the visitors~~ they were always curious to see what would happen.
5. When no one was watching, the children slid down the stairs on trays, and ~~the children~~ they roller-skated in the halls.
6. The President liked pets, so ~~the President~~ he let the children have dogs, cats, birds, rabbits, rats, guinea pigs, raccoons, a snake, and a pony.
7. One day, the children put the pony in the elevator so ~~the children~~ they could ride ~~the pony~~ it upstairs.
8. Since the children often played together, ~~the children~~ they were called "The White House Gang."

Page 117

Lines may vary.

Pages 118–119

Dishes: 28 feet
Drinks: 28 feet
Salads: 34 feet
Main Dishes: 52 feet
Vegetables: 44 feet
Fruits: 24 feet
Breads: 30 feet
Desserts: 40 feet

1. main dishes
2. fruits
3. dishes and drinks
4. salads by 4 feet
5. vegetables by 4 feet
6. Yes. The table for dishes has the same perimeter as drinks, but they have different lengths and widths.

Mind Bender: There were 14 women, 10 men, 7 boys, and 5 girls.

Answer Key

Page 120
1. ask-invite
2. practice-rehearse
3. booming-loud
4. perfect-ideal
5. greet-welcome
6. important-eventful
7. ability-talent
8. bright-colorful
9. unique-special
10. wild-ferocious

Page 121
1. Hundreds of ducks flew over the pond.
2. Melanie's cat chased the ball of yarn.
3. The wooden bucket holds a gallon of water.
4. Fred's car had a flat tire.
5. Hot dogs are Myron's favorite food.
6. My book is about pirates.

Other answers will vary.

Pages 123
Answers will vary. Check your child's sentences.

Page 124
1. $\frac{4}{9}$
2. $\frac{3}{8}$
3. $\frac{5}{6}$
4. $\frac{7}{12}$
5. $\frac{2}{11}$
6. $\frac{5}{14}$
7. $\frac{4}{7}$

Page 125
1. 8 x 3 = 264
2. 61 x 5 = 305
3. 53 x 9 = 477
4. 82 x 4 = 328
5. 95 x 8 = 760
6. 49 x 8 = 392

Page 126
1. 2 x 6 = 12; 6 + 12 = 18 games
2. 23 + 16 = 39; 39 x 2 = 78 cans
3. 6 + 7 = 13; 15 − 13 = 2 daisies
4. 6 + 3 = 9; 9 x 2 = 18 marbles
5. 9 + 7 = 16; 36 − 16 = 20 cookies
6. 42 − 7 = 35; 35 + 4 = 39 cards

Page 127
Story plans will vary.

Page 128
1. flip
2. slide
3. turn
4. flip
5. flip
6. slide
7. turn
8. flip

Page 129
1. sentence
2. not a sentence
3. sentence
4. sentence
5. not a sentence
6. not a sentence
7. not a sentence
8. sentence
9. sentence
10. not a sentence

Pages 130–131

Dad's sunglasses float because their density is less than the density of water.

Page 132
1. 40 + 8
2. 100 + 20 + 0
3. 100 + 20 + 5
4. 200 + 30 + 6
5. 70 + 9
6. 200 + 60 + 1
7. 400 + 30 + 5
8. 300 + 70 + 2
9. 300 + 0 + 3
10. 100 + 90 + 7

Page 133
Answers will vary. Places should be named and described. Three reasons for protecting the places should be listed.

Page 134
O = 37 U = 41 T = 104 S = 114 R = 36
E = 79 N = 89 H = 17 M = 66

MOUNT RUSHMORE

Page 135
Verbs: shines, grow, attack, gobble
Nouns: park, sun, trees, ladybugs
Adjectives: big, tall, harmful
Adverbs: brightly, quickly

Page 136
1. 9
2. 17
3. 2
4. 86
5. 158
6. 119
7. 54
8. 8
9. 3

Page 137
1. fiber
2. fiber
3. protein
4. starch
5. protein
6. fat

Pages 138–139

Stop. c
What a huge fountain! e
Who wants pizza? q
The dolphins and beluga whales leaped into the air. s
How high is the Ferris wheel? q
I thought the view would be better. s
This horse has a silky nose. s
The breeze from Lake Michigan is refreshing. s
Look both ways before you cross Lake Shore Drive. c
Have the Cubs ever won a World Series? q

Page 140

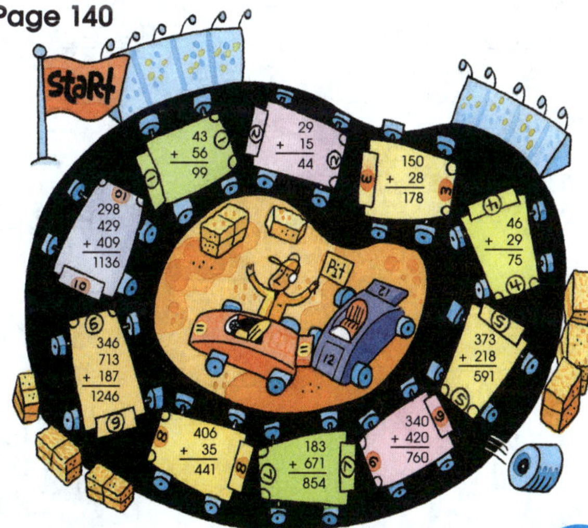

Answer Key

Page 141

The ~~S~~tars of football shine at the Pro Football Hall of Fame in canton, ohio. the Hall of Fame opened on september 7, 1963. Every year, the league names a few of its ~~B~~est players to the Hall of Fame. there, visitors can ~~S~~ee pictures of these players, their ~~U~~niforms, and their equipment.

Page 142

1. 2
2. Grand Island
3. about 4-5 miles
4. city
5. 2
6. Lake Erie, Lake Ontario

Page 143

1. opened
2. use
3. closes
4. continue
5. constructed
6. will read

Page 144

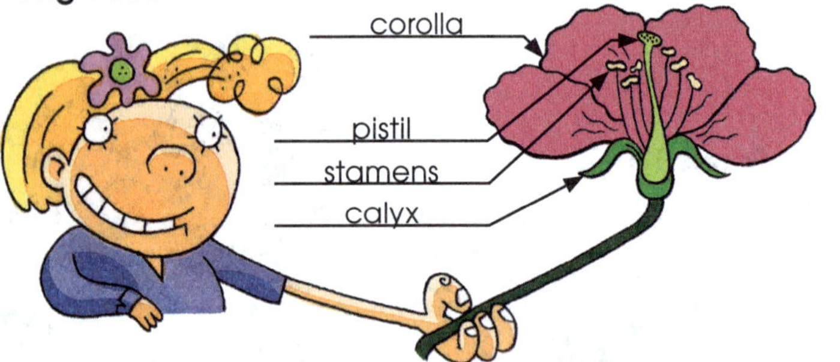

So that new plants can grow from seeds.

Page 145

6
1
3
2
5
4
7

Page 146

2 Chrysler Building, 1,046 feet
3 Citigroup Center, 915 feet
1 Empire State Building, 1,250 feet
4 GE Building, 850 feet

400 feet taller

Page 147

1. Brooklyn, Williamsburg
2. Verrazano-Narrows
3. Queensboro
4. George Washington

Page 148

1. Philadelphia is nicknamed "Philly" and "The City of Brotherly Love."
2. Independence Hall, where the Declaration of Independence was adopted, is located in Philadelphia, Penn., and is open for tours.
3. America's first pretzel bakery opened in Lititz, Penn., in 1861.
4. Mr. LaRose ate six pretzels on their visit to Philadelphia.
5. They bought a box of pretzels for their friend, Dr. Banks.
6. The LaRose family is leaving Philadelphia, Penn., tomorrow at 9:00 a.m.

Page 149

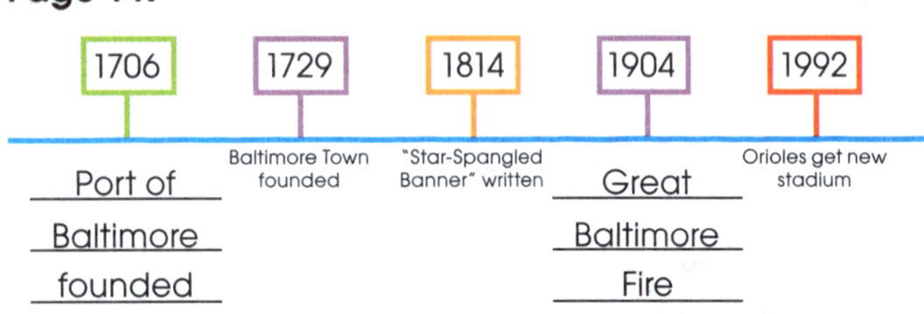

Pages 150–151

1. antonyms
2. homophones
3. synonyms
4. antonyms
5. homophones
6. homophones
7. synonyms
8. synonyms
9. antonyms
10. antonyms

Page 152

1. 34
2. 52
3. 205
4. 538
5. 305
6. 797
7. 298
8. 326

Page 153

Page 154

1. Branson
2. Joplin
3. St. Louis
4. New Madrid
5. (5,E) (4,F) (6,H) (1,H)

Answer Key

Page 155
Paragraphs will vary, but should include three facts from the page.

Pages 156–157
83 + 130 + 32 + 146 + 38 = 429 miles
88 + 131 + 99 + 30 + 119 = 467 miles
88 + 131 + 92 + 32 + 146 + 38 = 527 miles

Answers will vary. One possibility is:
Memphis → Selmer → Fayetteville → Murfreesboro → Lebanon → Knoxville → Gatlinburg:
88 + 131 + 54 + 32 + 146 + 38 = 489 miles

Answers will vary. One possibility is:
Memphis → Corinth → Decatur → Huntsville → Chattanooga → Cleveland → Cherokee:
95 + 96 + 24 + 104 + 30 + 119 = 468 miles

Page 158
looked, thought, drank

found, swung, brought

rowed, bit, came

pecked, ran, won

Peter

Page 159

Page 160
Big Pine Key = 35
Grassy Key = 54
Indian Key = 64
Key Largo = 81
Key West = 0
Long Key = 56
Seven Mile Bridge = 42
Stock Island = 12
Summerland Key = 16
Windley Key = 72

Page 161
1. probe
2. satellite
3. station
4. shuttle
5. orbit
6. rover

universe

Pages 162–163
1. pelican, panther, deer
2. turtle, manatee, alligator, anhinga

Pages 164–165

Page 166
1. civil rights
2. She refused to give up her seat on the bus.
3. boycott
4. Answers will vary.

Page 168
1. 3
2. 7
3. 6
4. 8
5. 9
6. 9
7. 9
8. 9
9. 7
10. 8
11. 9
12. 8

Page 167
1. Mardi Gras is an ancient festival, but people still enjoy it.
2. New Orleans, Louisiana, has a big Mardi Gras celebration.
3. People celebrate with food, music, parties, and parades.
4. Musicians play, and colorful floats roll down the street.
5. Riders on the floats throw coins, necklaces, and toys.
6. The LaRose family met some people from Berlin, Germany, at Mardi Gras.
7. The people from Berlin spoke English, so the two families enjoyed the parade together.
8. Then they went to a restaurant where they ate crayfish, gumbo, and jambalaya.

Page 169

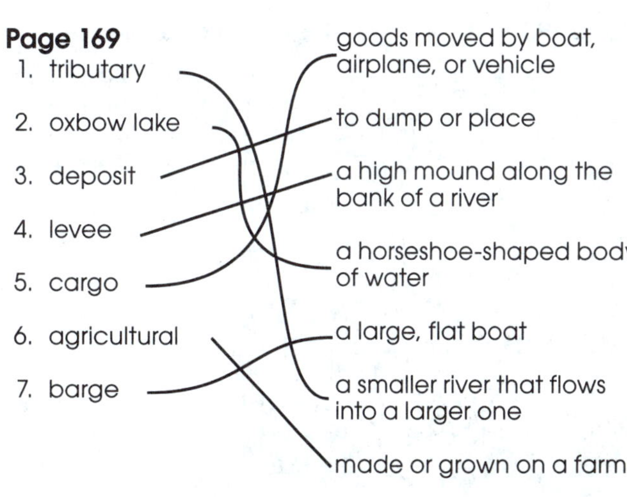

1. tributary
2. oxbow lake
3. deposit
4. levee
5. cargo
6. agricultural
7. barge

goods moved by boat, airplane, or vehicle
to dump or place
a high mound along the bank of a river
a horseshoe-shaped body of water
a large, flat boat
a smaller river that flows into a larger one
made or grown on a farm

Answer Key

Page 170

duck/goose — duckling/gosling
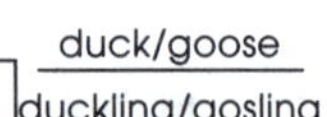

m frog — tadpole

deer — fawn
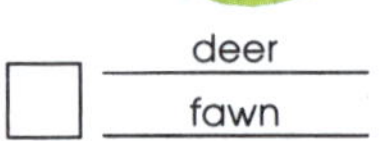

bear — cub

m butterfly — caterpillar

Page 171

1. 10:25 2. 7:40 3. 1:00
4. 6:30 5. 9:25 6. 3:05
7. 10:30 8. 10:55 9. 2:55

Page 172

Answers will vary. Possible sentences include:

1. Dad's van had a flat tire.
2. Peter's canteen is leaking.
3. The kites' tails are long and colorful.
4. Mom saw a lizard's footprints.

Page 173

1. trapezoid - 1 line
2. rectangle - 2 lines
3. circle - many lines
4. pentagon - 5 lines
5. triangle - 3 lines
6. parallelogram - no lines
7. square - 4 lines
8. octagon - 8 lines
9. 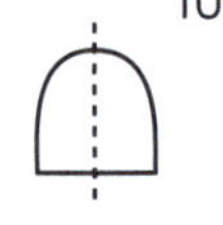
10. 

Page 174

1. their
2. His
3. their
4. it
5. His
6. She
7. Her
8. Her

Page 175

1. flip
2. slide
3. turn
4. flip
5. turn
6. flip
7. slide
8. flip

Page 176

Page 177

1. wind scorpion
2. black cactus longhorn beetle
3. trapdoor spider
4. wind scorpion
5. thistledown velvet ant
6. black cactus longhorn beetle

Page 178

1. It's
2. It's
3. It's
4. its
5. it's
6. its
7. its
8. It's

Page 179

1. 78°F 2. 20°F 3. 92°F 4. 53°F
5. 101°F 6. 18°F 7. 59°F 8. 80°F

Page 180

1. f+o 2. f 3. f 4. o
5. f 6. f+o 7. f
8. f 9. f 10. o

Page 181

Lumber: instrument, telephone pole
Pulp: bag, tissue, book
Chemicals: ink, shirt, paint, cement block

Page 182

Paragraphs will vary, but should include a topic sentence, supporting details, and a conclusion.

Page 183

Page 184

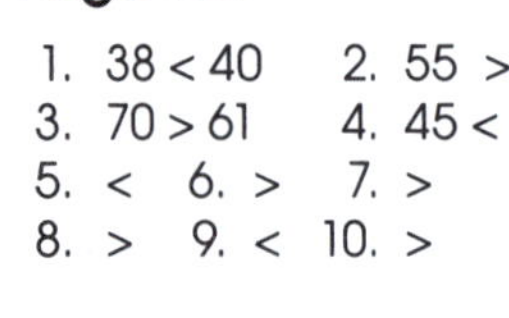

1. 38 < 40 2. 55 > 43
3. 70 > 61 4. 45 < 54
5. < 6. > 7. >
8. > 9. < 10. >

Page 185

1. 41, 42, <u>43</u>, 44, <u>45</u>, <u>46</u>, 47, <u>48</u>, <u>49</u>, 50
2. 87, <u>88</u>, 89, <u>90</u>, 91, <u>92</u>, <u>93</u>, 94, <u>95</u>, 96
3. 66, <u>67</u>, <u>68</u>, 69, <u>70</u>, <u>71</u>, 72, <u>73</u>, 74, <u>75</u>
4. <u>73</u>, 74, <u>75</u>, <u>76</u>, 77, <u>78</u>, 79, <u>80</u>, 81, <u>82</u>
5. <u>36</u>, <u>37</u>, 38, <u>39</u>, <u>40</u>, 41, <u>42</u>, <u>43</u>, 44, <u>45</u>
6. 19; 21; 36; 47
7. 33; 56; 65; 76
8. 17; 32; 46; 59
9. 19; 26; 39; 89
10. 37; 63; 67; 73

Page 186

1. 7, 2, 5, 7 2. 6, 9, 6, 3
3. 9, 5, 4, 9 4. 0, 6, 6, 0
5. 13, 7, 6, 13 6. 5, 13, 8, 8
7. 16, 9, 7, 16 8. 8, 12, 8, 4

Answer Key

Page 187

1. 6 + 8 = 14
   8 + 6 = 14
   14 − 6 = 8
   14 − 8 = 6
2. 4 + 9 = 13
   9 + 4 = 13
   13 − 4 = 9
   13 − 9 = 4
3. 7 + 8 = 15
   8 + 7 = 15
   15 − 7 = 8
   15 − 8 = 7
4. 5 + 7 = 12
   7 + 5 = 12
   12 − 5 = 7
   12 − 7 = 5
5. 5 + 9 = 14
   9 + 5 = 14
   14 − 5 = 9
   14 − 9 = 5
6. 8 + 9 = 17
   9 + 8 = 17
   17 − 8 = 9
   17 − 9 = 8
7. 6 + 9 = 15
   9 + 6 = 15
   15 − 6 = 9
   15 − 9 = 6
8. 9 + 0 = 9
   0 + 9 = 9
   9 − 9 = 0
   9 − 0 = 9
9. 7 + 7 = 14
   14 − 7 = 7

Page 188

1. 30 2. 90
3. 20 4. 60
5. 60 6. 30
7. 40 8. 80
9. 30 10. 40
11. 60 12. 30
13. 60 14. 90
15. 20 16. 50
17. 30 18. 40
19. 40 20. 70
21. 20 22. 10
23. 90 24. 80

Page 189

1. $\begin{array}{r}20\\+20\\\hline 40\end{array}$ 2. $\begin{array}{r}70\\-20\\\hline 50\end{array}$

3. $\begin{array}{r}80\\-50\\\hline 30\end{array}$ 4. $\begin{array}{r}50\\+30\\\hline 80\end{array}$

5. 90 6. 50
7. 10 8. 70
9. 90 10. 70

Page 190

1. 9	2		2. 7	5		3. 6	4. 5
6			4			5. 3	3
	6. 7	7. 6		8. 9	2		
	9. 4	3		0		10. 9	1
11. 8			12. 9		13. 6		
14. 3	3		5		15. 5	1	

Page 191

1. 59 2. 55 3. 24 4. 89 5. 25
6. 58 7. 44 8. 59 9. 99 10. 82
11. 54 12. 104 13. 188 14. 108 15. 117
16. 99 17. 76

Page 192

1. 43 2. 15 3. 39 4. 61
5. 1 6. 45 7. 8 8. 42
9. 49 10. 38 11. 49 12. 9
13. 55 14. 36 15. 27 16. 65

Page 193

90, 65, 51, 46, 60
45, 9, 50, 76, 75
95, 98, 56, 99, 90
46, 45, 76, 90
AFRICAN BUSH ELEPHANT

Page 194

1. 3 hundreds, 7 tens, 8 ones
   300 + 70 + 8
   378
2. 1 hundred, 9 tens, 6 ones
   100 + 90 + 6
   196
3. 5 hundreds, 7 tens, 0 ones
   500 + 70 + 0
   570
4. 3 hundreds, 0 tens, 9 ones
   300 + 0 + 9
   309

Page 195

1. 7 hundreds + 4 tens + 9 ones
2. 5 hundreds + 1 ten + 4 ones
3. 9 hundreds + 3 tens + 0 ones
4. 3 hundreds + 9 tens + 8 ones
5. 6 hundreds + 0 tens + 7 ones
6. 500 + 60 + 2
7. 900 + 50 + 3
8. 300 + 70 + 0
9. 600 + 10 + 7
10. 100 + 0 + 9

Page 196

1. 314 < 413
2. 324 > 224
3. 231 < 249
4. 264 > 240
5. < 6. > 7. >
8. > 9. < 10. <

Page 197

1. 111, 112, 113, 114, 115, 116, 117, 118, 119, 120
2. 307, 308, 309, 310, 311, 312, 313, 314, 315, 316
3. 555, 556, 557, 558, 559, 560, 561, 562, 563, 564
4. 710, 720, 730, 740, 750, 760, 770, 780, 790, 800
5. 872, 874, 876, 878, 880, 882, 884, 886, 888, 890
6. 319; 351; 721; 976
7. 572; 711; 807; 999
8. 237; 700; 702; 724
9. 418; 788; 808; 896
10. 381; 789; 813; 987

Page 198

1. 500 2. 700 3. 600
4. 300 5. 800 6. 200
7. 500 8. 400 9. 800
10. 300 11. 600 12. 200
13. 300 14. 600 15. 600
16. 400 17. 500 18. 400
19. 140 20. 250
21. 670 22. 470
23. 490 24. 560

Page 199

1. 700 + 200 = 900 2. 700 − 100 = 600
3. 500 − 100 = 400 4. 500 + 300 = 800
5. 600 6. 600
7. 200 8. 800
9. 900 10. 900

Page 200

1. 800 2. 750 3. 621 4. 400
5. 918 6. 900 7. 834 8. 910
9. 862 10. 600 11. 700 12. 820
13. 897 14. 850 15. 835 16. 800

Page 201

1. 659 2. 588 3. 492 4. 568 5. 870
6. 595 7. 244 8. 816 9. 374 10. 437
11. 399 12. 912 13. 837 14. 873 15. 986
16. 506 17. 935

Page 202

1. 112 2. 131 3. 210 4. 207
5. 148 6. 76 7. 542 8. 62
9. 105 10. 207 11. 745 12. 321
13. 45 14. 305 15. 550 16. 235

Page 203

785, 700, 518, 318, 888
685, 885, 418, 585, 618
800, 785, 700, 318, 685
885, 418, 618
SALTWATER CROCODILE

Page 204

1. 3 thousands, 1 hundred, 8 tens, 5 ones
   3,000 + 100 + 80 + 5
   3,185
2. 4 thousands, 2 hundreds, 0 tens, 7 ones
   4,000 + 200 + 0 + 7
   4,207

Answer Key

Page 205

1. ones
2. hundreds
3. thousands
4. thousands
5. tens
6. ones
7. 8, 1 9 (1)
8. (4), 2 7 5
9. 1, (2) 4 3
10. 9, 4 (7) 0
11. (5), 4 3 7
12. 9, (7) 5 1

Page 206

2	6	8			3	9	7
9		4	7	8	0		3
5		3	3	3	3		9
9	0	3	5		6	2	2
			4			5	
6	7	8		5	3	9	0
8	1	2	6		1	9	0
5		2	5	5	0		

Page 207

1. >, thousands
2. <, hundreds
3. >, ones
4. <, tens
5. <, tens
6. >, thousands
7. >, tens
8. 675; 6,075; 6,507; 6,705
9. 987; 4,279; 4,297; 7,942
10. 56; 506; 6,052; 6,502

Challenge: 9,631

Super Challenge:

1,369	3,169	6,139	9,136
1,396	3,196	6,193	9,163
1,639	3,619	6,319	9,316
1,693	3,691	6,391	9,361
1,936	3,916	6,913	9,613
1,963	3,961	6,931	9,631

Page 210

4	0	8		6	8	4
1		1	8		8	
2	0	4		6	5	6
		3	9	4		0
7	2		4	3	0	6
1	9	8		2		

Page 208

1. 5,863 2. 6,385 3. 5,813
4. 9,022 5. 9,004 6. 8,106
7. 6,683 8. 8,852 9. 7,932
10. 8,113 11. 7,621 12. 8,173

Page 209

1. 1,084 2. 3,074 3. 294
4. 1,103 5. 1,855 6. 2,301
7. 2,722 8. 4,073 9. 2,404
10. 3,116 11. 3,740 12. 2,207

Page 211

1. (add) 86 shells
2. (subtract) 18 shells
3. (add) 60 starfish
4. (subtract) 8 starfish

Page 212

1. 2 x 4 = 8 2. 2 x 5 = 10
3. 2 x 6 = 12 4. 3 x 6 = 18
5. 2 x 8 = 16 6. 2 x 7 = 14

Page 213

1. 2, 4, 6, 8, 10, 12, 14, 16, 18
2. 3, 6, 9, 12, 15, 18, 21, 24, 27
3. 1, 2, 3, 4, 5, 6, 7, 8, 9
4. 0, 0, 0, 0, 0, 0, 0, 0, 0

Page 214

1. 4, 8, 12, 16, 20, 24, 28, 32, 36
2. 5, 10, 15, 20, 25, 30, 35, 40, 45

3. 20 4. 0
5. 9 6. 20
7. 35 8. 21
9. 5 10. 32
11. 18 12. 45
13. 14 14. 10
15. 12 16. 16
17. 18 18. 28

Page 215

1. 6, 12, 18, 24, 30, 36, 42, 48, 54
2. 7, 14, 21, 28, 35, 42, 49, 56, 63

3. 3 4. 0 5. 2
6. 24 7. 27 8. 8
9. 9 10. 7 11. 6
12. 6 13. 1 14. 6

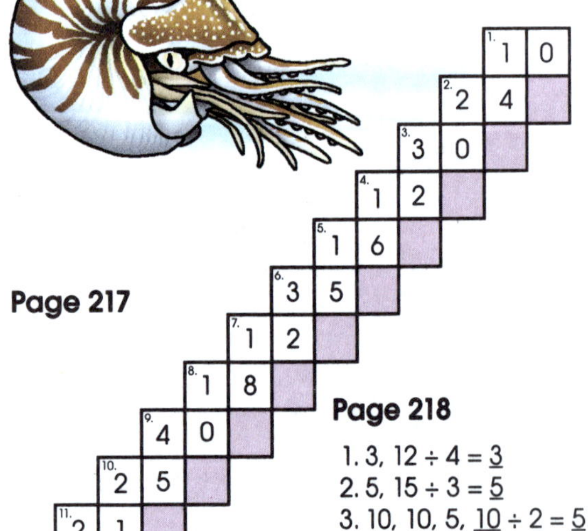

Page 217

1. 10
2. 24
3. 30
4. 12
5. 16
6. 35
7. 12
8. 18
9. 40
10. 25
11. 21
12. 24
8

Page 216

1. 8, 16, 24, 32, 40, 48, 56, 64, 72
2. 9, 18, 27, 36, 45, 54, 63, 72, 81

0 + 9 = 9
1 + 8 = 9
2 + 7 = 9
3 + 6 = 9
4 + 5 = 9
5 + 4 = 9
6 + 3 = 9
7 + 2 = 9
8 + 1 = 9

x	0	1	2	3	4	5	6	7	8	9
0	0	0	0	0	0	0	0	0	0	0
1	0	1	2	3	4	5	6	7	8	9
2	0	2	4	6	8	10	12	14	16	18
3	0	3	6	9	12	15	18	21	24	27
4	0	4	8	12	16	20	24	28	32	36
5	0	5	10	15	20	25	30	35	40	45
6	0	6	12	18	24	30	36	42	48	54
7	0	7	14	21	28	35	42	49	56	63
8	0	8	16	24	32	40	48	56	64	72
9	0	9	18	27	36	45	54	63	72	81

Page 218

1. 3, 12 ÷ 4 = 3
2. 5, 15 ÷ 3 = 5
3. 10, 10, 5, 10 ÷ 2 = 5
4. 12, 12, 3, 12 ÷ 4 = 3
5. 18, 6, 18 ÷ 3 = 6
6. 24, 4, 24 ÷ 6 = 4

Page 219

1. 4, 8 ÷ 2 = 4
2. 5, 10 ÷ 2 = 5
3. 7, 14 ÷ 2 = 7
4. 6, 12 ÷ 2 = 6
5. 1, 2, 3, 4, 5, 6, 7, 8, 9

Page 220

1. 4, 12 ÷ 3 = 4
2. 5, 15 ÷ 3 = 5
3. 6, 18 ÷ 3 = 6
4. 7, 21 ÷ 3 = 7
5. 1, 2, 3, 4, 5, 6, 7, 8, 9

Page 221

1. 1, 2, 3, 4, 5, 6, 7, 8, 9
2. 1, 2, 3, 4, 5, 6, 7, 8, 9

3. 2 4. 2
5. 5 6. 3
7. 5 8. 7
9. 4 10. 4
11. 5 12. 9
13. 2 14. 2
15. 4 16. 6
17. 7 18. 7

Answer Key

Page 222

1. 1 2 3 4 5 6 7 8 9
2. 1 2 3 4 5 6 7 8 9
3. 6 4. 7
5. 7 6. 9
7. 30 8. 42
9. 7 10. 7
11. 6 12. 6

Page 223

1. 1 2 3 4 5 6 7 8 9
2. 1 2 3 4 5 6 7 8 9
3. 40 4. 4 5. 63
6. 3 7. 7 8. 28
9. 42 10. 36 11. 8
12. 5 13. 56 14. 8
15. 49 16. 9 17. 8
18. 36 19. 1 20. 6

Page 224

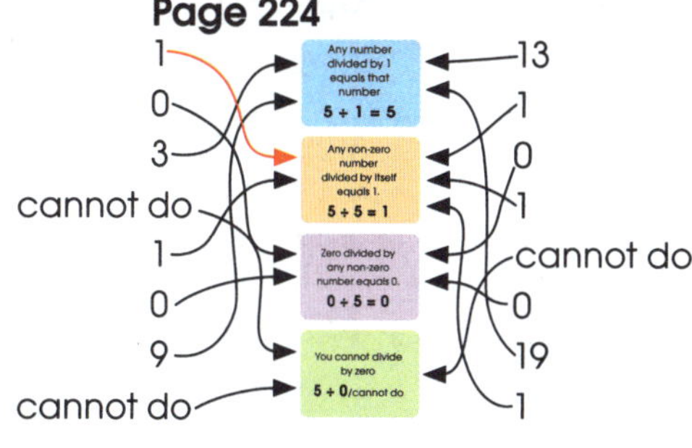

Page 225

1. $4\overline{)32}$ = 8 2. $2\overline{)18}$ = 9
3. $7\overline{)28}$ = 4 4. $6\overline{)48}$ = 8
5. 6 6. 5
7. 9 8. 6
9. 8 10. 1
11. 7 12. 8 13. 8
14. 7 15. 7 16. 3
17. 9 18. 7 19. 0

Page 226

1. 15, 5, 3, 15
2. 9, 2, 18, 9
3. 42, 7, 6, 6
4. 9, 3, 27, 9
5. 6, 30, 5, 5
6. 56, 8, 7, 56
7. 6 x 9 = 54
54 ÷ 6 = 9
54 ÷ 9 = 6
8. 9 x 8 = 72
72 ÷ 9 = 8
72 ÷ 8 = 9
9. 8 x 0 = 0
0 ÷ 8 = 0

Page 227

1. 16 2. 0 3. 45 4. 32 5. 30
6. 7 7. 9 8. 7 9. 9 10. 8
11. 35 12. 49 13. 54 14. 5 15. 63
16. 0 17. 9 18. 6 19. 8 20. cannot do
21. 28 ÷ 7 = 4 stickers

Page 228

1. 87 2. 72 3. 192 4. 52
5. 64 6. 165 7. 108 8. 36
9. 488 10. 364 11. 141 12. 819
13. 196 14. 272 15. 240 16. 98

Page 229

1. 954 2. 820 3. 2,448
4. 1,896 5. 256 6. 2,331
7. 700 8. 2,032 9. 858

8	2	8	5	8	7	9
5	2	7	1	2	1	3
2	1	0	8	8	5	2
0	3	0	2	4	9	5
3	2	4	4	8	5	6
2	2	3	3	1	4	7

Page 230

1. 3 R1 2. 3 R3 3. 2 R1 4. 9 R1 5. 3 R4
6. 4 R4 7. 3 R6 8. 8 R3 9. 5 R5 10. 5 R5
11. 4 R3 12. 6 R3 13. 8 R2 14. 7 R2 15. 8 R4
16. 7 R1 17. 7 R6 18. 3 R8 19. 9 R3 20. 7 R2

Page 231

1. 14 R2 2. 36 3. 11 R1 4. 15 5. 12 R2
6. 23 R2 7. 31 R2 8. 43 9. 15 R1 10. 11 R3
11. 62 R1 12. 68 R1 13. 39 14. 44 R2 15. 26

Page 232

1. 108 feet
2. 2,800 pounds
3. 680 pounds

Page 233

1. 3 birds
2. 5 loaves
3. 5 bananas
4. 7 lions

Page 234

1. (divide) 3 pounds
2. (multiply) 27 cards
3. (divide) 7 babies
4. (divide) 16 flowers

Page 235

1. 7 books
2. 18 books
3. 26 stickers
4. 16 stuffed animals

Page 236

1. 276; 277; <u>278</u>; 279; <u>280</u>; <u>281</u>; 282; <u>283</u>
2. 3,425; <u>3,426</u>; 3,427; <u>3,428</u>; 3,429; <u>3,430</u>; <u>3,431</u>; 3,432
3. < 4. < 5. >
6. < 7. > 8. <
9. 66; 67; 70; 76
10. 575; 579; 597; 759
11. 3,283; 3,287; 3,318; 3,481
12. 80 13. 70 14. 350
15. 500 16. 800 17. 500
18. 843
19. 2,508

Page 237

1. C 2. C
3. C 4. D
5. C 6. A
7. D 8. B

Page 238

1. 90 2. 30
3. 300 4. 600
5. 121 6. 36 7. 748 8. 326 9. 150
10. 521 11. 570 12. 691 13. 1,743 14. 3,825
15. 301 16. 543
17. 87 stamps
18. 83 stamps

Page 239

1. D 2. C
3. A 4. A
5. B 6. C
7. D 8. C

Page 240

1. 42 2. 0 3. 56
4. 7 5. 54 6. 35
7. 54 8. 104 9. 90
10. 5 11. 7 12. 8
13. 9 14. 0 15. cannot do
16. 9 R1 17. 10 R2 18. 13 R3
19. 88 cards
20. 9 stickers

Page 241

1. C 2. A
3. B 4. C
5. D 6. D
7. C 8. A

Page 242

1. 5 + 5 = 10
2 groups of 5 = 10
2 x 5 = 10
2. 3 + 3 + 3 + 3 = 12
4 groups of 3 = 12
4 x 3 = 12
3. 3 + 3 + 3 = 9
3 groups of 3 = 9
3 x 3 = 9
4. 2 + 2 + 2 + 2 = 8
4 groups of 2 = 8
4 x 2 = 8

Answer Key

Page 243

1. 3 x 4 = 12
2. 4 x 6 = 24
3. 5 x 2 = 10
4. 4 x 8 = 32
5. 4 x 5 = 20
6. 3 x 7 = 21

Page 244

1. 16; 2 x 8 = 16
2. 15; 5 x 3 = 15
3. 28; 4 x 7 = 28
4. 18; 3 x 6 = 18
5. 20; 4 + 4 + 4 + 4 + 4 = 20
6. 21; 7 + 7 + 7 = 21
7. adding

Page 245

1. 8; 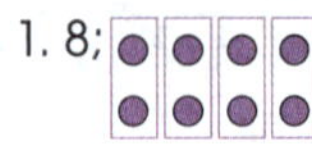 8; 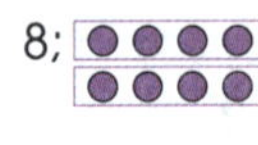

2. 15; 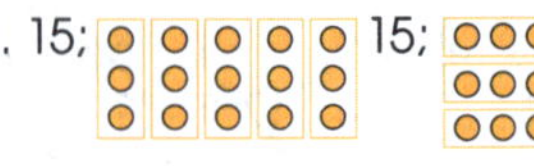 15;

3. 12; 12; 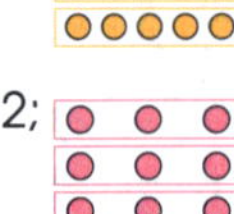

Page 246

1. 2 + 2 + 2 + 2 + 2 + 2 = 12
   6 x 2 = 12
2. 3 + 3 + 3 + 3 = 12
   4 x 3 = 12
3. 2 + 2 + 2 + 2 + 2 = 10
   5 x 2 = 10
4. 9 + 9 + 9 + 9 = 36
   4 x 9 = 36

Page 247

1. 1, 4, 1 x 4 = 4
2. 4, 0, 4 x 0 = 0
3. 8 4. 4 5. 0
6. 0 7. 7 8. 0
9. 6 10. 0 11. 0

Page 248

0	0	0	0	0	0	0	0	0	0
0	1	2	3	4	5	6	7	8	9

1. 0
2. that number
3. 3 4. 0
5. 5 6. 0
7. 8 8. 0
9. 6 10. 0
11. 4 12. 0
13. 9 14. 0
15. 5 16. 0 17. 4 18. 0 19. 0 20. 9 21. 0
22. 8 23. 0 24. 37 25. 43 26. 0 27. 60 28. 0

Page 249

1. 2, 4, 6, 8, 10, 12, 14, 16, 18, 20
2. 3, 6, 9, 12, 15, 18
3. 4, 8, 12, 16, 20
4. 5, 10, 15, 20

Page 250

1. 2, 4, 6, 8, 10, 12, 14, 16, 18
2. 3, 6, 9, 12, 15, 18, 21, 24, 27
3. 4, 8, 12, 16, 20, 24, 28, 32, 36
4. 5, 10, 15, 20, 25, 30, 35, 40, 45
5. 10, 20, 30, 40, 50, 60, 70, 80, 90

Page 251

1. 4
2. 16
3. 10
4. 14
5. 2
6. 12
7. 18
8. 6
9. 8

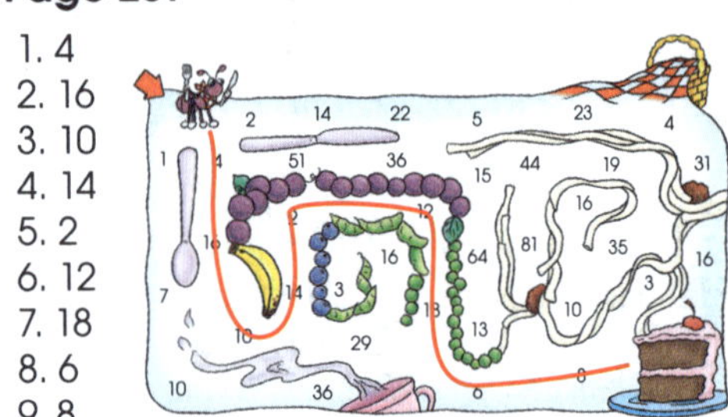

0	2	4	6	8	10	12	14	16	18

Page 252

1. 12 2. 3 3. 15
4. 18 5. 24 6. 6
7. 21 8. 27 9. 9
10. 3 x 5 = 15
11. 3 x 7 = 21
12. 3 x 6 = 18
13. 3 x 9 = 27

0	3	6	9	12	15	18	21	24	27

Page 253

1. 2 x 4 = 8
2. 3 x 5 = 15
3. 4 x 7 = 28
4. 3 x 6 = 18
5. 4 x 2 = 8
6. 5 x 6 = 30
7. Circle picture.
   2 x 3 = 6
8. Do not circle picture.
9. Circle picture.
   2 x 4 = 8

Page 254

1. 4 2. 12 3. 28
4. 20 5. 36 6. 16
7. 24 8. 8

A TENNIS BALL

0	4	8	12	16	20	24	28	32	36

Page 255

1. 15 2. 5 3. 25 4. 40
5. 30 6. 10 7. 35 8. 30
9. 20 10. 45 11. 20 12. 35
13. 5, or 0

0	5	10	15	20	25	30	35	40	45

Page 256

1. 3, 2, 6
2. 5, 5, 25
3. 0, 1, 0
4. 2, 4, 8
5. 5, 0, 0
6. 4, 3, 12
7. 3, 3, 9
8. 1, 5, 5

Page 257

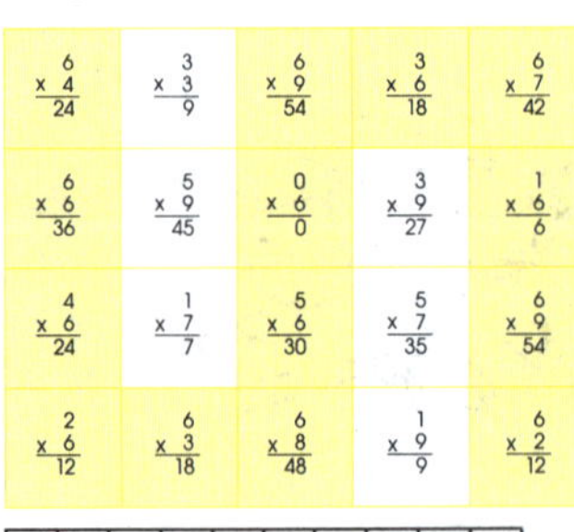

6 x 4 = 24	3 x 3 = 9	6 x 9 = 54	3 x 6 = 18	6 x 7 = 42
6 x 6 = 36	5 x 9 = 45	0 x 6 = 0	3 x 9 = 27	1 x 6 = 6
4 x 6 = 24	1 x 7 = 7	5 x 6 = 30	5 x 7 = 35	6 x 9 = 54
2 x 6 = 12	6 x 3 = 18	6 x 8 = 48	1 x 9 = 9	6 x 2 = 12

0	6	12	18	24	30	36	42	48	54

Page 258

1. 28 2. 63 3. 14
4. 42 5. 21 6. 35
7. 0 8. 56 9. 49

A GOLDFISH

0	7	14	21	28	35	42	49	56	63

Page 259

Across

1. 35
2. 16
3. 56
5. 24
6. 32
8. 48
9. 14
11. 32
12. 0

Down

1. 36
2. 14
4. 63
5. 28
7. 21
8. 42
10. 40

					1. 3	5					
				2. 1	6		3. 5	4. 6			
			5. 2	4				6. 3	7. 2		
		8. 4	8						9. 1	10. 4	
	11. 3	2								12. 0	

Page 260

1. 24 2. 48 3. 32
4. 64 5. 8 6. 72
7. 40 8. 56 9. 16

A BABY ELEPHANT

0	8	16	24	32	40	48	56	64	72

Page 261

1. 27, 45, 63, 9, 72, 0, 54, 18
2. 36, 54, 27, 0, 45, 63, 81, 72

0	9	18	27	36	45	54	63	72	81

Answer Key

Page 262

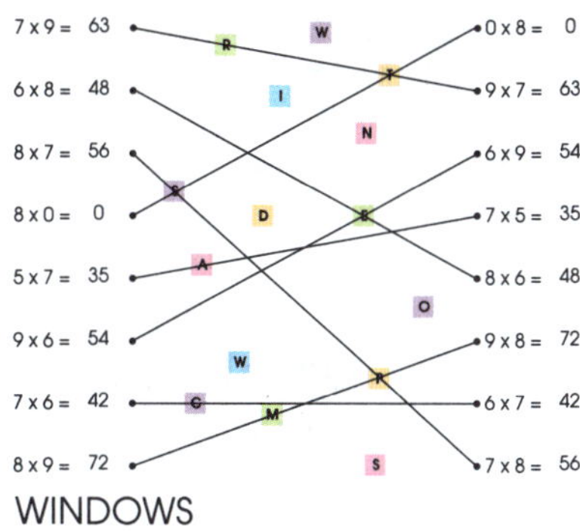

WINDOWS

Page 263

x	0	1	2	3	4	5	6	7	8	9
0	0	0	0	0	0	0	0	0	0	0
1	0	1	2	3	4	5	6	7	8	9
2	0	2	4	6	8	10	12	14	16	18
3	0	3	6	9	12	15	18	21	24	27
4	0	4	8	12	16	20	24	28	32	36
5	0	5	10	15	20	25	30	35	40	45
6	0	6	12	18	24	30	36	42	48	54
7	0	7	14	21	28	35	42	49	56	63
8	0	8	16	24	32	40	48	56	64	72
9	0	9	18	27	36	45	54	63	72	81

28, 18, 12, 40
10, 18, 40, 28
12, 42, 10, 42
A DIAMOND

Page 264

Page 265

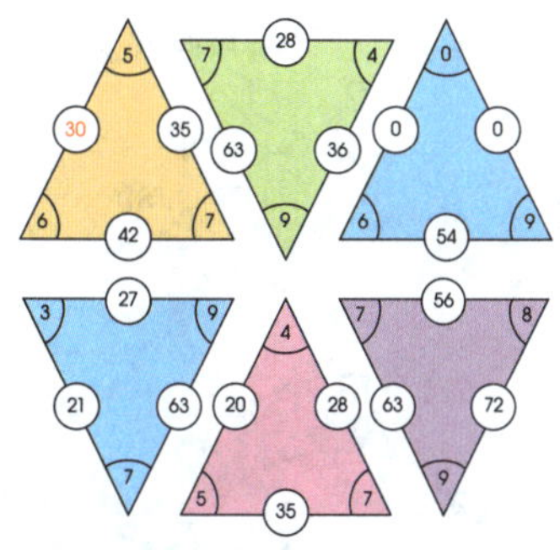

Page 266

1. 16, 20, 24, 21
2. 15, 24, 25, 32
3. 28, 36, 21, 48
4. 45, 6, 18, 36
5. 24, 14, 40, 56
6. 63, 64, 18, 0
7. 28, 54, 48, 63
8. 81, 0, 32, 54
9. 40, 49, 24, 56
10. 45, 35, 0, 72
11. 16, 42, 45, 28
12. 27, 0, 72, 0

Page 267

1. 5 2. 6 3. 9 4. 6
5. 2 6. 3 7. 7 8. 4
9. 8 10. 9 11. 1 12. 8
A FLYING PIZZA

Page 268

1. 60 2. 40
3. 10 4. 30
5. 50 6. 80
7. 70 8. 0
9. 20 10. 90
11. 0

0	10	20	30	40	50	60	70	80	90

Page 269

1. 33 2. 77
3. 99 4. 44
5. 22 6. 88
7. 55 8. 11
9. 0 10. 66

11	17	1	28	11	7	77
5	11	4	44	16	48	11
55	32	63	11	0	0	3
0	11	8	88	11	38	33
24	9	56	71	1	15	41
65	99	36	23	11	2	22
18	11	6	66	43	0	17

0	11	22	33	44	55	66	77	88	99

Page 270

1. 24 2. 60 3. 48
4. 96 5. 12 6. 84
7. 72 8. 108 9. 36
A PORCUPINE

0	12	24	36	48	60	72	84	96	108

Page 271

x	0	1	2	3	4	5	6	7	8	9	10	11	12
0	0	0	0	0	0	0	0	0	0	0	0	0	0
1	0	1	2	3	4	5	6	7	8	9	10	11	12
2	0	2	4	6	8	10	12	14	16	18	20	22	24
3	0	3	6	9	12	15	18	21	24	27	30	33	36
4	0	4	8	12	16	20	24	28	32	36	40	44	48
5	0	5	10	15	20	25	30	35	40	45	50	55	60
6	0	6	12	18	24	30	36	42	48	54	60	66	72
7	0	7	14	21	28	35	42	49	56	63	70	77	84
8	0	8	16	24	32	40	48	56	64	72	80	88	96
9	0	9	18	27	36	45	54	63	72	81	90	99	108
10	0	10	20	30	40	50	60	70	80	90	100	110	120
11	0	11	22	33	44	55	66	77	88	99	110	121	132
12	0	12	24	36	48	60	72	84	96	108	120	132	144

Page 272

1. Calvin found 46 rocks in total.
2. Jamie saw 53 birds in all.

Page 273

1. Stephanie has a total of 36 dolls in her collection.
2. Dalton has 53 baseball cards in all.
3. They counted a sum of 90 flowers.
4. Adam found 120 twigs altogether.
5. Krista saw 30 animals in all.
6. They caught a total of 91 fish.

Page 274

1. The difference between their throws was 2 feet.
2. John kicked the ball 19 more times yesterday.

Page 275

1. Sue delivered 11 more newspapers than Tom.
2. Jennifer sold 16 more candy bars than Patti.
3. Kim has 59 cartwheels left to do.
4. The difference between their times was 3 seconds.
5. Elliot has 34 hits left to do.

Answer Key

Page 276

1. add; There are 625 children in our school altogether.
2. subtract; They painted 3 more pictures on Tuesday.
3. add; They brought 70 pennies in all.
4. subtract; There were 87 pieces of chalk left unbroken.

Page 277

1. 34 butterflies
2. 5 spiders
3. 33 more grasshoppers
4. 28 more brown ants
5. 239 flies
6. 38 insects

Page 278

1. \$1.64 + \$0.35 = \$1.99
2. \$5.00 – \$0.25 = \$4.75
3. \$1.72 + \$1.18 = \$2.90
4. \$3.01 + \$0.45 = \$3.46
5. \$2.60 – \$0.55 = \$2.05

Page 279

1. 110 minutes
2. 6 more tubas
3. 555 miles
4. 9 more flutes
5. 60 more uniforms
6. 58 songs

Page 280

1. 60 people
2. 72 tickets

Page 281

1. 77 hours
2. 100 whistles
3. 36 times
4. 70 questions

Page 282

1. 8 nails
2. 7 screwdrivers

Page 283

1. 8 pieces of wood
2. 7 saws
3. 6 holes
4. 7 wrenches

Page 284

1. There are 21 ribbons altogether.
2. She spent 150 hours in training.
3. There were 72 helmets.

Page 285

1. 80 golfers
2. 296 miles
3. 312 glasses
4. 48 bikers
5. 384 friends

Page 286

1. 114 knee pads
2. 57 hours
3. 54 planes
4. 60 chairs

Page 287

1. She pulled 8 carrots from each row.
2. They had 8 vases.
3. There were 3 rose bushes in each row.

Page 288

1. He would have 7 bags.
2. He pulled 5 onions from each row.
3. There were 9 rows.
4. There are 5 plants in each row.
5. He picked 9 apples from each tree.

Page 289

1. 30 ÷ 5 = 6 dolls
2. 81 ÷ 9 = 9 laps
3. 24 ÷ 12 = 2 postcards
4. \$14.50 ÷ \$0.29 = 50 stamps

Page 290

1. 7 x 13 = 91 stamps
2. 40 ÷ 5 = 8 letters
3. 48 x 9 = 432 letters
4. 15 x 3 = 45 pen pals
5. 72 ÷ 9 = 8 postcards
6. 63 ÷ 9 = 7 houses

Page 291

1. 55 x 5 = 275 miles
2. 81 ÷ 9 = 9 postcards
3. 125 x 7 = 875 pictures
4. 9 x 32 = 288 bears
5. 12 ÷ 4 = 3 shirts
6. 25 ÷ 5 = 5 cable cars

Page 292

1. $\frac{1}{3}$
2. $\frac{3}{5}$
3. $\frac{2}{7}$
4. $\frac{1}{2}$

Page 293

1. $\frac{3}{8} + \frac{2}{8} = \frac{5}{8}$
2. $\frac{1}{3} - \frac{1}{3} = 0$
3. $\frac{4}{5} - \frac{1}{5} = \frac{3}{5}$

Page 294

1. She picked $\frac{3}{9}$ ($\frac{1}{3}$) of a bushel more on Wednesday than Thursday.
2. She dug $\frac{3}{4}$ of the garden altogether.
3. She has $\frac{6}{16}$ ($\frac{3}{8}$) of the garden more to plant.

Page 295

1. Todd bought $\frac{5}{8}$ of a yard of fabric.
2. Mom has $\frac{6}{12}$ ($\frac{1}{2}$) of an hour more to paint.
3. She has $\frac{2}{7}$ of a roll of wallpaper left.
4. It took $\frac{1}{3}$ of a can of paint more for the chair.
5. He used $\frac{3}{4}$ of a cup of paste altogether.
6. The difference is $\frac{6}{18}$ ($\frac{1}{3}$) of a yard.

Page 296

1. spaghetti
chicken
pizza

Page 297

1. 4′5″
4′7″
4′2″
2. 9
10
11
8

Page 298

1. 40 x 3 = 120; 120 – 90 = 30 minutes
2. 208 ÷ 4 = 52 balls; 52 x 3 = 156 balls
3. 4 x \$3.75 = \$15.00; \$15.00 + \$4.50 = \$19.50
4. 6 x \$1.50 = \$9.00; \$10.00 – \$9.00 = \$1.00

Page 299

1. in-line skating
2. biking
3. 6 children
4. 6 children
5. Jamar and Janet
6. 2 children

Page 300

1. Ramona
2. 24 days
3. 18 days
4. 6 days

Page 301

1. Todd
2. 30 tickets
3. 90 tickets
4. 20 tickets
5. 10 tickets